T0042834

A PATH
TO PEACE

A Brief History of Israeli-Palestinian
Negotiations and a Way Forward
in the Middle East

GEORGE J. MITCHELL
AND ALON SACHAR

SIMON & SCHUSTER PAPERBACKS

NEW YORK   LONDON   TORONTO   SYDNEY   NEW DELHI

Simon & Schuster Paperbacks
An Imprint of Simon & Schuster, Inc.
1230 Avenue of the Americas
New York, NY 10020

First Simon & Schuster paperback edition November 2017

SIMON & SCHUSTER PAPERBACKS and colophon
are registered trademarks of Simon & Schuster, Inc.

For information about special discounts for bulk purchases,
please contact Simon & Schuster Special Sales at 1-866-506-1949
or business@simonandschuster.com.

The Simon & Schuster Speakers Bureau can bring authors to your live event.
For more information or to book an event contact the
Simon & Schuster Speakers Bureau at 1-866-248-3049
or visit our website at www.simonspeakers.com.

The opinion and characterizations in this piece are those of the authors and do not
necessarily represent official positions of the United States government.

Interior design by Ruth Lee-Mui
Interior maps by Barak Paz

Manufactured in the United States of America

10   9   8   7   6   5   4   3   2   1

Library of Congress has cataloged the hardcover as follows:

Names: Mitchell, George J. (George John), 1933- author. | Sachar, Alon, author
Title: A path to peace : a brief history of Israeli-Palestinian negotiations and a way
forward in the Middle East / George J. Mitchell, Alon Sachar.
Description: New York : Simon & Schuster, 2016. |
Includes bibliographical references and index.
Identifiers: LCCN 2016027278 (print) | LCCN 2016040659 (ebook) | ISBN
9781501153914 (hardcover : alk. paper) | ISBN 9781501153938 (Ebook)
Subjects: LCSH: Arab-Israeli conflict--Peace. | Palestinian Arabs--Politics and government.
Classification: LCC DS119.7 .M585 2016 (print) | LCC DS119.7 (ebook) | DDC
956.9405/4--dc23
LC record available at https://lccn.loc.gov/2016027278

ISBN 978-1-5011-5391-4
ISBN 978-1-5011-5392-1 (pbk)
ISBN 978-1-5011-5393-8 (ebook)

ALSO BY GEORGE J. MITCHELL

The Negotiator: A Memoir

Making Peace

*Not for America Alone: The Triumph of
Democracy and the Fall of Communism*

World on Fire: Saving an Endangered Earth

*Men of Zeal: A Candid Inside Story
of the Iran-Contra Hearings*
(with Senator William S. Cohen)

CONTENTS

Contents

ACKNOWLEDGMENTS

The writing of a book is ordinarily a lonely pursuit. This book was not, because I was assisted by Alon Sachar. Alon now practices law in San Francisco, but from 2006 to 2012 he worked in the Near Eastern Affairs Bureau of the U.S. Department of State. From January 2009 to May 2011 I served as the U.S. special envoy for Middle East, and Alon was a valued member of my small staff. He has an encyclopedic knowledge of the Middle East, in particular the recent history of Israel and the Palestinians.

The laws of Israel regarding land use are as complex as they are consequential. Among other things, I relied on Alon to penetrate and explain them to me. I knew I had made the right choice when, at one of the many meetings we held with Israeli officials, they asked Alon to confirm their understanding of their own bureaucracy and laws.

I also relied on the knowledge and judgment of other members of my talented staff: David Hale, now the U.S. ambassador to Pakistan, previously ambassador to Jordan and Lebanon, served as my deputy and later succeeded me as envoy; Fred Hof, a retired army officer, is a widely respected expert on Israel-Syria issues; Mara Rudman, was also a deputy envoy and my chief of staff and later served as the Assistant Administrator for the Middle East at the Agency for International Development; and Payton Knopf, a career foreign service officer at the time whose understanding of the issues and of the mechanics of diplomacy and whose communication skills are first-rate. While I served as envoy, Jeff Feltman headed the Near Eastern Affairs Bureau; he had previously served in Jerusalem and as ambassador to Lebanon and is now the United Nations Undersecretary General for Political Affairs. Although he was not a member of my staff, I regularly benefited from his wise advice and counsel. Dan Shapiro, now the U.S. ambassador to Israel, and Prem Kumar were then on the staff of the National Security Council at the White House; they were extremely knowledgeable and helpful. Although only Alon worked with me on this book and the views expressed herein are ours alone, the combined knowledge of these colleagues made this book possible. What I learned from them continues to inform my views, and I thank each of them and all of the other members of my staff.

I am indebted to Jonathan Karp and his outstanding team at Simon & Schuster. Megan Hogan edited this book with skill and tact. Thanks also to Maureen Cole, Cary Goldstein, Stephen Bedford, Richard Rhorer, Lisa Healy, Ruth Lee-Mui, Jackie Seow, Lisa Erwin, Kristen Lemire, and Allison Har-Zvi.

Finally, I thank my family—my wife, Heather; our children, Andrew and Claire; and my daughter, Andrea, and her son, Ian—for their continued love and support.

When two people combine to write, readers may occasionally be uncertain about whose words they are reading. To be clear, *we* signals our joint writing; *I* signals that the words are mine.

George J. Mitchell

Mount Desert Island, Maine

July 2016

I knew little about George Mitchell when President Obama appointed him as his Special Envoy for Middle East Peace. I was too young to appreciate the significance of the Good Friday Agreement he negotiated in Northern Ireland in the 1990s; or the fifteen years he served as U.S. senator, including six as majority leader; or of the myriad other high-profile matters he had worked on since leaving the Senate, including efforts to rid Major League Baseball of steroids to overcoming the stain of corruption from the Olympic games. He has led a major international law firm and served on the board of several Fortune 500 companies. All this from a man who put himself through college and law school and grew up in the most humble of circumstances: his father was a janitor and his mother, an immigrant to the U.S. at the age of eighteen, worked in textile mills.

There are those who call Mitchell "the judge," alluding to his former stint as a federal judge, his infamous poker face, and his regular deployment of the Socratic method on issues big and small. With a lifetime (or, rather, several lifetimes) of accomplishment, he is most proud of his service to the people of Maine, the reason I and so many others continue to call him Senator.

This is who Senator Mitchell was when he was appointed Special Envoy. Unlike so many others in the policy world, he did not seek out a high-level appointment to make a name for himself. That he had many times over. Indeed, with a wife and two young children at home, as well as a comfortable private-sector career, his appointment came at a high personal cost. But Senator Mitchell is a life-long public servant, ultimately and entirely dedicated to the American people. He accepted a direct request from the president and secretary of state because he felt it was his duty to say yes despite the cost. Yes to a job that no one before him had succeeded in, yes to a push that would expose him to a great deal of criticism, and yes to likely failure. It has been the single greatest honor of my life thus far to work for and be mentored by Senator Mitchell.

The work I have poured into this book is dedicated to my parents Dina and Avram Sachar. They have persevered through hardship, live life with optimism and humor, and dedicate everything they have to their family. I have also been grounded by the unwavering love and support of my partner, Dave Guarnieri. I am honored and privileged to have him by my side. Finally, I have benefited from the wisdom and support of many individuals in writing this book, including: Danny Abraham, Benjamin Caspi, Alex Djerassi, David Hale, Payton Knopf, Yoni Komorov, Jonathan Prince, Julia Reed, Mara Rudman, Nicole Shampaine, Ann Ungar, and Rick Waters.

Alon Sachar
San Francisco
August 2016

A PATH TO PEACE

INTRODUCTION

"**T**his is the saddest day of my life since becoming prime minister."[1] The leader of Israel was referring to the moment the U.S. ambassador to his country delivered a letter informing him that the president was days away from unveiling a sweeping proposal for peace between Israel and the Palestinians. The president's speech was to be delivered from the Rose Garden of the White House. The world would be watching.

The ambassador, in the most uncomfortable of diplomatic circumstances, was instructed by the White House to hand-deliver the letter to the prime minister, who was vacationing with his wife in northern Israel. It was their first vacation together in years, and they were caught off guard. The prime minister's response was blunt: "Please inform the president that I have read his letter and am most unhappy both with its content and its implications. I have also listened very carefully to your oral message and am extremely upset by its contents. You may tell the president and the secretary of state that I am astonished that your government did not see fit to indicate that such an initiative was in the making or to consult with the government of Israel at any stage of its elaboration. This is entirely unacceptable."[2]

The prime minister tried to buy time to consult with his cabinet, to consider his response, and to reshape the initiative. But the president refused. To the contrary, he moved the speech up by two days; having sent copies of the proposal to the leaders of Egypt, Jordan, and Saudi Arabia, the president worried that its contents would prematurely reach the media and undermine the impact of his speech.

When the prime minister was informed that the speech would proceed despite his objection and that he had even less time to consider his reaction, his outrage grew, and he asked the ambassador, "Is this the way to treat a friend? Is this the way to treat an ally? Your government consorts with our despotic enemies and yet you choose to ignore us on a matter of vital import to our future. What kind of discourse is this between democratic peoples who purport to cherish common values? Is this the way to make peace? We do not deserve this kind of treatment."[3]

Harsh words from the leader of one friendly country to the ambassador of another. But the outrage and bitter response were not from Benjamin Netanyahu to a proposal made by Barack Obama, as you might suppose. This was Menachem Begin responding to Ronald Reagan in 1982.

The United States has long had strategic, moral, and domestic political reasons for its support of Israel. Even though the personal relationship between Obama and Netanyahu has been strained, U.S.-Israeli policy disagreements are neither new nor unusual. Despite the exceedingly close ties between the two countries, strong and often public disagreements between presidents and prime ministers have been common. We will describe some of those disagreements, and some agreements as well.

In 2001, amid the Second Palestinian Intifada, as chairman of an international commission on violence in the Middle East, I met several times with Yasser Arafat, president of the Palestinian Authority. On one occasion, described later in more detail, I urged him to resume negotiations with Israel. He insisted that he too wanted an agreement but that it had to be acceptable to the Palestinian people. Many felt, of course, that the proposals made by Israeli prime minister Ehud Barak at Camp David and later by President Bill Clinton should have been acceptable. But there were no further negotiations during Arafat's lifetime.

Nearly a decade later I returned to the Middle East as President Obama's special envoy. I met frequently with the Palestinian president Mahmoud Abbas, most often in his office in the presidential compound in Ramallah. We usually began with lunch, attended by about a dozen people, half or more members of his cabinet or staff, half or fewer members of my staff or that of the U.S. consul. During and after lunch we had a general discussion, after which Abbas and I, sometimes alone, sometimes with one aide each, moved to a small meeting space adjacent to his office. There most of what may be called our business took place.

Now eighty-one, Abbas has been active in Palestinian politics for most of his adult life. His views have evolved over time, as did those of the organizations he now leads: the Palestine Liberation Organization and the Palestinian Authority. For more than a quarter-century he has been the most prominent and vocal Palestinian advocate of their current policy, which recognizes Israel, opposes violence against Israel, and favors peaceful negotiations to achieve an independent Palestinian state.

On several occasions I said essentially the same thing to Abbas that I had said to Arafat, urging him to negotiate with Israel. In response Abbas said he wanted a peace agreement, but he offered many reasons for his reluctance to enter direct negotiations: the devastation of the recent Gaza war had aroused strong negative emotions; he deeply distrusted Netanyahu; and Israeli settlements continued to expand. The Kadima-controlled Israeli government under Ariel Sharon, Ehud Olmert, and Tzipi Livni had withdrawn settlers from Gaza. The Likud-controlled government under Netanyahu included settlers and others on the Israeli Right who had said repeatedly that there should never be a Palestinian state in the West Bank; they believe that all of the West Bank is and should always be an integral part of Israel. Both societies are now divided between those who favor and those who oppose a two-state solution.

I also met often with Netanyahu. As with Abbas, our meetings usually involved an initial discussion with a dozen or more officials, followed by a smaller group, occasionally just the two of us, in his personal office. Like all Israeli leaders, Netanyahu's primary goal, repeated often in our discussions, is to preserve Israel's security. On the question of whether peace can best be achieved by a two-state solution, his position has fluctuated between strong opposition and tepid support. Most recently he said he favors it but that the time was not yet right. In each of his meetings with me, and in many public comments, Netanyahu has expressed a desire for an agreement with the Palestinians and his willingness to meet and negotiate personally with Abbas. They met four times in September 2010; along with Secretary of State Hillary Clinton, I was present at those discussions and will describe them in what follows.

Based on these experiences I reached the conclusion that

Netanyahu and Abbas have very different visions of peace and the two-state solution. Netanyahu does not believe that Abbas has the personal or political strength necessary to gain approval of and implement an agreement with Israel. Abbas believes that Netanyahu is not sincere or serious about making an agreement with the Palestinians and does only as much as he deems necessary to placate the United States. Since both men assume that negotiations will not succeed, neither has any incentive to take the political risks that will inevitably be required to make an agreement possible.

The reluctance of the leaders is understandable, but, as we describe in the chapters of this book, that reluctance is contrary to the immediate and long-term interests of the people they represent. We believe those interests—on both sides—will be best served by an agreement that accepts Israel's existence and provides its people with reasonable and sustainable security behind defensible borders and at the same time creates a sovereign, independent, nonmilitarized Palestinian state. That has been and remains the basis for and the objective of U.S. policy under both Republican and Democratic presidents. We support that policy.

As the dominant world power the United States has relationships with almost all of the countries in the world. It is natural and understandable that each of our allies wants us to adopt and pursue policies favorable to their interests. But many of those countries have disagreements among themselves, in some cases devolving into war. As a result there is an inevitable tension in our relationships, a balancing that requires a combination of consistency and ingenuity in U.S. statesmanship. That is a delicate task, calling for knowledge, strength, skill, and tact, especially since our primary objective is and must be defending and advancing our national interest.

Nowhere is this task more obvious, or more difficult, than in the Middle East. The United States invaded Afghanistan in 2001 and Iraq in 2003, where we remain deeply engaged. In 2010 the Arab Spring erupted, bringing hope and a sense of renewal. That hope has dissipated, and now the people of the region struggle through the misery of seemingly unending war, displacement, and upheaval. If anything the Arab Spring has reminded us of the harsh reality of history: that the removal by revolution of an oppressive regime does not guarantee better governance or a better life. Russia under the czars and then Stalin is a prime example. In the United States it took years to achieve a somewhat equitable and stable political order. Indeed, the American experiment continues to this day.

The complexity of the Middle East is illustrated by the tangle of our relationships there in 2016: We oppose the Assad regime in Syria, and we also oppose ISIS, which is fighting the Assad regime. The Syrian Kurds join us in opposing ISIS, but are being attacked by Turkey, one of our allies. We also combat ISIS in Iraq, where we are joined by Shia militias who are supported by Iran, whom we oppose. In Afghanistan we oppose the Taliban, who receive some support from Pakistan, another of our allies. Pakistan meanwhile has fought several wars with India, another of our allies.

Israel is and will remain our closest ally in the region. But we also are allied with many Arab and Muslim countries. During both Republican and Democratic administrations we have maintained a naval base in Bahrain and a large facility in Qatar. For decades we have had close relationships with Turkey, Egypt, Saudi Arabia, and the United Arab Emirates, pillars of the Sunni Muslim world. Oman played a key role in helping to arrange the negotiations that led to the nuclear agreement between Iran and the United States, China, Russia, Britain, Germany, and France. We have a close relationship with Indonesia, the largest Muslim-majority country in the world.

Of the 7.4 billion people on earth today, 23 percent, about 1.6 billion, are Muslim. Sometime after midcentury the total population will reach 9.6 billion, and 31 percent, or about 3 billion, will be Muslim.[4] To put that in perspective: 3 billion was the total world population as recently as 1960. In the twenty-first century what happens in the Muslim world will affect everyone, in particular the dominant world power, the United States. The regional projections are daunting for Israel. By midcentury the number of Israeli Jews is estimated to be 12.5 million at most,[5] while the number of Arabs will be around 600 million.[6]

The United States has a clear and compelling national interest in remaining involved in the Middle East and in doing all we can to reduce violence and upheaval and to combat radical Islamic extremism. As of this writing, the U.S. remains heavily engaged in the region, working to protect the American people from acts of terrorism; to ensure Israel's security, to resist Iran's drive for regional hegemony, to defeat ISIS in Iraq and Syria, to help other Arab countries resist terrorism and achieve stability, to stabilize Iraq, and to defeat the Taliban in and stabilize Afghanistan, among other objectives. Inevitably there will be many more years of disruption, and no single policy or action can solve all of the region's problems. But a peaceful resolution of the Israeli-Palestinian conflict would be a significant step that might enable some of the countries, including Israel and Saudi Arabia, to cooperate in opposing their common foes: Iran and terrorist organizations, those supported by and those opposed to Iran.

We recognize the daunting difficulty of finding a resolution to the Israeli-Palestinian conflict. We acknowledge the long litany of failed past efforts. We are especially mindful of the current complexities in the region that work against an early resolution. It is of course easier to describe the problem than to prescribe a solution.

We are not certain that we know what to do, but we are certain of what we and everyone else should not do: we must not lapse into despair at the difficulty, and we must avoid inaction. For that reason we present what we believe to be a realistic path to peace. We explain why we believe that is through a two-state solution. At the very least we hope to stimulate debate and to renew movement toward negotiations. All of us who care about the region and its people, in particular Israelis and Palestinians, must do whatever we can to advocate and work for an end to that conflict.

In the Middle East history is an ever-present part of daily life. Walking the streets of its modern cities does not dull the sensation of walking on the same ground once trod by Moses and Abraham, by Jesus Christ, and by the Prophet Mohammed. Proposals for the future, intended to help solve the problems of the present, cannot fairly be evaluated without some knowledge of the past. We do not offer a comprehensive retelling of that history in this book; instead we describe the modern history of the Israeli-Palestinian conflict, highlighting those events that led to the prevailing attitudes in each society today. We hope this concise narrative will enable the reader to better understand our suggested path to peace.

1

LEADERS IN DISAGREEMENT

The exchange between Begin and Reagan—the "saddest" of the Israeli prime minister's life—took place in 1982. Reagan's timing was not random. Israel had just withdrawn the last of its troops from Egypt's Sinai Peninsula in accordance with the peace treaty between the two nations. Two months after the withdrawal the Israeli Army invaded Lebanon in an effort to push out Arafat and his Palestine Liberation Organization. From there the Palestinians had launched attacks on Israel's northern cities and towns. Israel's military operation in Lebanon lasted for months, ending only with U.S. mediation and when the PLO agreed to leave Lebanese territory.

With Israel out of the Sinai, the violence in Lebanon reduced, a pro-Western government set to be inaugurated in Beirut, and the PLO on the run, President Reagan decided to adopt a "fresh start" initiative. He hoped to capitalize on what suddenly appeared to be a favorable regional environment. The core of the initiative was a comprehensive diplomatic solution to Israel's conflict with the Palestinians and its Arab neighbors, to be achieved in part by providing autonomy for Palestinians in parts of the West Bank.[1]

But Begin immediately and categorically rejected the Reagan Plan. Relinquishing control of any of the West Bank was antithetical to his ideological commitment to Israeli control of biblical Jewish lands, and he had just paid a heavy price to push the PLO away from Israel's northern borders. Palestinian autonomy, Begin worried, would bring them right back.

U.S. and Israeli policy disagreements have existed since the relationship first began. President Harry Truman (1945–53) is often celebrated for initiating our close and strategic partnership with Israel. But that good relationship was not a foregone conclusion in the decades following Israel's independence.

From the outset of his administration, President Truman concerned himself with the plight of Jewish refugees, the survivors of Hitler's Final Solution who remained stranded in dilapidated displaced persons camps in Europe. Israelis have never forgotten that he was the first world leader to recognize their fledgling state, just eleven minutes after their 1948 declaration of independence. "At our last meeting," recalled David Ben-Gurion, a founding father of Israel and its first prime minister, "I told [Truman] that as a foreigner I could not judge what would be his place in American history; but his helpfulness to us, his constant sympathy with our aims in Israel, his courageous decision to recognize our new State so quickly and his steadfast support since then had given him an immortal place in Jewish history. As I said that, tears suddenly sprang to his eyes. And his eyes were still wet when he bade me goodbye."[2]

The early years of the U.S. relationship with Israel took place within the context of the cold war. With Soviet influence entrenched in eastern and central Europe, Asia, and beyond, the United States believed it urgent to prevent the Soviets from gaining a foothold in the Middle East. Even with his sympathies, Truman's decision to recognize Israel was not easy or automatic; because he feared that either Israel or the Arab states would be pushed into the arms of the Soviets his initial inclination was for a binational arrangement in which Jews and Arabs would coexist. Therefore his decision to recognize Israel surprised even some of the most senior officials in his administration.[3]

One day after Israel's declaration of independence, Egypt, Jordan, Syria, Lebanon, and Saudi Arabia[4] began military action against the new state. This first of several Arab-Israeli wars lasted ten months; Israel was ultimately victorious, and without U.S. military assistance as Truman had imposed an arms embargo on both sides. The policy of pursuing balance in America's relationship with the Arab states and Israel continued for decades.

In 1956 President Dwight Eisenhower did what today is unimaginable: he threatened to break off ties with Israel altogether. This crisis in relations followed a combined surprise attack by France, Britain, and Israel to gain control of the Suez Canal, which had just been seized and nationalized by Egypt's president Gamal Abdel Nasser. Because the Canal provided the shortest route for ships traveling between Europe and Asia, its geopolitical significance at the time, and even today, cannot be overstated.

France and Britain had their own reasons for initiating the war, not least of which was to protect their influence and interests in the region. The British government was the largest shareholder in the Suez Canal and British and French shippers among its largest patrons. Israel believed Nasser's populism and celebrity status posed a threat to its existence. Nasser had become the charismatic face of pan-Arab nationalism, positioning himself as the leader who would unite the Arab world and destroy Israel. To that end, Egypt had for years supported a steady stream of Palestinian guerrilla attacks into Israel, and enforced a blockade against Israel's southern port city on the Red Sea. Following Egypt's nationalization of the Canal, Nasser banned its use by Israel.

Eisenhower worried that armed conflict would enhance Soviet influence in the Middle East. Though wary of Nasser and his arms deals with the Soviet Union, Eisenhower disfavored war and preferred a diplomatic solution to the Suez crisis. He immediately and unambiguously cautioned the British and the French against armed conflict. When they did not heed his warning and proceeded to involve Israel in their plans, Eisenhower was shocked and angered. With the Soviet Union threatening to engage militarily in support of Nasser, Eisenhower scrambled to end the war in a way that preserved regional balance. But by then Israeli forces had taken full control of Sinai.

Over strong objections from the Israelis, Eisenhower pushed through a United Nations resolution calling for their full and immediate withdrawal. He warned Israel that failing to comply with the resolution would "impair the friendly cooperation between our two countries."[5] Eisenhower went so far as to threaten to cut off U.S. assistance to Israel, to seek Israel's eviction from the UN, and to withhold U.S. support in the event of an attack by Soviet-allied forces. Ben-Gurion desperately sought a meeting with the president to explain his position, that Israel was reluctant to simply withdraw its forces without clear assurances of its security and its continuing right to navigate the Canal and other international waters. But Eisenhower refused to meet until after Israel agreed to withdraw. Ben-Gurion complied, but bitterly.[6]

The Suez crisis was the lowest moment in U.S. relations with Israel. Efforts to prevent the Middle East from becoming yet another cold war arena had failed, for the Soviet Union made inroads. Cairo, Baghdad, and other Arab capitals drew closer to Moscow.

In the land of King David, Israel believed that resisting Arab Goliaths would require a giant ally of its own. And America came to view Israelis as partners in curbing and offsetting Soviet influence. Under the Kennedy and Johnson administrations Israel received its first large-scale shipments of sophisticated American weapons systems, including antiaircraft missiles, tanks, and jet fighter planes. The sales were intended to help Israel maintain its defenses against the larger and better armed Arab states still bent on its destruction and also to counterbalance Soviet arms pouring into the region. In return Israel provided the United States with intelligence information about Soviet weapons systems and the USSR's posture in the Middle East.

President John F. Kennedy told Israel's foreign minister Golda Meir, "The United States has a special relationship with Israel in the Middle East really comparable only to what it has with Britain over a wide range of world affairs." He was the first president to speak of this "special relationship" by name. But he also said, "For us to play properly the role we are called upon to play, we cannot afford the luxury of identifying Israel . . . as our exclusive friends . . . and letting other countries go."[7] To preserve its influence in the region, the United States also supplied certain Arab states, such as Jordan, with arms.[8]

Tension developed when the United States feared Israeli actions might destabilize the balance in the region, as when Kennedy and Ben-Gurion clashed over Israel's nuclear program. Kennedy worried about a broader nuclear arms race; Ben-Gurion viewed the arms race as inevitable absent U.S.-Soviet détente and was determined to own the ultimate weapon of deterrence before his neighbors could. Frustrated, Kennedy warned Israel in a bluntly worded letter that U.S. support "would be seriously jeopardized" and that Israel risked isolation from the West if it pursued nuclear weapons. The disagreement ultimately played a role in Ben-Gurion's resignation as prime minister.[9] By the time President Lyndon Johnson assumed power, Israel had agreed to allow American inspectors to examine its nuclear capability.[10]

As have many other U.S. presidents, Johnson had deep and emotional ties to the Jewish state. He spoke of his admiration for Israel's commitment to democratic values and of the "gallant struggle of modern Jews to be free of persecution." When asked by Soviet premier Aleksei Kosygin why the United States supported Israel, a country of only 3 million people, when there were 80 million Arabs, Johnson replied, "Because it is right."[11]

Johnson was the first U.S. president to host an Israeli prime minister at the White House and the first to directly supply Israel with offensive military weapons. Like his predecessors, Johnson was in part reacting to Soviet moves in the Middle East. He worried that an imbalance in power between the Israelis and the Arabs would invite an Arab attack and instigate a regional war that would threaten U.S. interests. But close ties between Johnson and Israel did not mean the absence of disagreement.

In 1966 the West Bank was under the control of Jordan. Although they tried, Jordanian forces could not prevent Palestinian guerrilla groups from launching attacks against Israel. One land mine killed three Israeli soldiers and provoked a heavy Israeli cross-border response with tanks and hundreds of troops. It was meant as a show of strength and a warning to Palestinian militants against continued attacks. However, Johnson was deeply troubled by Israel's action and was critical in public; he worried that the move undercut King Hussein of Jordan, America's closest Arab ally at the time, so he joined the Soviet Union in support of a UN Security Council resolution that deplored the move and warned of further Security Council action were it to be repeated.

Even during the escalation that led to the Six-Day War in 1967 Johnson warned Israel against making any rash moves. In the preceding years Nasser had continued calling for a united Arab war against Israel, organizing a coalition of states under his direct or indirect control. He gave speeches to crowds of tens of thousands extolling the virtue of ridding the Middle East of the Jewish state and reinstated a blockade against Israel in the Straits of Tiran.[12] When he ordered a massive buildup of Egyptian forces in the Sinai Peninsula, Israel launched a preemptive and decisive strike against Egypt. At Nasser's request, Jordan, Syria, Iraq, and Lebanon joined the conflict, with broad support across the Middle East, initiating a multifront war from the south, north, and east.

The all-out, regional war that Johnson feared had become a reality, but his concern that the United States would be drawn in turned out to be unfounded. By the war's end Israel had captured the entire Sinai Peninsula from Egypt, the West Bank from Jordan, and the Golan Heights from Syria. Unlike Eisenhower, Johnson would not force the Israelis to withdraw without security guarantees. His administration viewed Israel's greatly strengthened position as leverage for a peace treaty with the Arabs.

But instead of peace the decade following the Six-Day War saw even greater escalation of hostilities. The Arabs issued their infamous Three No's—"No peace with Israel, no recognition of Israel, no negotiations with Israel"—and Israel would not agree to retreat from its more fortified positions.

President Richard Nixon assured his counterpart, Prime Minister Golda Meir, of his desire to see "a strong Israel because he did not want the United States to have to fight Israel's battles."[13] He felt that the Arabs, and Nasser specifically, would not make peace with Israel until they realized they could not destroy it. So as long as he was president, he promised, "Israel would never be weak militarily."[14] The country had to have "a technological military margin to more than offset her hostile neighbors' numerical superiority."[15]

Yet, at least initially, the Nixon administration blocked arms supplies, to Israel's frustration. Nixon's hope was to slow down the arms race, even as the Soviet Union was undertaking a massive rearmament of Egypt, even sending in military personnel. In the years following the Six-Day War, Nasser had engaged in a war of attrition against Israel; a constant barrage of attacks on Israeli positions in the Sinai met with fierce Israeli retaliation.

Nasser died of a heart attack in 1970. By then the Nixon administration had secured a cease-fire between Egypt and Israel, though both remained on edge. Anwar Sadat, Nasser's successor, began to loosen ties with the Soviets to see what he could get out of the United States in return. He also was more receptive to U.S. overtures for peace. When the Nixon administration saw an opening and pursued a diplomatic initiative, Meir equivocated. She feared that a full withdrawal from the Sinai, one of Sadat's conditions, would leave Israel far too vulnerable. "I understand the difficulties Israel faces in exchanging something concrete—territories—for promises and guarantees," Nixon told the Israelis in March 1973. "But you should remember that your pipeline of military supplies is liable to dry up. Under no circumstances will that happen as long as I am president of the United States. But I won't serve forever."[16]

In September 1973, on the Jewish High Holiday of Yom Kippur, Egypt and Syria launched a surprise coordinated attack on Israel. During the first weeks of that war Nixon withheld arms from Israel in the hope that a military stalemate would lead to a peace agreement. But as the Egyptians were gaining the upper hand in Sinai and the Soviets were not reciprocating his restraint, Nixon acknowledged that an Israeli defeat was intolerable. According to his national security advisor, Henry Kissinger, "The judgment was that if another American-armed country were defeated by Soviet-armed countries, the inevitable lesson that anybody around the world would have to draw is to rely increasingly on the Soviet Union."[17]

Nixon initiated a large-scale operation to arm the Israelis despite concerns over a possible Soviet response. "We are going to get blamed just as much for three planes as for three hundred," he told Kissinger.[18] So he ordered the military to "use every [plane] we have—everything that will fly." The United States flew 567 airlift missions, delivering over 22,000 tons of supplies, with another 90,000 tons of arms delivered to Israel by sea.[19] Even before the full arms supply reached them, Israel was beginning to gain the upper hand. With U.S. help, Israel was able to hold off the Syrians and push beyond the Sinai Peninsula toward Cairo.

Without consulting Israel, however, Kissinger met with his Soviet counterpart to secure a cease-fire. The two superpowers eventually agreed on a Security Council resolution to end the hostilities, which the Israelis felt was premature. Israel had suffered high casualties in the Yom Kippur War and feared that anything short of a clear victory would leave them vulnerable to continued Arab aggression. Yet, despite those concerns, Israel complied with the cease-fire.

In the months following the war Kissinger engaged in urgent shuttle diplomacy in an effort to forge a lasting peace agreement between the Israelis and the Arabs, in no small part in hope of reducing Soviet influence in the region. Little progress was made by the time the Watergate scandal forced Nixon to resign. And although Israel ultimately staved off the combined Arab forces, Prime Minister Meir was blamed for being ill prepared for the war and resigned.

She was succeeded by Yitzhak Rabin. When President Gerald Ford first welcomed Rabin to the White House, in 1974, he made clear that the United States "continue[d] to stand with Israel," promising, "We are committed to Israel's survival and security. The United States for a quarter of a century has had an excellent relationship with the State of Israel. We have cooperated in many, many fields—in your security, in the well-being of the Middle East, and in leading what we all hope is a lasting peace throughout the world."[20] Kissinger became Ford's secretary of state and continued to pursue an agreement between Israel and Egypt. He believed the "Soviets [would] be happy" if there were no such agreement.[21]

Rabin faced intense internal opposition to the U.S. proposals. His cabinet calculated that the withdrawals Kissinger was requesting of Israel did not match the security concessions being requested of Egypt; in fact Cairo would not even agree to declare an official end to hostilities. But Kissinger trusted that Sadat wanted to make progress with U.S. help, shifting Egypt away from Soviet influence. He believed Israel's stance was harming U.S. interests as well as its own. This prompted the Ford administration to undertake a public "reassessment" of U.S. relations with Israel. Ford wrote to Rabin to "express [his] profound disappointment over Israel's attitude in the course of the negotiations" and insisted,

"Failure of the negotiations will have a far-reaching impact on the region and on our relations."[22]

By the end of Ford's presidency, in 1975, Kissinger had managed to secure the Sinai Interim Agreement,[23] in which Egypt and Israel agreed that the conflicts between them would "not be resolved by military force but by peaceful means." Israel committed to moving its forces farther away from the Suez Canal and accepted the creation of a UN buffer zone. To secure Rabin's support, the United States provided Israel with substantial security assurances, including $2 billion in aid and a commitment for annual assistance thereafter. Every president since has honored that commitment.

A full-fledged peace agreement between Israel and Egypt followed, in 1979. Most historians have come to believe that were it not for Egypt's success in the 1973 War, this peace treaty would not have happened. The war not only tempered Israel's confidence but also helped elevate Sadat's status and legitimacy throughout the Arab world, enabling him to embark on his historic visit to Jerusalem and to become the first Arab leader to make peace with Israel.

Nearly a year after the signing of the historic treaty on the White House lawn, President Jimmy Carter emphasized in the strongest possible terms, "Our aid for Israel is not only altruistic; indeed, our close relationship with Israel is in the moral and the strategic interest of the United States." Carter was referring not just to America's support for a Jewish homeland, but to the importance of the relationship amid the cold war and to regional stability and ongoing intelligence and defense cooperation. "There is a mutual relationship and there is a mutual benefit and there is a mutual commitment, which has been impressed very deeply in my mind and also in the minds of the leaders of my Government and the Government of Israel."[24]

Notwithstanding those remarks, Carter had a sometimes tense
relationship with the Israelis. His administration wanted to build
on the success of the Israel-Egypt peace agreement with a comprehensive settlement between Israel and all the Arab states that
would include resolution of the Palestinian issue. In 1977 Prime
Minister Rabin, who would later become the face of Israel's peace
movement, objected when Carter became the first U.S. president
to speak of a Palestinian homeland as part of a comprehensive
peace accord. And after Israelis elected Menachem Begin as prime
minister later that year, their first right-wing leader in history,
Begin and Carter often clashed on the Palestinian issue and on
Israeli settlements.[25]

Even before assuming the presidency, Reagan viewed the strategic partnership with Israel with some urgency. The fall of America's ally in Iran to the Islamic Revolution, he said, "has increased
Israel's value as perhaps the only remaining strategic asset in the region on which the United States can truly rely; other pro-Western
states in the region, especially Saudi Arabia and the smaller Gulf
kingdoms, are weak and vulnerable."[26] Reagan pursued a number
of initiatives aimed at broadening and strengthening the U.S.-
Israeli partnership: he entered into the Strategic Cooperation
Agreement, formed the Joint Political Military Group, initiated
a series of joint military exercises, and built two American War
Reserve Stock facilities in Israel. Also during Reagan's tenure the
United States entered into a free trade agreement with Israel, and
provided $1.5 billion in loan guarantees, in which the United
States served as a guarantor of Israeli debt, enabling them to bor-
row funds at lower interest rates than otherwise possible. Perhaps
most important, Reagan worked with Congress to grant Israel
major non-NATO ally status.

Reagan is now viewed as being staunchly pro-Israel, yet there

were many moments of deep tension between the two countries during his presidency. In 1981, for instance, when Israel
launched a covert military attack against an Iraqi nuclear facility to prevent Iraq from acquiring a nuclear weapon, Reagan's
administration criticized Israel and suspended promised deliver-
ies of F-16 fighter planes. Fearing accusations of collusion with
Israel, Reagan supported a UN Security Council resolution that
condemned Israel's actions as a "clear violation of the Charter of
the United Nations and the norms of international conduct." A
few months later Israel's Knesset ratified the Golan Heights Law,
which officially extended Israeli law into Syrian territory captured in the 1967 War. But the United States considered this to
be occupied territory, so the Reagan administration suspended
the Strategic Cooperation Agreement and again delayed the ship-
ment of F-16s.

Begin and Reagan also clashed over Israel's invasion of Lebanon in 1982. Israel's goal was to deny the PLO space for launching continued attacks in the north of Israel. Though Reagan was
sympathetic, he believed the invasion of Lebanon went too far. As
Israeli forces encircled Beirut, Reagan told Yitzhak Shamir, Israel's
foreign minister, "If you invade West Beirut, it would have the
most grave, most grievous consequences for our relationship."[27]
And, as previously noted, once the 1982 war in Lebanon ended,
Begin reacted harshly to Reagan's proposed "fresh start" initiative
for regional peace through Palestinian autonomy.

By the time President George H. W. Bush assumed office, the
First Palestinian Intifada had erupted in the West Bank and
Gaza. In his first meeting with Yitzhak Shamir, who was now
prime minister, Bush affirmed that the United States was "un-
shakable in our commitment to Israel."[28] Early in his term, Bush

and Secretary of State James Baker were occupied with events in Europe and the elevation of Mikhail Gorbachev, who would turn out to be the Soviet Union's last leader. But the administration continued the political and military dialogues with Israel initiated by Reagan; helped Israel reestablish diplomatic relations with several dozen African and Asian countries; secured the release of hundreds of thousands of Jews from Ethiopia, Syria, and the Soviet Union; and increased assistance to Israel to cover damage inflicted by the barrage of scud missiles launched by Saddam Hussein during the First Gulf War.

While Bush supported continued high levels of military assistance to Israel, he also supported a number of UN Security Council resolutions condemning Israeli actions against Palestinians during the Intifada. Baker said bluntly, "Now is the time to lay aside, once and for all, the unrealistic vision of greater Israel. Israeli interests in the West Bank and Gaza—security and otherwise—can be accommodated in a settlement based on [UN Security Council] Resolution 242. Forswear annexation. Stop settlement activity. Allow schools to be reopened. Reach out to the Palestinians as neighbors who deserve political rights."[29]

Withdrawal from the West Bank and Gaza, though, was inconceivable to Israelis at the time. Resolution 242 called for an exchange of land for peace. But many Israelis argued that 242 did not apply to the West Bank or Gaza, that Israel's peace agreement with Egypt and withdrawal from Sinai was enough. Baker's comments were discomforting to Israel and to many of its supporters.

Following the First Gulf War, Bush and Baker resumed efforts that had begun under Reagan to launch a dialogue between Israel and the Palestinians. Arab-Israeli diplomacy was no longer seen through the lens of the cold war, but it mattered no less. Prime Minister Shamir's initial response to meeting with Palestinian leaders, though, was simply to say no.[30] At the time, the PLO, with Arafat as its chairman, was widely regarded as a terrorist organization, given a streak of airplane hijackings and bombings of Israeli and Jewish civilian targets worldwide. Eventually, following many efforts by Bush and Baker, Israeli and Palestinian representatives met at the Madrid peace talks of 1991.

No political agreements were reached at Madrid and significant disagreements between the United States and Israel on the peace process remained. Bush and Baker vigorously opposed settlement activity in particular. When Shamir's government persisted in creating and expanding settlements, Bush refused to support an Israeli request for an additional $10 billion in loan guarantees. When Shamir lost reelection in 1992, this was due in part to his strained relations with the United States.

Shamir's successor, a reelected Yitzhak Rabin, won on a platform of peace with Israel's Arab neighbors and with the Palestinians. In September 1993 President Clinton hosted Rabin and Arafat at a ceremony celebrating the first of several agreements known as the Oslo Accords, in which Israel began withdrawing from parts of the West Bank and Gaza and committed to further negotiations to end the conflict. And in 1994 Clinton presided over talks that led to peace between Israel and Jordan.

Clinton was widely admired and respected in Israel, which he called "a shining example for people around the world who are on the frontline of the struggle for democracy in their own lands." At a news conference with Rabin in 1993 he asserted, "Our relationship is also based on our common interest in a more stable and peaceful Middle East, a Middle East that will finally accord Israel the recognition and acceptance that its people have yearned for so long and have been too long denied. . . . I believe strongly in the benefit to American interests from strengthened relationships with Israel."[31] Yet even Clinton's relationship with Israeli leaders was at times strained.

Rabin was tragically assassinated in 1995 by a right-wing Israeli extremist opposed to his concessions in Oslo. In 1996, after a string of terror attacks against Israelis, Benjamin Netanyahu was elected prime minister on a platform of opposition to the Oslo Accords. Although after his election he pledged to adhere to Oslo's provisions, Netanyahu accused the Palestinians of violating its terms, thereby justifying his delayed implementation of Israeli requirements under the Accords. This gave rise to deep personal tension between him and Clinton. So strained were the relations that Netanyahu complained, "We are being vilified and scorned and misrepresented."[32] At one point he bypassed the president and went directly to Congress to garner support for his opposition to additional Israeli concessions. Thereafter meetings between the two leaders were publicly canceled.[33] Clinton eventually secured an Israeli-Palestinian agreement on Israel's partial withdrawals from the West Bank city of Hebron in 1997 and later to further withdrawals in the 1998 Wye Agreement, meant to resurrect the stalled Oslo Accords.

The subsequent failure of peace negotiations between Netanyahu's successor, Ehud Barak, and Arafat at Camp David in 2000 was followed by the Second Palestinian Intifada, a period of widespread violence. Arafat was blamed for the failed negotiations, and President George W. Bush sympathized deeply with Israeli anxiety over Palestinian suicide attacks, which were particularly resonant in America's new post-September 11 reality. "We will speak up for our principles," Bush said, "and we will stand up for our friends in the world. And one of our most important friends is the State of Israel. . . . At the first meeting of my National Security Council, I told them a top foreign policy priority is the safety and security of Israel.

My Administration will be steadfast in supporting Israel against terrorism and violence, and in seeking the peace for which all Israelis pray."[34] During Bush's presidency the United States committed to providing Israel with an average of $3 billion annually in security assistance as well as an additional $8 billion in loan guarantees.

Yet even the Bush administration did not always agree with Israel. In response to settlement activity, for example, Bush cut the amount of loan guarantees available by hundreds of millions of dollars. During the first year of the Second Intifada, to protest the use of U.S. equipment in the killing of Palestinian leaders that Israel accused of being involved in terror attacks, Bush imposed an arms embargo on spare parts for U.S.-made helicopters. At the same time he prepared to unveil a plan to help put the peace process back on track and to end the violence. While the plan was ultimately shelved following the attacks of September 11, Prime Minister Sharon accused Bush of selling out Israel to appease the Palestinians and other Arabs.[35] The White House angrily labeled Sharon's remarks "unacceptable."

In 2002 Bush became the first U.S. president to make the establishment of a viable Palestinian state an explicit foreign policy objective.[36] After unveiling his Roadmap for Peace, which, among other things, called on Israel to freeze settlement activity, he obtained a supportive UN Security Council resolution and united the international community behind his plan.

Too often in the never-ending political debate in our country, the attitudes of U.S. administrations toward Israel are expressed in binary terms, as either too close to or too distant from, too friendly with or too hostile toward Israel. The relationship is viewed in the same zero-sum terms that are used to describe the Israeli-Palestinian conflict.

Too many hold the view that President Obama has distanced the United States from Israel to the detriment of our relationship, Israel's interests, and Middle East peace. Some attribute this supposed distancing to an effort to improve relations with the Arab world. It is true that Obama came into office intent on improving America's strained relations with Arabs and Muslims. But he did not believe that doing so had to come at the expense of close relations with Israel.

To the contrary, in June 2009 he traveled to Cairo to deliver a much anticipated and widely televised speech, titled "A New Beginning." To the Arab audience gathered before him at Cairo's al-Azhar University, the millions watching on television, and to the entire Arab and Muslim world he hoped would hear him, Obama spoke of the deep relationship between the United States and Israel based on "cultural and historical ties, and the recognition that the aspiration for a Jewish homeland is rooted in a tragic history that cannot be denied. Threatening Israel with destruction—or repeating vile stereotypes about Jews—is deeply wrong, and only serves to evoke in the minds of Israelis the most painful of memories while preventing the peace that the people of this region deserve." He called on the Palestinians to "abandon violence" and "focus on what they can build." The broader Arab world, he said, should "recognize Israel's legitimacy and choose progress over a self-defeating focus on the past."[37] Those are words almost all U.S. presidents have used in speeches to Jewish organizations in the United States, but not directly to Arabs and Muslims.

Many Israelis and their U.S. supporters, however, did not hear those words, or if they did, they discounted them. They were concerned that President Obama spoke of centuries of discrimination, pogroms, and the Holocaust as the justification of Israel's existence, but did not mention the historical and ancient Jewish connection to the land—a critical component of their narrative. They read the press accounts that focused on the president's outreach to Muslims and were disappointed that he did not visit Israel on the same trip. In retrospect he should have done so, but some accused him of distancing himself from the Israeli people when he had done just the opposite.

During his tenure as president, Obama has provided Israel with unprecedented levels of military support with the intent to bolster Israel's security and ensure Israel's military superiority over its neighbors. Maintaining Israel's qualitative military edge, as the policy is known, has been the priority of successive U.S. administrations.

Under President Obama, the United States regularly conducts joint military exercises with the Israeli Defense Forces (IDF) and has provided Israel with over $23 billion in military aid.[38] Most of that aid is in accordance with the ten-year commitment President Bush made to provide Israel an average of $3 billion each year through 2018. Obama followed through with the commitment, pushed for an additional $225 million to help the Israelis expedite production and deployment of their Iron Dome missile defense system, and approved sales to Israel of the most sensitive and advanced American weapons systems, including the newly released F-35 fighter planes.[39] In September 2016, President Obama approved a new ten-year aid commitment, increasing America's annual assistance to Israel from $3 billion to $3.8 billion between 2019 through 2028. Israeli officials have repeatedly said that under Obama U.S.-Israeli security ties are the best they have ever been.[40] Obama is the first president in decades under whose tenure no UN Security Council resolution opposed by Israel has been passed.[41]

Israeli prime ministers not only have the weight of tragedy-ridden Jewish history to contend with, but they must deal with the reality that many Arabs prefer that Israel not exist at all. And as in all democratic societies, Israel's leaders must handle competing domestic concerns and interests, in their case amplified by a multiparty system that requires the government to be the product of a coalition of small political parties, often with competing agendas. As a result U.S. presidents inevitably confront Israeli counterparts who are not as amenable or agreeable as they would like. There always have been and always will be some disagreements.

However, those disagreements have accompanied the U.S.-Israel relationship since day one. They are mostly about strategy, tactics, and personalities, not about the fundamentals of America's relationship with Israel and our commitment to its survival as a Jewish and democratic state.

Obama, like most presidents before him, came into office fully aware that enhancing Israel's ability to secure and defend itself is morally sound and a necessary factor in improving relations between Israel and the Arabs. That was true when Israel made peace with Egypt and Jordan. It has been true in the many interim agreements Israel has signed with the Palestinians. It is equally true, however, that while every U.S. president since 1948 has pursued Arab-Israeli peace, none has been fully successful and all have emerged bruised.

2

EARLY CONFLICT

In early April 1920 Passover, Greek Orthodox Easter, and an annual Muslim procession from Jerusalem to Moses's tomb in Jericho all took place in the same week. The atmosphere in the Old City of Jerusalem, however, was anything but holy. A witness to the rioting and violence that week wrote that he left the scene with his "soul disgusted and depressed by the madness of mankind."[1] By the time authorities managed to restore order, five Jews and four Arabs had been killed; 216 Jews and 23 Arabs were injured; and some 300 Jews were evacuated from Jerusalem.

It is unclear what ignited the violence that week. Some said a Jew pushed an Arab carrying a flag, others that an Arab attacked an elderly Jewish pedestrian. What is clear, though, is that in the preceding years tension and violence between Jewish and Arab communities in the region had increased steadily. Those April

1920 Nebi Musa riots—Nebi Musa is Arabic for "the Prophet Moses"—were evidence of the growing clash of competing yet still nascent Jewish and Arab nationalist agendas. They were an indicator of the relentless conflict to come.

Though heavy with religious undertones, the Israeli-Palestinian conflict is not exclusively religious. Rather it is a conflict of competing nationalities and narratives, of a political and military struggle between two distinct communities over a stretch of land one-tenth the size of Colorado. Many books about the peace process refrain from delving deeply into the origins of the conflict, for good reason: it is hard to get right and even harder to describe in an objective manner.

Embroiled in conflict, both Israelis and Palestinians feel a need to constantly justify the legitimacy of their existence as independent peoples. And too often, doing so means denying the legitimacy of the other's aspirations or connections to the land both call home. History has become a weapon rather than a tool of understanding.

But some things are indisputable: both Israelis and Palestinians have suffered tremendous individual and collective trauma, and not just at the hands of one another. If we are ever to have peace, we must understand why Israelis and Palestinians feel as they do and how those beliefs inform their behavior—to ignore these realities is to render the politics of each side unintelligible and realistic policymaking impossible.

Prior to the twentieth century much of the world was dominated by empires, and what we know as the Middle East was no exception. For over four hundred years it was part of the Ottoman Empire, a Sunni Muslim government based in modern-day Turkey. At its height the empire surpassed its European rivals in power and wealth. Ottoman subjects were ethnically and religiously diverse, and their territory was vast, stretching from the Balkans through modern-day Iraq and from North Africa across the Arabian Peninsula.

Palestine under the Ottomans was not a defined territory but rather denoted the Holy Land embraced by Arabs and Jews alike. Prior to its demise, Ottoman Palestine was divided into three administrative regions: the north was under the provincial authority of Beirut, the south governed from Damascus, and the area surrounding Jerusalem was controlled directly by the Ottoman government in Istanbul.

Ottoman Palestine was, of course, the birthplace of Judaism, the site of the Kingdoms of Israel and Judah, and the First and Second Temples. Even after their forced exile from ancient Israel at the hands of the Roman Empire two thousand years ago, Jews maintained a consistent presence primarily, though not

DECLINE OF THE OTTOMAN EMPIRE

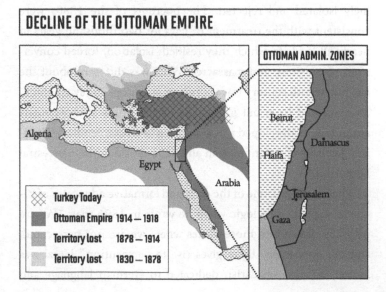

OTTOMAN ADMIN. ZONES

Algeria

Egypt

Arabia

Beirut

Damascus

Haifa

Jerusalem

Gaza

⊠ Turkey Today

Ottoman Empire 1914 — 1918

Territory lost 1878 — 1914

Territory lost 1830 — 1878

exclusively, in the four holy cities of Judaism: Hebron, Tiberius, Safed, and Jerusalem. But the territory was also home to many others, the descendants of those originating in the region or who arrived over the centuries with the conquests of competing empires. They included Canaanites, Philistines, ancient Egyptians, Assyrians, Babylonians, Persians, Greeks, Romans, crusaders, and others. Starting with the conquest and expansion of the Muslim Caliphates in the seventh century, Islam became the dominant religion of the region. By 1890, roughly 432,000 Muslims and 57,000 Christians lived in Ottoman Palestine.[2] The vast majority were culturally and linguistically Arab.

The first wave of new Jewish immigration took place largely as a response to anti-Jewish pogroms and ethnic cleansing in eastern Europe and Russia during the 1880s.[3] For Jews scattered there, the rising nationalisms of the nineteenth century led to increased exclusion and overt anti-Semitism. Even Jews who embraced secularism and sought assimilation found themselves increasingly isolated and rejected. The pogroms of the 1880s were consistent with the treatment of Jews for two thousand years in nearly all lands in which they resided: isolation, forced conversions, expulsions, and massacres. What was different about the late nineteenth century was the response. European Jewish thinkers, alienated from but influenced by the political movements around them, developed a new solution to an old problem: Zionism, Jewish self-determination and nationhood in their ancestral homeland.[4]

Theodor Herzl, one of the early and formative advocates of Zionism, explained its logic when he wrote in 1896 that: "We are naturally drawn into those places where we are not persecuted, and our appearance there gives rise to persecution." Herzl was himself an avid secularist, dedicated to German language and culture. In France, he spent four years as a reporter for a leading Viennese newspaper. Relentless anti-Semitism in Paris, and the rise of hostile demagogues in Vienna, caused Herzl to abandon his belief that liberal European ideals would help liberate and secure Jewish communities. While in Paris, amid the influx of Jewish refugees from the east, he observed a centuries-old cycle: Jews are driven from their homes, settle in friendlier territory, and later face expulsion again. "This is the case," he wrote, "and will inevitably be so, everywhere, even in highly civilized countries—see, for instance, France—so long as the Jewish question is not solved on the political level."[5]

By 1890, alongside the 489,000 predominantly Muslim Arabs living in Ottoman Palestine, there were roughly 43,000 Jews,[6] including some of the first Jews escaping from eastern Europe and Russia. The new Jewish arrivals—for Zionism was quickly and enthusiastically embraced by a minority of Jews who began organizing, raising funds, and lobbying governments for support—were as different from these existing Jewish populations as they were from the Arabs.

The early Zionists were generally secular. They saw their Jewishness as a cultural and ethnic identity grounded in their ancient history and connection to the land. They established new towns and institutions and focused relentlessly on nurturing a growing Jewish national consciousness both within and outside of Palestine. Still, different strands of Zionism with distinct, often adverse goals emerged. Some set statehood as their aim; others emphasized cultural revival in the biblical land of Israel over overt political independence; still others believed in Jewish-Arab socialist unity or the establishment of communal agricultural communities as the key to Jewish salvation.

By the end of Ottoman rule, some eighty-four thousand Jews

were in Palestine,[7] and many more in the diaspora began preparations for immigration. But as Jews continued to immigrate and as
their desire for self-determination, however defined, became apparent, the existing Arab population felt increasingly alarmed and
threatened.

A major factor in Arabs' apprehension was the newcomers'
land acquisition. Not surprisingly, scholars still debate the nature and scope of those purchases, but it is clear that much of the
land acquired by Jews was previously devoid of inhabitants and
uncultivated and required intensive rehabilitation. It is also clear
that earlier reforms within the Ottoman Empire had consolidated
landownership in the hands of distant, wealthier individuals, so
many of the Arab sellers were absentee landowners living in Cairo,
Damascus, or Beirut. They benefited from the sales, but most
local Arab farmers (*fellahin* in Arabic) did not. Jewish acquisitions
from those absentee owners, and the reality that local Arabs were
uninvolved and even at times excluded from new economic and
social enterprises, sparked divisions between the two groups.

There are also, of course, many accounts of Jewish and Arab
cooperation during this time. Some local Arabs, who still greatly
outnumbered Jews, saw the influx of immigrants from Russia and
Europe as an economic boon. And as ideas of autonomy began to
take hold in the wider Arab world, cooperation between Zionists
and Arab nationalists was not uncommon.

Arab nationalism intensified during the waning years of the
Ottoman Empire. Previously their identity had been grounded in
religion, family, clan or tribe, and locality. Most Arabs would have
considered themselves loyal subjects of the Ottoman Empire. But,
as with Jews, the spread of European ideals aroused robust Arab
nationalist dialogues. In 1908 a revolution modernized Ottoman
Istanbul, but many Arab intellectuals and elites considered the

new government too Turkish. Societies promoting greater Arab autonomy within the Ottoman Empire formed in Damascus, Beirut, Jerusalem, Cairo, and elsewhere in response. Their burgeoning nationalism intensified with the influx of Jews and Zionism. In 1913 delegates from these nationalist societies held the National Arab Congress in Paris to consider and advance their political aspirations. Zionist leaders were also in attendance. One year later, almost to the day, World War I broke out.

In the early years of that war Britain and France suffered huge losses on the battlefields. From the beginning those two governments sought help wherever they could find it, and they saw opportunity in the Middle East. But the alliances they entered into, and the conflicting promises they made during the war, raised both Arab and Jewish expectations of independence.

When the Ottomans sided with Germany during the war, persuading Arab inhabitants of the empire to revolt became an important British military objective. In addition to depleting Ottoman resources and precipitating the empire's collapse, an alliance with the Arabs would remake the balance of power in the region to favor Britain and France, particularly Britain, which already had a colonial presence in Egypt.

In 1915 the British high commissioner in Egypt, Henry McMahon, was dispatched to the Arabian Peninsula to encourage and negotiate the terms of an Arab revolt, well aware that Arabs were beginning to agitate for autonomy. Emir Hussein, the Hashemite Arab tribal leader in part of what is today Saudi Arabia, met McMahon with little hesitation. In a letter later confirming their agreement, McMahon wrote to Emir Hussein that the British government would "recognize and support the independence of the Arabs within the territories in the limits and boundaries proposed by" the emir, although some districts, "cannot be said to be purely Arab, and must on that account be excepted from the proposed limits and boundaries."[8] In 1916, under Hashemite leadership, thousands of Arab fighters attacked Ottoman army and military installations in the Arabian Peninsula and nearby territories, initiating a revolt that lasted until the collapse of the empire in 1918. The emir and his Arab allies believed that, in exchange, the British had committed to supporting Arab independence in the region, extending from modern-day Iraq through Syria and the Arabian Peninsula.

For years Zionists had sought a commitment from the British government, then still regarded as the dominant world power, to support a Jewish state in Palestine. Britain's interest in the Zionists, as with the Arabs, rose as its losses mounted in the war. Ironically the British prime minister David Lloyd George came to back a Jewish national homeland in part because he believed an age-old canard of inflated Jewish power. He later testified that he was motivated to back Zionist aims in order to encourage support for Britain from the United States and Russia, both of which had sizeable Jewish populations. Lloyd George's conversations with Zionist leaders culminated in 1917 with a letter from the British foreign secretary Lord Balfour to Baron Walter Rothschild, a leader of Britain's Jewish community. The letter expressed support for "the establishment in Palestine of a national home for the Jewish people," subject to its "being clearly understood that nothing shall be done which may prejudice the civil and religious rights of existing non-Jewish communities in Palestine, or the rights and political status enjoyed by Jews in any other country."[9]

Few documents have been subjected to the microscopic analysis accorded the Balfour Declaration or McMahon's letter to Emir Hussein in the century since they were issued. What does a Jewish "national home" mean? How could this be accomplished without "prejudice [to] the civil and religious rights of existing non-Jewish communities in Palestine"? What are the areas "not purely Arab" excluded from Britain's commitment to the Hashemite emir?

The apparently contradictory positions taken by the British government in the McMahon-Hussein negotiations and the Balfour Declaration were further complicated by the Sykes-Picot Agreement, signed in 1916 (and named after the British and French diplomats who negotiated it). Under the treaty's terms, Britain, France, and later Russia agreed to divide among themselves control of the lands of the Ottoman Empire once they won the war. Palestine, they agreed, would be under international administration. Although the agreement itself was subsequently repudiated, Britain and France received mandates from the League of Nations in 1922 to govern most of the region.

Modern-day Lebanon and Syria would fall under French

LEAGUE OF NATIONS MANDATES (1922)

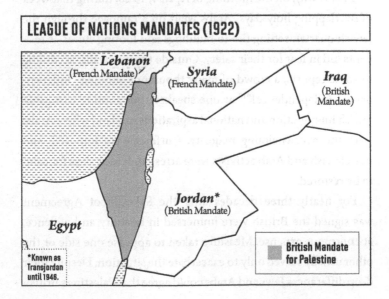

Lebanon (French Mandate)

Syria (French Mandate)

Iraq (British Mandate)

Jordan* (British Mandate)

Egypt

*Known as Transjordan until 1946.

British Mandate for Palestine

control; Israel, the Palestinian territories, and Jordan under the British. Initially the British planned to include modern-day Jordan within the boundaries of Palestine, but in trying to make good on McMahon's promise to the Hashemite emir, the British installed his son Abdullah as the king of Jordan and his other son, Faisal, as king of Iraq. Neither Iraq nor Jordan had previously existed as independent nations.

The establishment of the British Mandate for Palestine gave the territory—for the first time in history—specific borders and a single governing authority. Both Jews and Arabs within those borders would lay claim to it. The Arabs in Palestine were less unified in their goals than the Zionists came to be; many prominent Arab nationalists, for example, advocated for Palestine's inclusion in greater Syria. Still, whatever form they wanted for their independence, Palestinian Arabs agreed they did not want to be dispossessed by the Jews.

That is why, on the morning of April 4, 1920, during that week of overlapping holy days, Arabs went on a rampage through the Jewish quarter, setting fire to buildings and looting stores as residents hid in fear for their safety. Outside the city walls, according to some reports, a crowd of many thousands shouted "Independence! Independence!"[10] as one speaker after another castigated Jewish immigration and national aspirations in a land where Arabs were the overwhelming majority. Curfews were imposed, and both Jewish and Arab activists were arrested. It took days for calm to be restored.

For nearly three decades after the Sykes-Picot Agreement was signed the British were immersed in hostility and violence, at enormous expense. Measures taken to appease one side or the other usually served only to exacerbate the situation. Despite their deep differences Jews and Arabs could agree that Palestine's British rulers were illegitimate and their leadership biased, incompetent, or both. From the beginning of British control in Palestine in 1918 to the end of the official Mandate in 1948, the British struggled unsuccessfully to contain the tensions.

For the Zionists establishment of a Jewish state became all the more urgent after World War I. Worsening economies in Germany and Poland—not to mention the rise of Nazism and the pervasive anti-Semitic propaganda and anti-Jewish laws that accompanied it—sent ever-increasing numbers of Jews fleeing from Europe to settle in Palestine. But Arab trepidation rose alongside Jewish immigration; the violence of the Nebi Musa riots in 1920 paled in comparison to that of the 1930s. Thousands lost their lives. Several times, in response to violence and pressure, the British tried to limit Jewish entry to Palestine. This of course angered the Jewish inhabitants, who then more aggressively strengthened their own political and military institutions. A militia called Haganah (Hebrew for "defense") was created to protect the Jewish community in Palestine, the Yishuv, and to promote immigration; later it played a major role in Israel's War of Independence.

In 1936 the British established a commission to investigate the cause of unrest in Palestine. Lord Peel, the commission's leader and namesake, wrote that "Though the Arabs have benefited by the development of the country owing to Jewish immigration"— and indeed Arab immigration to Palestine was also on the rise— "this has had no conciliatory effect. On the contrary, improvement in the economic situation in Palestine has meant the deterioration of the political situation."[11] The Peel Commission ultimately attributed the cause of Arab rioting to

first, the desire of the Arabs for national independence; secondly, their antagonism to the establishment of the Jewish

National Home in Palestine, quickened by their fear of Jewish domination. Among contributory causes were the effect on Arab opinion of the attainment of national independence by Iraq, Trans-Jordan, Egypt, Syria and the Lebanon; the rush of Jewish immigrants escaping from Central and Eastern Europe; the inequality of opportunity enjoyed by Arabs and Jews respectively in placing their case before [His] Majesty's Government and the public; the growth of Arab mistrust; Arab alarm at the continued purchase of Arab land by the intensive character and the "modernism" of Jewish nationalism; and lastly the general uncertainty, accentuated by the ambiguity of certain phrases in the Mandate, as to the ultimate intentions of the Mandatory Power.[12]

Two years after the report's publication, in 1939, the British made a significant gesture to the Arabs by renouncing Britain's commitment to a Jewish national homeland in Palestine and restricting the number of Jews allowed to immigrate to the area to 75,000 over five years. For Jews the timing could not have been worse.

World War II was a turning point. The Yishuv and its leaders supported the Allies; some 5,000 fought alongside the British. The Arab states were split; some supported the Allies, including with a few thousand soldiers, but more supported the Axis powers. Most notable among the latter was Haj Amin al-Husseini, the grand mufti of Jerusalem, who spent the war years in Germany colluding with senior figures in the Nazi regime.

After the war, widespread international criticism of Britain's restrictions on Jewish immigration to Palestine, which had resulted in the rejection of countless Jews trying to flee the Holocaust, added to British discontent over the Mandate. It didn't help that at its peak the British military force in Palestine exceeded 100,000 troops—a huge expense for a country reeling from the cost of World War II. Discontent within Palestine was growing too. Several Jewish paramilitary factions, organized in response to the earlier Arab uprisings and what they viewed as passivity by the Zionist establishment, began a campaign of violence to force the British to withdraw; Menachem Begin and Yitzhak Shamir, both of whom would later be elected prime minister, were among the leaders of these groups. To the British these organizations were terrorists; to mainstream Zionists they were traitors. Their most publicized attack was the 1946 bombing of the British military headquarters at the King David Hotel in Jerusalem, in which ninety-one people died. In Britain the desire to withdraw intensified, and in 1947 the government announced that it would leave Palestine the following year and asked the United Nations to decide what should replace the British administration there.

On November 29, 1947, the UN General Assembly adopted Resolution 181, proposing that Britain's Mandate be replaced by a plan of partition under which there would be an independent Arab state, an independent Jewish state, and an international regime for the city of Jerusalem. Even though two-thirds of their allocated land was desert, Zionist leaders accepted the UN's Partition Plan; they were desperate to build their state and were focused on absorbing hundreds of thousands of refugees. But the Arabs viewed partition as fundamentally unjust. They believed they were the rightful inheritors of Ottoman lands and that partition prioritized Jewish self-determination over their own. The 600,000 Jews in all of Palestine in 1947 constituted only 30 percent of the total population, yet they received close to 60 percent of the land. Even just within territory allocated for the Jewish state, Palestinian Arabs accounted for some 45 percent of the population. Thus the UN

1947 UN PARTITION PLAN (RESOLUTION 181)

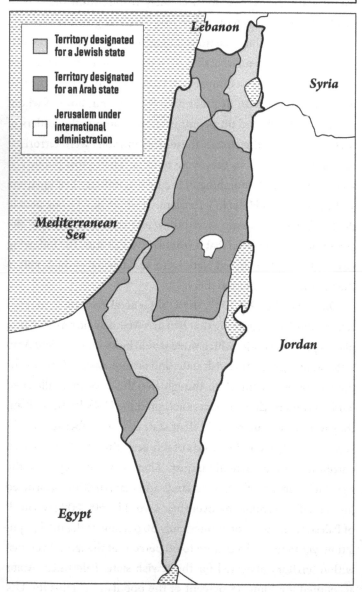

Territory designated for a Jewish state

Territory designated for an Arab state

Jerusalem under international administration

Lebanon

Syria

Mediterranean Sea

Jordan

Egypt

resolution triggered a civil war between Arabs and Jews in Palestine, in which surrounding Arab governments participated. Thousands were killed, including civilians.

Desperate to disengage, the British gradually withdrew their forces. When the last contingent left Palestine on May 14, 1948, David Ben-Gurion publicly proclaimed the establishment of the state of Israel within the borders set by the UN Partition Plan. The following day the surrounding Arab states together launched a war to reverse Palestine's partition and undo Israel's independence. Overnight Israelis transitioned from celebrating their independence to fighting for their lives.

Israel's military hardware was inferior and its troops were outnumbered by the Arabs many times over. But the Israelis were not defenseless; the previous decades of intercommunal violence had stimulated robust defense preparations, training, and the accumulation of weapons by Zionist organizations. The Haganah was reconstituted as the Israel Defense Forces, and members of fringe Jewish paramilitary groups were forced to disband and join the state's new army. One out of ten Jewish Israelis, many recently liberated from concentration camps in Europe, were mobilized to defend their new homeland. For the brand-new state of Israel the war was a desperate matter of survival or annihilation.

But the armies of the Arab states were uncoordinated, and their disunity crippled their war effort. When Ben-Gurion said he had a secret weapon and was asked to identify it he replied, "The Arabs." Midway through the war the Israelis managed to secure formidable weapons from Czechoslovakia, and by the following spring the IDF had prevailed on all fronts, pushing back the Arab armies and considerably expanding the territory under Israel's control. Once a truce was declared and armistice agreements with neighboring states were signed, Israel's portion of the former British Mandate had increased from 56 to 78 percent. No Palestinian state would emerge in the 22 percent that remained in Arab hands following the war. Instead, the Old City of Jerusalem and the West Bank were absorbed by Jordan and the Gaza Strip by Egypt.

For Israel victory was euphoric and liberating. For the Palestinians it was a national tragedy they still refer to as al-Nakba, "the catastrophe." During the war 710,000 Arabs living in Israel became refugees. To this day Palestinians tell of the making of their own diaspora: how they were systematically expelled from their homes by the IDF or fled when accounts spread of indiscriminate attacks on Arab villages. Many Palestinian refugees continue to hold on to keys to homes in villages that no longer exist.

The Israelis of course have a different perspective on what caused the Palestinian exodus. They point to the tens of thousands who began leaving even before the war broke out, encouraged by Arab states promising they could return once Israel was defeated. Some Israelis recite accounts of Jews pleading with their Arab neighbors to stay. They insist that instances of expulsion or intimidation were isolated, uncoordinated, and a tragic consequence of a war they did not start.

Relations between Israel and the Arab states remained entirely hostile for decades thereafter. Some 800,000 Jews living in Arab countries were expelled, fled, or left their homes during this period. With some exceptions, the Jews of the Middle East and North Africa had for centuries been treated at best as second-class citizens, often far worse. But amid war with Israel the Jews of the Arab world were no longer tolerated. The vast majority of these Jewish refugees found sanctuary in Israel. A smaller portion went to Europe, and even fewer to the United States.

Israel's victory over the Arabs in 1948 and 1956 fueled deep

RESULT OF THE 1948 WAR

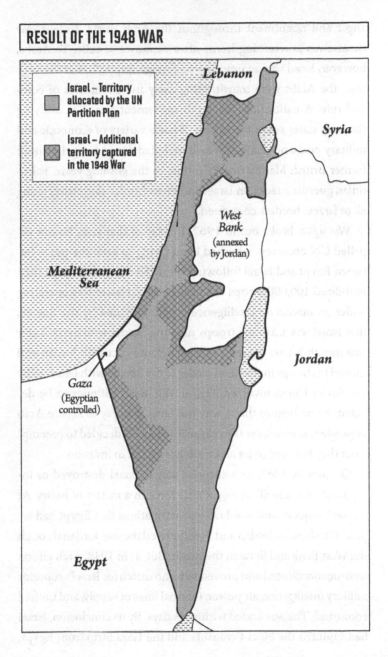

Israel – Territory allocated by the UN Partition Plan

Israel – Additional territory captured in the 1948 War

Lebanon

Syria

Mediterranean Sea

West Bank (annexed by Jordan)

Jordan

Gaza (Egyptian controlled)

Egypt

anger and resentment throughout the Arab world. Israelis saw themselves as returning home after centuries of exile. To Arabs, however, Israel was an unwelcome foreign imposition at the very time the Arabs were transitioning away from centuries of colonial rule. A nationalist, pan-Arab movement aimed at unifying the Arab states swept the region. It had a variety of economic and military goals, not least of which included recapturing the entire former British Mandate of Palestine. In the ensuing years, Palestinian guerilla attacks on Israel and cross-border skirmishes along all of Israel's borders continued.

War again broke out in 1967. In May of that year, Nasser expelled UN observers who had been trying to keep the peace between Egypt and Israel following the 1956 Suez War. Egypt then mobilized 100,000 troops in the peninsula. Nasser was operating under an inaccurate intelligence report provided by the Soviets that Israel was amassing troops near the border with Syria. Later that month Nasser signed a mutual defense pact with Jordan and moved his troops in the Sinai closer to the border with Israel. Why the Soviet Union involved itself in this way continues to be debated. Some believe that a war was seen as a way to secure Arab dependence. Whatever the reason, the Israelis decided to preempt what they believed to be an imminent Egyptian invasion.

On June 6, 1967, in a surprise attack, Israel destroyed or incapacitated nearly all of Egypt's air force in a matter of hours. At Nasser's request, and amid false proclamations that Egypt had repelled the Israelis, Jordan and Syria entered the war, Jordan through the West Bank and Syria in the north. But, as in 1948, Arab efforts were uncoordinated and proved to be no match for Israel's superior military intelligence, air power, internal lines of supply, and unified command. The war ended within six days. By its conclusion, Israel had captured the Sinai Peninsula and the Gaza Strip from Egypt,

RESULT OF THE 1967 WAR

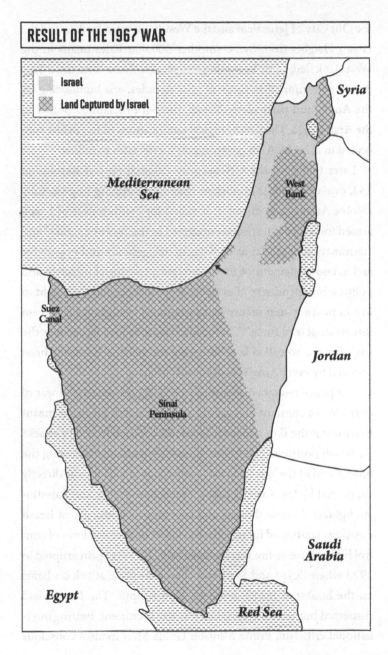

Israel

Land Captured by Israel

Syria

Mediterranean
Sea

West
Bank

Suez
Canal

Jordan

Sinai
Peninsula

Saudi
Arabia

Egypt

Red Sea

the Old City of Jerusalem and the West Bank from Jordan, and the Golan Heights from Syria. Another 300,000 Palestinians in the West Bank fled, some becoming refugees for the second time. This defeat, even more than those of prior decades, was humiliating for the Arabs, and particularly Nasser, the self-proclaimed unifier of the Arab world. The psychological ramifications of the defeat continued to echo for Arab governments for decades to follow.

Later that year, the UN Security Council passed Resolution 242, one of the most important resolutions aiming to peacefully resolve Arab-Israeli disputes. It called for "withdrawal of Israeli armed forces from territories occupied in the recent conflict" and "termination of all claims or states of belligerency and respect for and acknowledgment of the sovereignty, territorial integrity and political independence of every State in the area and their right to live in peace within secure and recognized boundaries free from threats or acts of force." The resolution continues to serve as the basis for the so-called land-for-peace model that has since been pursued by every American administration.

But peace remained elusive. In 1969, Egypt declared a war of attrition—a constant barrage of attacks on Israeli positions meant to wear out the IDF and push Israel out of Sinai. In reality attacks on Israeli positions had begun almost immediately following the official end of the war two years earlier. Egypt's effort was directly supported by the Soviet Union, several Arab states, and Palestinian fighters. Intense shelling and land and air raids against Israeli positions continued for months but failed to alter any lines of control before a cease-fire was declared in 1970. War again erupted in 1973 when Egypt and Syria launched a surprise attack on Israel on the holiest of Jewish holidays, Yom Kippur. The Israelis had suspected but were not certain a war was imminent. Fearing international criticism, Prime Minister Golda Meir made a conscious decision not to launch a preemptive strike, as Israel had done in 1967. To this day that decision is almost universally condemned in Israel. It took the IDF days to fully mobilize, while Egypt managed to push Israeli forces back from the frontiers of the Suez Canal. Despite the fact that Israel retained almost all of the Sinai and made advances even deeper into Egypt, the IDF's near-perfect military record was shattered.

Today, almost 100 years after the collapse of the Ottoman Empire, control of the Holy Land remains in bitter dispute. Palestinians continue to mourn a country that has yet to come into existence. Israelis continue to feel under siege and rejected by their neighbors. Both see themselves as victims.

3

MOVING IN OPPOSITE DIRECTIONS

The first decades of Israel's existence were difficult. Hostile neighbors remained intent on destroying the young state from the outside, while severe economic distress threatened it with collapse from within. The 1948 War required the participation of the entire nation. So did the absorption of the 700,000 Jewish refugees and immigrants who poured in from Europe and the Arab world in the first years of Israel's existence. Within three years Israel's Jewish population doubled. The overwhelming majority of these newcomers arrived with little more than a suitcase and the clothes on their back. Refugee camps and absorption centers were established throughout the country, though many lived in abject poverty in tents. These new Israelis spoke dozens of different languages but little, if any, Hebrew. Unemployment was high and Israel's foreign cash reserves for imports almost nonexistent. Striking the right balance between defense spending and caring for the basic needs of the population led to prolonged periods of government austerity. Many nonessential food items were banned; coupons were required for purchases; the government struggled to enforce rationing of 1,600 calories per citizen per day. U.S. assistance consisted almost entirely of desperately needed food aid. This precarious existence mobilized greater levels of support from the Jewish diaspora.

Especially after World War II Jews around the world wondered whether their communities would have suffered pogroms and genocide if a strong Jewish state with a formidable military had been in existence decades earlier. Many saw Israel as a sort of insurance policy they should invest and participate in, so there would always be a homeland to return to if their existence in the diaspora was ever threatened again. Most Jews decided not to move to Israel, but almost all embraced the goals of Zionism. As a result financial backing from Jews around the world, in the form of bond purchases and private donations, poured in. That support, as well as billions in reparations from the German government, helped pull Israel out of austerity and enabled considerable investment in the state's development.

Meanwhile the Palestinians too were struggling with a new reality, where one out of two was a refugee. Unlike Israelis, the Palestinians had no representative body to advocate for their needs and interests. Members of the same family were often split between host countries and refugee camps. From the beginning the Arab states made clear they had no intention of providing a haven for the Palestinians. Their goal was to overcome what they saw as the temporary setback of the 1948 war, to defeat Israel, and to eventually recover what they believed was rightfully their territory. With no one else providing for the needs of the Palestinian refugees, the

UN stepped in, establishing the Relief Works Agency (UNRWA—
"uhn-rah") in 1950 to spur Palestinian employment through work
programs in their new homes. UNRWA's long-term goal was for
Palestinian self-sufficiency to replace international emergency
aid. But that was a goal the Arab states generally opposed; they
championed the Palestinian cause but saw employment projects
as a means of integration into their societies and the prelude to
permanent resettlement, which directly undermined the objective
of Palestinian repatriation. The bulk of the UNRWA's work was
therefore restricted to aid distribution.

The Arab states would not allow Palestinian refugees to assimi-
late, and Israel prevented their return.

From Israel's perspective, the Arabs were to blame for the Palestinian refugee crisis, a view strongly contested by the Arabs. But
the Israelis were concerned about demographics: the return of
all 710,000 Palestinian refugees would erode the Jewish majority within the border lines drawn at the conclusion of the 1948
War. The 160,000 Palestinians who remained within the Jewish
state became Israeli citizens. Israel's Declaration of Independence
granted equality to Jews and non-Jews alike and promised protec-
tion of minority and religious rights. But Palestinian Israelis were
viewed as a security risk and until 1966 Arab population centers in
Israel were governed under martial law, which included curfews,
travel restrictions, and close monitoring. Aside from a limited
number of family reunifications, both Israel and the Arab states
generally forbade cross-border travel, and mail and phone connections were not readily available.

Arab countries bestowed their own mix of rights on the Palestinian refugees in their midst. Egypt, for instance, restricted Palestinian entry from Gaza. With Israel bordering the remainder of the
Strip, the Palestinians there were effectively stuck. Throughout

the region the refugees were largely separated from the host population economically, politically, and legally. Most relied on UNRWA for survival.

Jordan was the exception. In a move condemned by other Arab leaders, the Hashemite Kingdom granted full citizenship to Palestinians, including those living in its new West Bank frontier, more than doubling the country's population. Jordan's Palestinians became an integral part of society and had a transformational impact on the politics, socioeconomics, and culture of the kingdom. The capital city of Amman tripled in size by 1950 and Palestinians began to populate and build out urban centers throughout the country.

At the same time, on both banks of the Jordan River, hundreds of thousands remained in refugee camps, dependent on international assistance for basic sustenance. Clusters of Palestinian guerrilla fighters, known as Fedayeen, began to form in the region and engaged in cross-border skirmishes against Israel from Egypt's Sinai, Lebanon's south, and Jordan's West Bank. Many Fedayeen initially subscribed to Nasser's pan-Arabism, which viewed Palestine as a distinct but component part of a unified Arab homeland. But Yasser Arafat and several other Fedayeen fighters became increasingly agitated that Nasser and the other Arab leaders were not more aggressive against Israel, despite their fierce rhetoric. So in 1959 Arafat formed Fatah, a Palestinian nationalist group with an agenda distinct and independent from the pan-Arabists'. Fatah's stated aim was to liberate Palestine—to defeat and replace Israel—for the Palestinian people and by their own initiative. Almost immediately Fatah began to launch attacks on Israel.

When Israel captured the West Bank and Gaza Strip in 1967, most Palestinian Fedayeen and political groups lost whatever remained of their faith in the Arab states' resolve in fighting Israel.

The Jewish state's near instant victory over the Arabs, perhaps more than any other event, helped to solidify among Palestinians Arafat's independent brand of nationalism.

The Palestine Liberation Organization had been founded in 1964 with Nasser's help to represent the interests of the Palestinian people. When Arafat became chairman in 1968, he transformed the PLO into an umbrella organization of political and guerrilla groups. Fatah was devoutly socialist and the largest faction within the organization; other factions adopted different platforms. However, all the factions in the PLO agreed on Palestinian independence and determined opposition to Israel's existence through armed struggle. The PLO's charter declares that the "Zionist entity" is "null and void" and that "the claim of a historical or spiritual tie between Jews and Palestine [is] incompatible with the facts of history. . . . Judaism, being a religion, is not an independent nationality. Nor do Jews constitute a single nation with an identity of its own; they are citizens of the states to which they belong."

For the quarter-century following its formation, the PLO waged a relentless campaign of guerrilla warfare against Israel. It gained international infamy in the 1970s for commercial airplane hijackings, hostage taking, and the killing of civilians. Israelis and Jews around the world were targeted, but casualties often included others. One of the most publicized acts was the murder of Israeli athletes at the 1972 Olympic Games in Munich by a now defunct PLO faction called Black September.

Throughout the 1970s, Arafat's political and militant activism rendered him a household name across the world and a national hero of the Palestinian people. The Palestinian diaspora felt betrayed and forgotten. They hoped armed resistance would lead to a return to their homes and land they believed had been stolen and to reunions with loved ones separated by borders and status. The PLO, meanwhile, actively nurtured the Palestinian national identity throughout the region.

Even before the 1967 War, King Hussein of Jordan was worried about what Arafat's brand of independent Palestinian nationalism would mean for the Hashemite Kingdom, where Palestinian citizens were a majority. After 1967 Hussein watched with concern as the PLO's popularity and authority grew throughout his country; he was constrained in his response, however, in part by complicated intra-Arab politics. Egypt remained one of the PLO's most steadfast backers and, although Egypt and Jordan had fought Israel together in the Six-Day War, Nasser's pan-Arab populism viewed Jordan's monarchy with contempt. Following Nasser's death in 1970, Palestinian groups increasingly questioned the legitimacy of continued Hashemite rule in Jordan. After surviving several assassination attempts, Hussein embarked on an aggressive campaign to drive the PLO out of his country. The result was an intense civil war marked by combat between the Jordanian Army and thousands of Palestinian fighters in the streets of Amman and other urban centers in Jordan. Thousands died and many more were injured. The internal conflict nearly ignited a regional war when Syria threatened intervention on the PLO's behalf, and Israel announced that it would intervene to stop the Syrians. U.S. and Soviet naval forces were deployed to the region, prepared to back opposing sides. In 1971, one year after the campaign began, Jordan succeeded in expelling the PLO and thousands of its fighters and activists.

Weakened and in disarray, the Palestinian leadership regrouped in Lebanon. Bordering Israel to the north, Lebanon, a country of roughly two million people at the time, was home to several hundred thousand Palestinian refugees and therefore was a natural base of popular support. The PLO was assertive and had effective autonomy in its Lebanese enclaves; as in Jordan, the PLO presence resembled a state within the state. From their strongholds in west Beirut and the refugee camps, Arafat and the PLO continued to organize politically and coordinate attacks on Israel.

But Lebanon in the 1970s was divided along sectarian and political lines, as several factions vied for power. Some controlled militias that fought each other from time to time. In 1975 the violence spiraled into civil war among various coalitions of Lebanese militias and external influences; prominent in this mix were PLO paramilitary factions.

The IDF briefly entered southern Lebanon in 1978, pursuing a group of Fatah militants that had infiltrated Israel by sea and killed thirty-seven Israelis. In the following four years, amid the already complex Lebanese Civil War, Israel persistently targeted PLO positions but was unable to completely halt Palestinian attacks. So the IDF's strategy in 1982 was to lay siege to Beirut in order to force the PLO out of Lebanon. It took two months before Arafat and some 11,000 PLO fighters and political affiliates left Lebanon, as they had left Jordan in the prior decade. Arafat fled to Greece and then to Tunisia, where he regathered the PLO factions and reconstituted the organization's headquarters. Unlike in Lebanon or Jordan, however, the PLO's base in Tunisia was as far removed from the Palestinian people it represented as it was from the state of Israel it was determined to defeat.

Israel's economic performance in the first decades of its existence was as impressive as its military might. Its annual GDP growth averaged close to 10 percent in the 1950s and 1960s, at that time second in the world to Japan's rate. A 1968 World Bank mission described Israel's performance as an "economic miracle" enabled by an influx of foreign capital and "a capable and determined population with a broad base of well-educated and energetic people who proved able to overcome the difficulties of economic development with great ingenuity."[1] Israel signed free trade agreements with Europe in 1975 and with the United States in 1985.

Of course, Israel still faced serious challenges. Its economy slowed in the 1970s and 1980s as it contended with a tense security environment, extremely high defense spending, and rising inflation. Their "economic miracle" did not extend to the Palestinians in the West Bank and Gaza, where living standards had improved but lagged far behind that of Israelis. Israel's position overall, though, was strong and improving. Its 1979 peace agreement with Egypt ushered in a thaw in Arab-Israeli relations and resulted in an annual provision of robust financial and military assistance from the U.S. government, a practice that continues to this day.

The Palestinians, though, saw the Egyptian-Israeli agreement as an abandonment of their cause. While Egypt regained the Sinai Peninsula, the Palestinian people in Gaza and the West Bank remained under Israel's control and their refugees continued to languish in camps throughout the region. Throughout this period the possibility of relinquishing control over the West Bank and Gaza was not seriously considered by any mainstream Israeli political party.

Israel disagreed with the international consensus that the West Bank and Gaza Strip were occupied territories. The West Bank is the heart of biblical Judea and Samaria; religious and archaeological sites revered by religious Jews and secular nationalists dot its landscape. Israeli leaders asserted that the "land for peace" model of UN Security Council Resolution 242 was satisfied when Israel relinquished control of the Sinai Peninsula to Egypt in 1982.

Resolution 242, they argued, called for their withdrawal "from territories," not "from *the* territories," obligating them to return some but not all of the lands captured in 1967. They could not accept handing territory over to the Palestinians. The exhausting wars of attrition and Fedayeen guerrilla campaigns cautioned against Israeli territorial concessions just miles from Israel's population centers.

To retain control of the territories the Israelis began building settlements throughout the West Bank and Gaza Strip and invested heavily in infrastructure there. While almost all others viewed the territories as occupied under international law, Israel was determined to make the West Bank an inseparable part of the territory under its control. But of course they had built settlements and invested in the Sinai Peninsula before ultimately withdrawing in exchange for peace with Egypt. Many foreign policy analysts assumed that the same would happen with the West Bank when the right time and terms arose. In the decades following the 1967 War diplomacy was not focused on a Palestinian state; of greater concern were ending the instability of recurring Egyptian-Israeli wars, preventing a cold war escalation, and preserving the regional balance of power.

With a rapidly developing economy in Israel and a poorer Palestinian population in the West Bank and Gaza under Israel's control, the Palestinian economy became increasingly dependent on Israel. Soon after the 1967 War, Palestinians found low-skilled jobs in the Jewish state, including in construction of the very settlements they saw as expropriating their land. By the end of the 1980s over 40 percent of the Palestinian labor force crossed daily from the West Bank or Gaza into Israel. Markets in Palestinian towns were easily accessible to Israelis and became popular destinations for lower-cost consumer goods and services. The entirety of the British Mandate for Palestine prior to partition had essentially been reconstituted, this time under full Israeli control.

For some Israelis that had been the dream all along. When the UN revealed the proposed borders under its Partition Plan in 1947, Begin accused mainstream Zionist leaders who accepted it of betraying their cause. He had lost his mother, father, and sister in the Holocaust and believed that "the world will never pity slaughtered Jews."[2] Only through strength and control could Jews secure their own future; partition would leave Israel vulnerable to attack. The years of war with the surrounding Arab states validated Begin's beliefs. He had surprised many when, as prime minister, he overrode protests within his own coalition and gave up Sinai for peace with Egypt—but Sinai had never been part of the British Mandate. He had no inclination and felt no obligation to concede anything to the Palestinians.

The Israelis have built a strong, successful, and diverse state with sophisticated institutions and involved citizens. In 2015 the Organization for Economic Cooperation and Development ranked Israel as the fifth happiest country in the world, trailing only Denmark, Finland, Iceland, and Switzerland.[3] Israel's GDP has increased over tenfold since the 1980s, and its per capita income now rivals that of Europe. Today Israel boasts one of the most advanced economies in the world, responsible for groundbreaking technological innovations in fields as diverse as agriculture and medicine. Israelis take pride in the fact that their saturation of high-tech and start-up companies ranks just behind that of Silicon Valley and that their country boasts the third highest number of companies listed on the NASDAQ behind only the United States and China. Israel's universities are among the best in the world, and it has the highest number per capita of scientists and published scientific papers. The Jewish state is one of just ten countries to independently launch its own satellites into space.

Israel's military consistently ranks among the most powerful. There is little doubt that the nation could defeat its neighbors in conventional wars and that the IDF is the major power in the Middle East. Of course U.S. assistance has contributed greatly to Israel's military might, but so too has Israel's own investment in its homegrown defense capabilities. Indeed Israel's domestic defense industry is thriving, often producing equipment and technology sought by countries many times larger, including the United States. Compared to the circumstances that existed at the time of Israel's birth, its current economic prowess and military dominance are astonishing. It is hard to believe that the country was once dependent on food aid from the United States.

With respect to the Palestinian issue, however, a gap has developed between Israel and its major allies. The occupation has lasted for a half century and it has been humiliating for the Palestinians on an individual level and as a people. Israeli security measures in Palestinian territories—checkpoints, roadblocks, and the like—serve to protect Israel. But many of those measures are also in place to protect settlers scattered through the West Bank and have had an adverse effect on the Palestinian economy, restricting their movement and their access to lands for agriculture and for other purposes.

In the 1980s many in the United States and Israel considered a two-state solution to be extreme, even inconceivable. Arafat and the PLO fighters were regarded as terrorists and a threat to regional and international security, certainly not capable of governing a state. In 1982 President Reagan presented a peace plan that did not include statehood for Palestinians; instead it proposed limited Palestinian self-governance under the sovereignty of Jordan. But for Begin even limited Palestinian autonomy was unthinkable.

Two decades later George W. Bush became the first U.S. president to call for an independent Palestinian state in the West Bank and Gaza. Most other countries had reached that conclusion before then, but for the president of the world's superpower and Israel's closest ally to explicitly identify and support such a goal was a significant turning point. Since then even the parameters of that solution and the recognition of Palestine as an independent state are readily and repeatedly declared even by Israel's closest partners.

When the armistice lines were drawn at the conclusion of the 1948 War, Israel and the Arabs agreed that they were "not to be construed in any sense as a political or territorial boundary." Yet that is exactly what they have become. In 2009 the EU's Foreign Affairs Council declared that it "will not recognize any changes to the pre-1967 borders including with regard to Jerusalem, other than those agreed by the parties," with those "pre-1967" borders being the lines drawn at the conclusion of Israel's War of Independence, giving the West Bank and Gaza to the Arabs.[4]

In 2014 the European Parliament voted 498 to 88 to support recognition of the state of Palestine based on the 1967 lines, irrespective of a peace agreement or Israeli concessions. The British Parliament did the same in a 274 to 12 vote.[5] Those votes were nonbinding, but they nevertheless reveal a clear change in European and British positions from those of earlier decades. That same year Sweden recognized Palestine, the first major Western European government to officially do so. Since Prime Minister Netanyahu took power in 2009, twenty-seven more countries plus the Vatican have recognized Palestine. Today a total of 136 countries recognize Palestine; 160 recognize Israel.

Despite intense opposition by the United States and Israel, in November 2012, 138 countries voted for a UN General Assembly resolution that elevated Palestinian status in the UN to that of a nonmember observer state, a status shared only by the Vatican. And in September 2015, the UN General Assembly voted 119 to 8 (with 45 abstaining) to permit Palestinians to raise their national flag in front of UN headquarters in New York.[6]

When Begin rejected the Reagan Plan, he could not have imagined the extent to which, over the next few decades, as Israel became militarily dominant, a global consensus would coalesce not just around Palestinian autonomy, but unambiguously in favor of an independent, sovereign Palestinian state in the West Bank, East Jerusalem, and the Gaza Strip.

4

FROM MADRID TO CAMP DAVID

"We come to Madrid on a mission of hope to begin work on a just, lasting, and comprehensive settlement to the conflict in the Middle East." President George H. W. Bush was addressing Israeli and Arab leaders gathered at a peace conference in Madrid in 1991. "We come here to seek peace for a part of the world that in the long memory of man has known far too much hatred, anguish, and war."[1] Those are words that today could easily be repeated verbatim by any U.S. president, but sadly with more proof of concept, for in the intervening twenty-five years there has been much, much more of hatred, anguish, and war.

"Peace will only come as the result of direct negotiations, compromise, give-and-take," Bush continued. "Peace cannot be imposed from the outside by the United States or anyone else. While we will continue to do everything possible to help the parties overcome obstacles, peace must come from within."

Decade after decade the entire world has watched and shared in the highs and lows of Israeli-Palestinian peacemaking and war. Yet despite the setbacks, impasses, and violence, this conflict is not as cyclical as it may initially appear. There has been a steady movement toward finding common ground, each initiative and negotiation building on earlier efforts.

In Israel the Likud Party controlled the government almost un-interrupted from 1977 until 1992. Begin retired in 1983, leaving Yitzhak Shamir at the helm of their party. Like Begin's, most of Shamir's immediate family had been killed in the Holocaust, and his overriding belief was in peace through strength. To that end Shamir idealized the Greater Land of Israel from his earliest days as a Zionist activist and militant. He opposed territorial conces-sions as a matter of principle and even abstained from the vote approving Israel's treaty with Egypt and its return of the Sinai Pen-insula. Creating settlements throughout the territories, facts on the ground to ensure Israeli control, was a priority throughout his tenure. As prime minister Shamir scorned "land for peace," push-ing instead for "land and peace": Palestinian self-rule under Israel's control.

That possibility could not have been further from his mind, though, when the First Palestinian Intifada erupted in 1987. The uprising was sparked when an IDF truck patrolling a refugee camp in the West Bank collided with a vehicle, killing four Palestinian civilians. Protests reflecting grassroots resentment against Israeli rule quickly spread into civil disobedience, rioting, and violence throughout the Palestinian territories. Israel responded with an unprecedented deployment of tens of thousands of soldiers throughout the territories and in Palestinian cities. IDF troops equipped with armored vehicles and tanks clashed with Palestinians throwing Molotov cocktails and stones and burning tires on the street. Policies of mass arrests, curfews, and cuts in services proved ineffective.

In November 1988 the PLO unilaterally declared Palestinian statehood and—after a decade of maintaining a general policy of rejecting talks with Israel, its goal being to defeat and replace the Jewish state, not negotiate with it—called for direct negotiations with Israel based on UN Resolution 242, "land for peace." Among Western publics, including important Jewish constituencies in the United States, the Intifada seemed effective at evoking sympathy for the Palestinians and sustained criticism of Israel's occupation, unlike the earlier tactics of terror—premeditated shootings, bombings, and hijackings. In declaring statehood Arafat adopted and projected a more moderate image of the Palestinians. To this day Palestinians refer to their acquiescence to 242 as their historic compromise, the moment they accepted partition.

But the only thought Shamir detested more than relinquishing control of the territories was engaging with Arafat and the PLO to make it happen. On that most Israelis agreed. PLO attacks had aroused strong emotions.

"The PLO's [1988] decisions and the declaration of state," Shamir said in a written statement, "are a deceptive propaganda exercise, intended to create an impression of moderation and of achievements for those carrying out violent acts in the territories of Judea and Samaria."[2]

Even those who rejected Shamir's maximalist approach agreed that Arafat's flexibility in front of Western audiences was belied by contradictory remarks to the Arab world. Violence persisted. The

PLO charter continued to call for the Jewish state's destruction through armed struggle.

The U.S. position was less categorical. The Reagan administration initiated the first American contacts with the PLO in 1988 after it accepted Resolution 242. George H. W. Bush continued those contacts and actively began working to open a dialogue between Israel and the Palestinians. His efforts were put on hold when Saddam Hussein invaded Kuwait in 1990. Six months later the U.S.-led and Arab-backed coalition won a decisive victory and restored Kuwait's sovereignty.

The First Gulf War symbolized the steep decline of Soviet influence in the region. During the crisis Moscow chose not to back Saddam, though Iraq had been a close ally. If the advantages of cooperation with the United States had not been clear to Arab leaders before the war, they certainly were by the time the dust had settled. U.S. involvement was at an all-time high. Meanwhile the Palestinian position had deteriorated. Iraq had been providing the PLO with arms and cash. During the Kuwait conflict Arafat supported Iraq and opposed external interference. That infuriated the Gulf Arab states, who saw Saddam's aggression as unjustified and threatening. Once reliable PLO financial backers, they shunned Arafat and cut off the PLO financially.

The Israelis were stunned, but for a different reason: during his invasion of Kuwait, Saddam unsuccessfully attempted to draw Israel into the Gulf War in order to undermine its credibility among Arabs. He showered Israel with scud missiles, and no one knew whether they contained chemical weapons. Israelis grew accustomed to carrying a gas mask at all times.

Bush's hope was that the events surrounding the Gulf War and the First Palestinian Intifada would underscore the folly of continued conflict and soften Israeli, Palestinian, and Arab positions, which until then had made a negotiated settlement impossible. That is how and why the Madrid Conference was conceived.

Shamir initially resisted Bush's call for an international Arab-Israeli peace conference. He feared such a gathering would impose unfavorable terms on Israel, and he rejected any implication that Israel would give up territory. From Shamir's perspective, the Iraq War proved that the region's volatility had nothing to do with Israel and that leaders like Saddam were the very reason Israel needed the security buffer provided by the West Bank. Bush took the opposite view, insisting that Israel and the Palestinians needed to resolve their differences not just for their own sake but to promote greater stability and deter future regional wars.

In the face of Shamir's intransigence, the Bush administration turned up the heat by publicly calling on Israel to rethink its future and abandon the notion of Greater Israel. In response to Shamir's aggressive settlement expansion, Bush refused to consider loan guarantees Israel requested to help absorb the wave of incoming Jewish immigrants from the former Soviet Union.

Persistent U.S. diplomacy and considerable pressure eventually broke Shamir's resolve. He reluctantly agreed to attend the Madrid Conference in 1991, but contingent on a formula in which Palestinians were part of a Jordanian delegation and had no association with the PLO. He would not be seen negotiating with terrorists or appearing to entertain withdrawal. Arafat was in no position to demand otherwise.

In Madrid, with U.S. leadership, Israeli, Palestinian, and Arab state representatives would gather for the first time, aiming to resolve their differences diplomatically. Multiple tracks of negotiations were launched. Israel met bilaterally with the Jordanian-Palestinian delegation, Lebanon and Syria and engaged in multiparty negotiations on regional issues, like the environment, arms control, and economic development. Some of these discussions continued for several years, but none led to any tangible agreement. What Madrid did achieve was significant, although primarily psychological.

Israeli elections in 1992 were a disaster for the Right, and particularly for Likud, Israel's dominant right-leaning party, in no small part due to the shift in Israeli attitudes following the Madrid Conference. Israelis were tired of endless conflict, and many worried about losing favor with the United States and the major powers of Europe. The First Intifada continued, and the 1982 Lebanon operation had turned into a quagmire. The IDF remained fortified some twenty miles deep in Lebanon, uneasily maintaining a security buffer to prevent attacks on Israel's north.

Most Israelis, including many of the settlers, were not as averse to withdrawal as Shamir. But they had been under the impression that there was no partner for peace, that the Palestinians and the Arabs would never accept Israel's existence, even within more modest borders. Madrid showed Israelis a different side of the Palestinians: as diplomats speaking of peace rather than militants promoting conflict. Yitzhak Rabin, Israel's new Labor prime minister, was elected with a mandate from the public to set aside skepticism and test the limits of the Palestinians' desire for peace.

Within the Labor Party, however, Rabin was more hawkish than most. Preventing Arab threats to the Jewish state was his life's work. As a career IDF officer he had fought in nearly all of Israel's wars, even commanding the IDF to victory in 1967. But as defense minister during the First Intifada he saw that force alone was not effective. Later he would famously say, "We have to fight terror as if there were no peace talks, and we have to pursue peace as if there were no terror."[3]

Early on, Rabin cleared the path to direct negotiations with the PLO. Israel had been negotiating with the PLO indirectly all along for Palestinian representatives were not so discreetly taking their orders from Arafat throughout the entire Madrid process. The result of Rabin's direct engagement with Arafat was the Oslo Accords, a series of groundbreaking agreements named after the city where they originated as a secret initiative of the Norwegian government.

The first of the Oslo Accords was announced in 1993 with a carefully coordinated Declaration of Principles in which Israel and the PLO formally recognized one another. The PLO renounced terrorism and violence as well as the articles in their charter "which deny Israel's right to exist." Those provisions were "now inoperative and no longer valid." At the same time Rabin wrote to Arafat that Israel "decided to recognize the PLO as the representative of the Palestinian people and to commence negotiations with" the organization.

The United States was aware of but uninvolved in the secret Oslo talks. But once the concept of mutual recognition had been worked out, the parties agreed that U.S. involvement was critical to legitimizing the effort. Images of Clinton presiding over Rabin's uneasy handshake with Arafat on the White House lawn are now iconic. The PLO was no longer viewed by the U.S. and Israeli governments as an organization to be crushed; now it was considered an entity with which political deals, perhaps even peace, could be struck.

Along with mutual recognition, the parties agreed in 1993 that Israel would begin the process of withdrawal to create an interim Palestinian authority that could engage in self-rule in the West Bank and Gaza. That entity was referred to as "interim" because both parties envisioned negotiations to permanently settle

Israeli-Palestinian differences based on Resolution 242's model of land for peace. The Palestinian Authority would have its own legislature, ministries, police force, and tax base. Arafat was officially welcomed back from Tunis.

It was no small feat that the parties also listed core issues requiring political resolution: the status of Jerusalem, the disposition of refugees, security, and borders. But those inevitably contentious negotiations would be deferred to give time for Israelis and Palestinians to first establish cooperative and productive working relations. Initially Israel would withdraw incrementally to make room for Palestinians to learn how to govern themselves and especially to test their ability and determination to tackle real security threats. Negotiations were therefore fixed to begin no later than the third year and conclude no later than the fifth after the first Israeli withdrawals from Palestinian territories. In May 1994 Gaza and Jericho were selected for the trial run of withdrawals, triggering the five-year timeline for concluding negotiations.

In September 1995, with momentum in full force, the parties continued to refine the concept of Palestinian interim self-rule in a complex agreement known as Oslo Two. President Hosni Mubarak of Egypt and King Hussein of Jordan joined Arafat and Rabin in Washington to commemorate the stunning progress.

Oslo Two divided the West Bank and Gaza into three governing zones, labeled Areas A, B, and C, with varying degrees of Palestinian autonomy. Area A was drawn tightly around Palestinian cities like Ramallah, Jenin, Nablus, and Bethlehem. There the new Palestinian Authority would assume full civil and security control. Area B was primarily composed of Palestinian villages and other densely populated areas close to Area A cities and would be governed civilly by the Palestinian Authority; security would be a joint Israeli-Palestinian effort. In Area C, which represented the bulk of the West Bank, there was no change in status, and Israel retained full control of all civil and security responsibilities. Most of Area C was land Israel had already allocated for settlements and military use, though there were some Palestinian villages there as well. Rabin committed to completing the withdrawals from Areas A and B within three months and to negotiating additional withdrawals throughout the five-year interim period.

As a result of Oslo Two almost all Palestinians in the territories came under at least the civil control of the Palestinian Authority. Shortly after, the PA held elections to choose a legislature and president. To avoid any doubts about the PA's legitimacy, Israel permitted Palestinian residents in East Jerusalem to participate in the vote, even though PA jurisdiction was not extended over them. Arafat was elected president in a landslide. He also maintained his chairmanship of the PLO, which to this day functions in parallel with the PA. The two bodies are intrinsically linked, and distinctions are often blurred. Each has its own assembly except that the PA's responsibilities are limited to daily governance in Areas A and B, while the PLO represents the interests of all Palestinians worldwide. Israel cooperates with the PA on the ground but negotiates with the PLO.

Rabin's four-year term was to expire in October 1996, just under a year after Oslo Two was signed. But his territorial and political concessions sparked fierce debate well before the normal campaign season. Among the most extreme settler and right-wing nationalist groups Rabin was portrayed as a traitor to the Jewish people. Demonstrators blocked intersections and heckled him when he appeared in public. At some rallies his face was superimposed over Hitler's, and his effigies were burned in protest.

But Rabin was not deterred. "I was a military man for 27 years,"

OSLO TWO & WEST BANK DIVISIONS

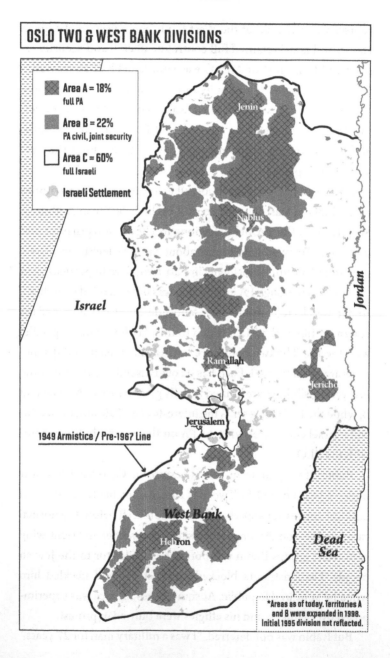

Area A = 18%
full PA

Area B = 22%
PA civil, joint security

Area C = 60%
full Israeli

Israeli Settlement

Israel

Jordan

Jenin

Nablus

Ramallah

Jericho

Jerusalem

1949 Armistice / Pre-1967 Line

West Bank

Hebron

Dead Sea

*Areas as of today. Territories A and B were expanded in 1998. Initial 1995 division not reflected.

he told 100,000 Israelis gathered in Tel Aviv on November 4, 1995. They were at a pro-peace rally meant to counter the vocal opposition on the Right. "I fought so long as there was no chance for peace. I believe that there is now a chance for peace, a great chance. We must take advantage of it for the sake of those standing here, and for those who are not here—and they are many." His ultimate hope was that the Israeli electorate would see that the risks of withdrawal were worth the goal of ending the violence. "In a democracy there can be differences," Rabin continued, "but the final decision will be taken in democratic elections, as the 1992 elections which gave us the mandate to do what we are doing, and to continue on this course."[4]

As Rabin left the rally and walked to his motorcade, a fellow Israeli Jew, a right-wing ideologue who opposed any concessions of land to the Palestinians, shot him in the back from just a few feet away. The prime minister died at a hospital shortly afterward.

Until the country could hold elections to replace Rabin, Shimon Peres took over as prime minister and vowed to continue the course Rabin had set, which was also very much his own. He had always subscribed to a political and practical Zionism criticized by the Right as weak and dangerous. Throughout Likud rule from 1977 to 1992 Peres led the Labor Party and supported territorial moderation. He was one of Israel's earliest advocates of engagement with the Palestinians and withdrawal from the territories. As Rabin's foreign minister, Peres was Oslo's main architect. He was expected to win easily in the elections, now moved up by five months to May 1996.

Israelis, even those uncomfortable with Rabin's embrace of Arafat, were shaken by the assassination. Oslo's staunchest political opponents were accused of generating a violent atmosphere with their extreme and vitriolic attacks on the prime minister, and at the center of the firestorm was Benjamin Netanyahu.

Born in Israel, Netanyahu spent significant portions of his youth in suburban Philadelphia because of his father's academic career. He served in an elite IDF Special Forces unit and moved between military service in Israel and academic studies in the United States, including at MIT and Harvard. After his brother Yonatan was killed in a hostage rescue mission in 1976, Netanyahu became more politically active. He joined the Likud Party in 1988 and rose through the ranks quickly, becoming party leader in 1993, succeeding Shamir, who resigned following Rabin's 1992 election.

Netanyahu warned of the grave dangers of the Oslo Accords and spoke at many of the opposition rallies. He believed that Arafat and the PLO could not be trusted. Like Shamir, he viewed their moderation as a tactic to gain a foothold in the Middle East, from which they would seek Israel's destruction. As far back as 1977, shortly after his brother's death, Netanyahu had expressed the commonly held view that "the real core of the conflict is the unfortunate Arab refusal to accept the State of Israel." Referring to Egyptian and Jordanian rule from 1948 to 1967, he emphasized that "for 20 years the Arabs had both the West Bank and the Gaza Strip, and if self-determination, as they now say, is the core of the conflict, they could have easily established a Palestinian state."[5]

Throughout his 1996 campaign for prime minister, Netanyahu decried the political and territorial concessions of Oslo as empowering Palestinian terrorists and undermining Israel's security needs. That message originally resonated mostly with his conservative party's followers, but after a number of suicide bombings were carried out in Israel just prior to and following the Oslo Two agreement, more and more Israelis began to share

Netanyahu's dire assessment. Then, in one nine-day period two months before the elections, four separate attacks in Jerusalem and Tel Aviv claimed the lives of sixty-one Israelis and injured hundreds of others.

Exit polls had predicted a Peres victory, but Netanyahu edged him out by 30,000 votes, less than 1 percent of votes cast. One famous catchphrase in Israel stated that the country "went to sleep with Peres and woke up with Bibi."[6]

The Clinton administration's involvement in the peace process was primarily supportive, but with the election of Netanyahu, Clinton moved quickly to ensure Oslo's survival.

Though he was disparaging of Oslo, Netanyahu knew that renouncing the agreement would be disastrous for Israel. So he assured Clinton that he would respect the commitments of prior governments so long as Arafat and the PLO did so too. In his first meeting with Clinton, Netanyahu described a string of PLO transgressions that had to be remedied before his government would reengage. One of the earliest he identified was the PLO's failure to revise its national charter, which continued to call for "the liquidation of the Zionist presence in Palestine." Arafat had renounced those provisions during the 1993 Declaration of Principles, but altering the national charter required approval by two-thirds of the PLO, a threshold Arafat had not yet tried to meet.

Arafat and the PLO had a violent past; the PA's performance on security was shaky; and compliance with Oslo was imperfect at best. It was not wrong to point out the discrepancies. But neither had Israel fulfilled all of its Oslo Two promises, including the release of Palestinian prisoners. Clinton worried the relationship between the two sides would regress. At stake weren't just the Oslo Accords; this was a test of the resilience of Israel's peace treaties with Egypt and Jordan. Clinton could not be certain that both would continue to support reconciliation with Israel in the face of stagnation on the Palestinian front.

One of the first challenges Clinton faced was Netanyahu's insistence on renegotiating Israeli withdrawals from Hebron, where 450 Israeli settlers lived among hundreds of thousands of Palestinians. Peres had agreed to the withdrawals but deferred implementation until after the elections. Arafat resented the precedent that renegotiation would set but acquiesced after a month of impasse and American encouragement.

Early into the negotiations, Netanyahu approved the opening of an ancient tunnel in the Old City of Jerusalem, running underground from the Western Wall alongside the outer edge of the Temple Mount/Haram al-Sharif—the most sensitive and contentious site in the Israeli-Palestinian conflict. The Temple Mount/Haram al-Sharif has been under Muslim administration for centuries. Palestinians, and the broader Arab world, are hypersensitive to any moves by Israel that appear threatening to Muslim control. Prior Likud governments had withstood the pressure to open the tunnels, anticipating Arab and Muslim outrage and fearing demonstrations and violence. That is exactly what followed Netanyahu's move. Among the Palestinian protestors clashing with Israeli forces were armed PA police officers from the West Bank. Netanyahu was incensed. Shoot-outs with Palestinian police validated the concerns he had expressed during his election campaign. Arafat blamed Netanyahu for the provocation. Many analysts suggested the move was intended to offset criticism from the Right over his PLO engagement, a tactic Netanyahu would repeat many times.

Negotiations over Hebron were affected by more than the rioting in Jerusalem. In 1929, during the pre-state Arab riots, some seventy Jews were killed in Hebron, and the Jewish community that had been there for centuries was evacuated. A small number of ideologically committed settlers had since returned to be close to the Tomb of the Patriarchs, the burial site of Abraham, Sarah, Isaac, Rebecca, Jacob, and Leah. The site revered by the Abrahamic faiths had previously been off-limits to Jewish worshippers for hundreds of years. The historic ill treatment of Jews in Hebron was part of the narrative of Jewish persecution and therefore resonated across Israel's political spectrum.

In January 1997, three months after negotiations began and with a firm push from Clinton, Netanyahu and Arafat finalized the Hebron Agreement. Israel withdrew from 80 percent of the city; the settlers and some 30,000 Palestinians would remain under Israeli control in the remaining 20 percent; and the Tomb of the Patriarchs would be open to Jewish and Muslim worshippers alike.

For Netanyahu, meeting face-to-face with Arafat during the Hebron Agreement negotiations was no small gesture; he had criticized the Palestinian leader his entire political life. Even more remarkable was that a prime minister from the Likud, the party of Begin and Shamir, actually reached an agreement with the PLO and withdrew from territory.

The January 1997 Hebron Agreement was followed by a protracted period of negotiations over the unspecified additional Israeli withdrawals envisioned by Oslo Two. Clinton insisted on keeping alive some momentum in that process, even if it had slowed down. After nearly two years of provocation, blame, and violence, the parties finally reached an agreement, announced in September 1998, following a summit organized by Clinton on Wye River Plantation, Maryland. Netanyahu agreed to withdraw from an additional 13 percent of the territories in phases, increasing the total amount of pre-1967 territory under PA control from 27 to 40 percent. Perhaps most significant, Area A, the territory under full PA civil and security control, would double in size.

Netanyahu had been elected prime minister with only a narrow margin. In addition to the Likud, his only option to govern with a majority backing of Israel's Knesset was in alliance with small ultra-right and religious parties. Many of them tolerated his negotiations with the PLO but were outraged by the additional territorial concessions, all the more so given Netanyahu's own accusations that Arafat and the PA were soft on combating terrorism. Meanwhile the Left, whose support was essential to passing Wye River in the Knesset, criticized Netanyahu for moving too slowly, thereby risking collapse of the Oslo process altogether. Indeed, within just two months of the Wye River agreement, he had already suspended its implementation, claiming that Arafat and the PA had not lived up to their commitments. Facing criticism from all sides and finding governing close to impossible, Netanyahu set new elections for May 1999, over a year ahead of schedule.

Arafat also felt squeezed. While Netanyahu did eventually commit to making territorial concessions, they were hardly sufficient to appease many within the PLO, whose hopes were raised by Oslo and who continued to agitate for Palestinian independence. Wye River left Palestinian enclaves surrounded entirely by areas under Israeli control. Palestinians could not travel between their own cities without Israel's compliance. That may have been acceptable in the initial phases, but this was four years on. Furthermore many of Israel's criticisms of the PA's performance, especially on security, were justified and in the PA's own interest to address. But Netanyahu's public enumeration of PA shortcomings only rendered real reform more politically difficult to implement, lest Arafat be accused of accepting Israeli orders. This tension was high given the widespread perception that Netanyahu was deliberately delaying implementation of the Oslo agreement. The five-year timeline for concluding final status negotiations was set to expire in May 1999, just prior to Israel's elections. But the negotiations had not even begun.

Labor's candidate in the 1999 elections was Ehud Barak, one of Israel's most decorated soldiers. He had served as interior minister in the Rabin government and foreign minister for Peres. In the run-up to the election, Barak aligned himself with smaller, left-leaning parties; one of his campaign promises was to end Israel's occupation of the security buffer the IDF had maintained in southern Lebanon for close to fifteen years. That occupation had come at a heavy price, with scores of Israeli soldiers killed. Another priority was to resume implementation of the Wye River withdrawals that Netanyahu had agreed to, then froze. With this platform Barak defeated Netanyahu by a 12 percent margin, and in the Knesset his bloc controlled close to three times as many seats as the Likud.

Within a year of the election withdrawal from Lebanon was complete, and Barak and Arafat had met to work out the details of the Wye River withdrawals; they also set a one-year target for a final Israeli-Palestinian peace agreement. Barak hoped to end the incrementalism of the Oslo Accords; he suggested that concessions should be done within sight of the final goals and the assurance of an end to the conflict, as another interim agreement would mean there was no end in sight for either Israel or the Palestinians. Arafat concurred.

The Oslo Accords envisioned final status negotiations between the parties, but what those negotiations would look like or result in was not specified, only that both parties were committed to resolve a set of core issues to end the conflict between them. Except for a brief time during Peres's last moments as prime minister in 1996, Israeli and Palestinian officials had not discussed the breadth of issues before them. Not much had changed, however. The prominent issues identified back in 1993 were essentially the same that Barak and Arafat set out to resolve in 2000: Jerusalem, borders, refugees, and security.

All the issues between Israel and the Palestinians are contentious, but Jerusalem may be the most difficult. In the center of Jerusalem the walled Old City is divided into four uneven quarters: one Jewish, one Muslim, one Christian, and one Armenian. Within the Old City and its immediate vicinity are countless sites with competing religious, historical, and national claims. Several, like the Temple Mount/Haram al-Sharif, the Western Wall, and the Dome of the Rock, are physically overlapping or adjacent to one another and therefore particularly sensitive. The 1947 UN Partition Plan envisioned that the Old City and its surrounding urban areas would be governed by an international regime, but between 1948 and 1967 the Old City and everything to its north, south, and east, referred to as East Jerusalem, was under Jordanian control. Israel's Jerusalem consisted of the urban neighborhoods immediately to the west of the Old City. Palestinians claim full sovereignty over East Jerusalem because the territory was not part of Israel prior to 1967; they have more than their national interest at stake because of Jerusalem's deep religious and cultural significance to Arabs and Muslims worldwide. For Muslims, Jerusalem, and more specifically the Haram al Sharif, is the site from which Muhammad ascended into heaven and was given the second of five pillars in Islam, to pray five times a day. At the same time secular and religious Israelis regard Jerusalem as their united and indivisible capital, its stones the same that were walked on by

MAP OF GREATER JERUSALEM

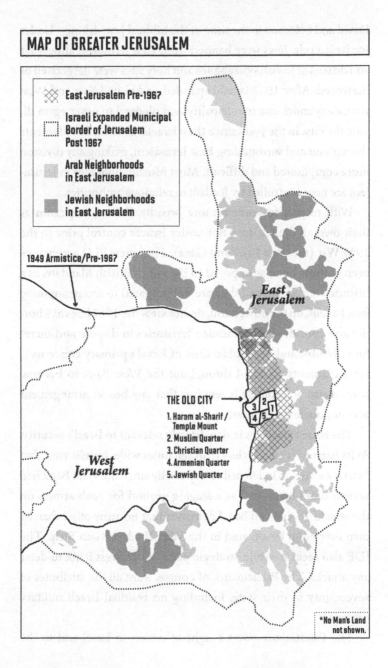

⬲ East Jerusalem Pre-1967

Israeli Expanded Municipal
Border of Jerusalem
Post 1967

Arab Neighborhoods
in East Jerusalem

Jewish Neighborhoods
in East Jerusalem

1949 Armistice/Pre-1967

East Jerusalem

THE OLD CITY
1. Haram al-Sharif /
   Temple Mount
2. Muslim Quarter
3. Christian Quarter
4. Armenian Quarter
5. Jewish Quarter

3 2 1
4 5

West Jerusalem

*No Man's Land
not shown.

David and Solomon in the time of the biblical Jewish kings. Under Jordanian rule, Jews were banned from East Jerusalem altogether and dozens of Jewish synagogues and holy sites were desecrated or destroyed. After 1967 Israel expanded and united East and West Jerusalem under one municipality and pledged to never again divide the city. In the years since then Israelis have built settlements throughout and surrounding East Jerusalem, making any division more complicated and difficult. Most Muslim holy sites in Jerusalem are now controlled by Jordanian religious authorities.

With respect to borders more broadly, Palestinians claim as their own all the territory not under Israel's control prior to the 1967 War (the West Bank and Gaza). They view PLO acceptance even of those lines, as opposed to the entire British Mandate, as a historic concession, and they are not prepared to accept anything less. Israelis, on the other hand, do not view the 1967 lines as a border and consider the Palestinian territories in dispute and therefore divisible and negotiable. One of Israel's primary concerns is for settlements scattered throughout the West Bank to become permanent; accordingly it requires that any border arrangement accommodate that interest.

The issue of borders is also directly relevant to Israel's security. At its narrowest Israel is less than ten miles wide. Israelis view that "narrow waist" as indefensible, especially since the West Bank had several times been used as a staging ground for Arab armies on the attack. To that end Israel demands that no army other than its own ever again be situated in the West Bank or Gaza Strip. The IDF also seeks to retain strategic parts of the West Bank to deter any attacks. The Palestinians, of course, want all the attributes of sovereignty in their state, including no residual Israeli military presence.

The Palestinians assert a right of return to Israel and to the

Palestinian territories for some 5 million refugees—those displaced in 1948 and 1967 and their descendants. Today one-third, some 1.5 million people, remain in fifty-eight official refugee camps run by the UN in Jordan, Lebanon, Syria, and the Palestinian territories. As generations of Palestinians grow up stateless, often impoverished and reliant on aid, much of their national narrative remains tied to their continued displacement. Israel, of course, opposes a right of return to Israel for Palestinians, which it views as a tactic to undermine Jewish self-determination. Israelis deny that they systematically expelled Palestinians during the 1948 War and blame the Arab states for creating and sustaining the refugee problem. That they remain one of the largest, longest-lasting refugee populations in the world underscores for Israelis the view that the Arab world preserves Palestinian refugee status as a bargaining chip in negotiations. Israelis also point to the fact that at least as many Jews living in Arab countries were expelled or intimidated into leaving their homes following Israel's independence and subsequent wars. The vast majority of them settled in Israel and were absorbed into society, and today nearly two-thirds of Israel's Jewish population are descendants of those Jewish refugees. Palestinians disavow the equivalence of their refugees with Jewish refugees from Arab lands, pointing out that they were not involved in Jewish displacement but that Israel was involved in theirs.

On July 11, 2000, Clinton hosted Barak and Arafat at Camp David for final status negotiations on these core issues. Heading into the talks the parties were far apart. Barak insisted there would be no withdrawal to the 1967 lines, no division of Jerusalem, and no evacuation of settlements; he would not accept a Palestinian right of return to Israel and would require that the West Bank and Gaza Strip be demilitarized. Arafat's positions were the mirror opposite: he insisted on full withdrawal of Israel and its settlers behind the Green Line, including in East Jerusalem, where Palestine would declare its future capital, and he could not accept an agreement without the right of return to Israel for Palestinian refugees.

In an effort to encourage candidness and flexibility, the parties accepted the principle "Nothing is agreed until everything is agreed." This principle allows negotiators to discuss and make proposals on core issues without being locked in to them before knowing the nature of the full agreement and assessing the potential offsets for their concessions. So when Clinton announced a stalemate two weeks after the summit began, although technically nothing had been agreed to, Barak and Arafat had actually broached topics previously considered off-limits and had moved significantly toward closing the gaps between them.

In his press conference announcing the deadlock, Clinton praised Barak's effort: "The prime minister moved forward more from his initial position than Chairman Arafat, particularly surrounding the question of Jerusalem."[7] Barak himself criticized Arafat for hesitating to take "the historic decisions that were needed in order to put an end to [the conflict]." When reports of Barak's offer to Arafat trickled out to the press, Barak faced considerable criticism; he feared losing support in the Knesset and being forced into new elections with nothing positive to show from his embrace of negotiations. Arafat later said the United States and Israel had ganged up on him throughout the talks. He and Barak met again in late September to revive discussions, but within days an incident in Jerusalem's Old City ended the negotiations.

On September 28 Ariel Sharon, the Likud leader, visited the Temple Mount/Haram al-Sharif surrounded by hundreds of Israeli police officers. The question of sovereignty over the site was at the heart of the Israeli-Palestinian impasse in Camp David, and

Palestinians were indignant at the display of Israel's power and its claim over Jerusalem's holiest site. The following day, after their Friday prayers, Palestinians began hurling stones at Jews worshipping at the Western Wall. In the ensuing fog of confusion, intensity, and close contact, Israeli police responded with live fire, killing several Palestinians. By early October armed Palestinian police officers and settlers had joined in the violence. The Second Palestinian Intifada had begun.

Israelis came to believe that Arafat had planned the Second Intifada; that he never intended to conclude an agreement at Camp David but rather used the summit to show defiance of Israel and the United States; and that his incitement of Palestinians to violence was in an effort to rally international sympathy and support. For his part Arafat blamed Sharon and Israel for provoking and escalating the conflict, which he viewed as a conspiracy to undermine his authority and an effort by Barak to silence his critics. An international commission established to investigate the causes of the Second Intifada found no evidence to support either charge.[8]

Clinton spent his final months in office trying to secure an end to the violence and prevent the total collapse of the peace process. On December 23, 2000, he presented his own parameters for a peace agreement to bridge substantive gaps between the two positions. Clinton proposed a contiguous Palestinian state on roughly 95 percent of the West Bank and the entire Gaza Strip. The 5 percent of excluded West Bank territory would enable Israel to keep 80 percent of its settlers in place. Israel would compensate the Palestinians with its own territory around Gaza. Those land swaps would be equal to roughly 1 to 3 percent. Jerusalem would be divided along ethnic lines: Israel would have sovereignty in West Jerusalem and the Jewish neighborhoods in East Jerusalem;

the Arab neighborhoods of East Jerusalem would be allocated to the Palestinian state. As for the Old City, Palestine's sovereignty would extend over the Muslim and Christian quarters, both predominantly Arab, as well as to the Dome of the Rock; Israel would gain sovereignty over the Jewish quarter and the Western Wall. The Haram al-Sharif would be Palestine's and the Temple Mount below it Israel's, a horizontal split.

With respect to refugees, Clinton emphasized the need to "adopt a formulation on the right of return that will make clear that there is no specific right of return to Israel itself but that does not negate the aspiration of the Palestinian people to return to the area." An international commission would help with the effort, and Israel would acknowledge the "moral and material suffering caused to the Palestinian people by the 1948 war and the need to assist the international community in addressing the problem."[9]

On security Clinton proposed an "international presence that can only be withdrawn by mutual consent." Israel would maintain three early-warning facilities in the West Bank and keep a fixed presence in the Jordan Valley for thirty-six months, after which it could remain for an additional thirty-six months under the authority of the international force. Palestine would be a nonmilitarized state.

"This is the best that I can do," Clinton concluded. "Brief your leaders and tell me if they are prepared to come for discussions based on these ideas. If so, I would meet them next week separately. If not, I have taken this as far as I can. These are my ideas. If they are not accepted, they are not just off the table, they also go with me when I leave office."[10]

Barak's cabinet endorsed the proposal with reservations that Clinton said were "within [his] parameters": "It was historic: an

Israeli government had said that to get peace, there would be a Palestinian state in roughly 97% of the West Bank" and all of Gaza. Arafat also accepted the parameters, though with reservations that Clinton said were inappropriate. Clinton left the White House and took the parameters with him. He later wrote in his memoirs, "Arafat's rejection of my proposal after Barak accepted it was an error of historic proportions."[11]

Barak too was in his final days in office; sensing the imminent collapse of his government, he called for new elections in February 2001. Amid failed negotiations and the Second Intifada, the Likud's Sharon easily defeated him and became prime minister. Sharon was considered one of Israel's greatest soldiers and military strategists. He had opposed all previous peace efforts and was a staunch advocate for settlement expansion, even encouraging settler groups to disregard the law by building settlements without seeking permission. Israelis elected him to crush the intifada.

The Second Intifada was far more destructive than the First. Suicide bombings in Israel became a regular occurrence, as did IDF strikes throughout the Palestinian territories. Amid the violence the diplomatic breakthroughs of the 1990s unraveled, including those that brought Arafat out of exile and gave him control over Palestinian cities and other population centers. Hundreds of checkpoints were erected, and sweeping curfews took effect. Israel reentered areas of the West Bank and Gaza from which it had previously withdrawn. Palestinian officials charged with fighting terror were unable to do anything, and some joined in the violence themselves. Israel's relations with surrounding Arab countries, which had been slowly and unofficially improving, crumbled. Perhaps worst of all, the optimism and hope for peace that had built up in the prior decade turned into despair and anger. Even

Israelis on the Left, lifelong advocates of peace and moderation, disparaged Arafat's intentions and leadership.

Before the meetings at Camp David and the outbreak of the Second Intifada, Israel and the international community were generally willing to overlook Arafat's flaws, believing he was the only man capable of striking a deal on behalf of the Palestinians. It was an uncomfortable truth, then, that he led the PLO during its most violent years of existence. But Arafat had earned legitimacy on the world stage, and in Israel, when he accepted Israel's right to exist in 1993. And he persuaded most of the Palestinian people to his reformed, more moderate views.

That perception changed again: now Arafat was portrayed as defiant, annoyed with the West and even some powerful Arab states for the pressure they put on him to accept the Clinton Parameters. During the intifada he condemned the terror and violence, speaking words of peace and reconciliation on the international stage, but at home he encouraged violence against Israel.

As president, Arafat had established several overlapping security and intelligence services; each answered to him. This divide-and-rule strategy aimed to encourage internal competition, to command loyalty, and to ensure that no other individual could become powerful enough to challenge his authority. He often paid the members of the various security services in cash. Corruption was widespread. His PA security forces had a revolving-door approach to terrorists: arresting them through the front door, releasing them through the back. When, in January 2002, the Palestinians were caught smuggling fifty tons of weapons into the territories by ship, many world leaders criticized Arafat.

President George W. Bush was clear about the need for a new Palestinian leadership. In a speech in June 2002 he said, "I call on the Palestinian people to elect new leaders, leaders not compromised by terror. . . . And when the Palestinian people have new leaders, new institutions and new security arrangements with their neighbors, the United States of America will support the creation of a Palestinian state whose borders and certain aspects of its sovereignty will be provisional until resolved as part of a final settlement in the Middle East."[12]

Arafat was under enormous pressure to reorganize his government and to name a deputy who would loosen his grip on the PA and its funds. His answer was to appoint Mahmoud Abbas as prime minister of the Palestinian Authority in March 2003. It was the first time Arafat had agreed to share power with anyone since becoming chairman of the PLO in 1968. But Abbas was selected precisely because Arafat did not regard him as a direct threat. The two were founding members of the Fatah Party in the 1950s. They differed, however, in that Abbas's role within Fatah and the PLO had been predominantly diplomatic and nonviolent; he was among its first members to call for direct negotiations with Israel.

Sharon was also under pressure throughout the intifada. His aggressive antiterror campaign, which included erecting a separation barrier in the West Bank and establishing checkpoints and roadblocks, seemed to be effective in restoring security. But even though incidents of terrorism had subsided, Sharon was unable to achieve pre-intifada levels of calm. He pledged to fight terrorism until the end, but there was no end in sight. And Sharon was getting less credit for ending the violence than blame for causing alienation toward Israel with his heavy military approach in the Palestinian territories. Many of Israel's military operations caused extensive destruction to Palestinian infrastructure and high numbers of civilian casualties. The IDF laid siege to Arafat's compound in Ramallah, basically imprisoning him inside. When the separation barrier under construction twisted through the West

Bank to protect many of the largest settlements on the Israeli side and cut some Palestinians off from their agricultural land, the international community interpreted this as Israel's attempt to unilaterally draw the border outside of negotiations with Palestinians.

What emerged from Bush's June 2002 speech was the Roadmap for Peace, a phased, performance-based plan for getting to the unambiguous goal of Palestinian statehood. The shell of that state would need to be in place before Palestinians were granted sovereignty and independence, and they would need to prove themselves capable of self-governance. The international community rallied behind Bush's approach; in April 2003 the Quartet for Middle East peace—the United States, the European Union, the UN, and Russia—adopted the Bush Roadmap as its own. By then Israel and the PA had also accepted the Roadmap.

Many declared that President Bush's support of Palestinian statehood was simply stating the obvious, but no previous U.S. president had made Palestinian statehood an official U.S. position. Even Clinton, who had operated on the assumption that the Palestinians would get their own state, chose not to get ahead of the parties' own agreements. Also remarkable was that Bush secured support for the two-state goal from Sharon, a father of the settler movement whose political base was in the Likud Party, which categorically opposed Palestinian statehood and pointed to the intifada as validation for their opposition to territorial concessions. Sharon's base had elected him to reverse Barak's march toward a Palestinian state. Two years after coming to office, Sharon shocked the world and especially Israelis by calling Israel's presence in the West Bank and Gaza a "terrible thing" and saying, "You may not like the word, but what's happening is occupation."[13]

The Roadmap had three phases. The first called on the Palestinians to immediately end violence and incitement to violence;

to reform, professionalize, and restructure their security services; to resume security cooperation with Israel; and to enact political reforms to end corruption and cronyism. Phase I also called on the Israelis to again withdraw to the positions they held before the intifada as part of the Oslo Process, to give the PA space to reform and operate, and to freeze all settlement activity. Phase II focused on the transition to Palestinian statehood, following the cessation of violence and Palestinian political reforms. It called for "ratification of a democratic Palestinian constitution, formal establishment of [the] office of prime minister, consolidation of political reform, and the creation of a Palestinian state with provisional borders." Phase III called for negotiations to establish a Palestinian state within five years and the normalization of relations between Israel and the surrounding Arab states.

The sequencing of the Roadmap and the marginalization of Arafat's role were critical for Sharon. Shortly after he accepted the Roadmap and its goal of two states, he declared, "Israel can no longer be expected to make political concessions until there is proven calm and Palestinian governmental reforms. . . . The achievement of true and genuine coexistence must be a precondition to any discussion on political arrangements."[14] In other words, he interpreted the sequential nature of the document as relieving Israel of any immediate requirement, at least until the Palestinians got their house in order.

But when the parties met to discuss Roadmap implementation, the situation on the ground had not improved. Suicide bombings continued; Arafat made only cosmetic changes in PA governance; Israel continued to conduct raids in the parts of the West Bank it was supposed to leave; and settlement construction continued.

Realizing that Arafat had no intention of relinquishing control,

Prime Minister Abbas resigned in frustration in September 2003. By resigning Abbas exposed Arafat's intransigence and delivered a harsh blow to the hope of PA reform and the spirit of progress set forth in the Roadmap. It took until 2007 to get the process back on track.

In September 2004 Sharon rallied support for unilateral disengagement from the Gaza Strip, where 8,000 Israeli settlers lived among a million and a half Palestinians. He argued that Israel's continued presence in Gaza was untenable. When he faced uncompromising opposition from the ranks of his own Likud Party, he gathered like-minded leaders and formed his own centrist party, Kadima, to proceed with his agenda. Kadima drew members from both the Labor Party and the Likud by projecting an image of cautious pragmatism and a commitment to Israel's security. The withdrawal was set for the following summer.

Arafat died in November 2004, inflaming already tense intra-Palestinian conflicts. In January 2005 Abbas was elected PA president after running on a platform of reform. He set out to consolidate the numerous and competing security services Arafat had created and to assert PA control over independently armed groups operating throughout the Palestinian territories. The international community lauded Abbas's determination to disarm militias and moved to provide him with hundreds of millions of dollars in financial and technical support. (Since the beginning of the Oslo process the United States had provided close to $1.5 billion in assistance to the Palestinians.)

But the Palestinian fundamentalist group Hamas had boycotted the elections, claiming that the PA and the PLO were illegitimate; throughout the 1990s Hamas had gained supporters who were tired of Arafat's cronyism and corruption. While the PLO was generally secular in its orientation and political goals, Hamas sought to establish an Islamic government in all of the former British Mandate for Palestine. Founded during the First Palestinian Intifada as an offshoot of the Muslim Brotherhood in Egypt, Hamas opposed the PLO's renunciation of armed struggle and its recognition of Israel and the establishment of the PA; it wanted an Islamic state, had reliable backers in the Arab and Muslim world, and provided services that the PA didn't or couldn't provide. The 1996 bombings that preceded and likely influenced Netanyahu's election as prime minister were not Hamas's first attacks on Israel, but they were the most dramatic and destructive thus far.

After Abbas took control of the PA, the intifada began to taper off. In March 2005 Fatah, Hamas, and other, smaller Palestinian factions reached an agreement to end the violence between them and committed to a conditional truce with Israel. With calm mostly restored and Abbas committed to reform, the Bush administration significantly increased assistance levels, as did many European countries. For the first time the White House permitted tens of millions of dollars in direct budget support to Abbas's PA government rather than channel money to projects and NGOs, bypassing the PA. U.S. military personnel were appointed to advise Abbas in his efforts to reform and professionalize the PA security services.

Israel's disengagement was initially born out of the belief that with Arafat at the helm of the PA, Israel had no partner for peace and therefore had to go it alone. Upwards of 60 percent of Israelis now supported withdrawal from Gaza. Though many of the settlers resisted, even barricading themselves inside their homes, Israel's withdrawal was completed in August 2005. Disengagement took on new meaning as an early test of the PA's ability to assert itself, monopolize the use of force, and govern responsibly.

There was cautious optimism for the future. Israel had firmly committed to the two-state solution and had withdrawn from Gaza. The Palestinians had a leader dedicated to nonviolence and reform. The challenge remaining was implementation. Hamas had gained extensive power and appeal among Palestinians, and they and other Palestinian militant groups would not simply disarm themselves. Abbas's agenda of reform and consolidation would require new laws, new powers, political compromise, and considerable force.

As a condition of the 2005 Fatah-Hamas truce, Abbas agreed to hold PA legislative elections, which had not taken place since the inaugural election establishing the body in 1996. So in January 2006 Palestinians throughout the West Bank, the Gaza Strip, and East Jerusalem voted. Hamas, which had never before participated in an election, was included on the ballot to ensure the outcome would appear legitimate and fair, but Abbas was confident Fatah would win, and the Bush administration agreed.

However, the vote proved disastrous for the reform agenda. Because the Fatah Party could not overcome internal rivalries, it ran multiple candidates, splitting the vote and allowing Hamas to win by a plurality; it took 74 of the 132 seats in the Palestinian Legislative Council, while Fatah captured only 45. The results shocked the Middle East. For the first time, and in one of the Arab world's most transparent and free elections, monitored by foreign observers, an Islamist party had won.

Israel immediately signaled that it would not cooperate with or engage the PA if Hamas ran any part of the government. The Quartet also conditioned their engagement on Hamas's renouncing violence, recognizing Israel, and accepting previous Israeli-PLO agreements. Hamas refused.

The PA was in crisis. Abbas was still the president, and he

refused to work with Hamas, as did the other elected Fatah representatives. Part of their motivation was the likelihood that the flow of Western financial aid, essential to covering PA salaries, electric bills, and and ensuring other basic services, would dry up if Hamas refused to accept the Quartet's conditions. If anything, Abbas consolidated more authority to prevent the appearance of collusion. His prior reforms had placed the security services under the command of the PA interior minister. After the election Abbas returned those security forces to their previous place: under the president's control.

Suddenly, unexpectedly, just months before his term expired, Prime Minister Sharon was permanently incapacitated by a stroke. The Kadima Party persevered in the already scheduled March 2006 election, and Ehud Olmert took over both Sharon's campaign and his platform of unilateral Israeli actions to preserve a Jewish majority—in other words, more withdrawals. Olmert, who had served as mayor of Jerusalem for years and was a long-standing member of the Likud before switching to Kadima, won the election and became prime minister. With Hamas and Fatah unable to agree on how or whether to form a government, he pledged action irrespective of whether there was a Palestinian partner he could engage.

On June 25, shortly after Olmert took office, Hamas militants from Gaza sneaked into Israel through a tunnel, killed two soldiers, and kidnapped another, Gilad Shalit. Militants from Gaza had been firing occasional mortars and rockets into Israel for years, but the cross-border raid escalated the tension. Israel initiated a naval blockade of Gaza and, less than one year following withdrawal, reentered the Strip. Israeli ground troops searched for Shalit. They struck Hamas and other militant targets and arrested dozens of Hamas members, government officials, and recently elected legislators. Hamas launched more rockets that reached deeper and more accurately into southern Israel than previously. The conflict threatened to spiral out of control. Three weeks after Shalit's capture, militants from Hezbollah, an Iranian-backed Shia terrorist organization in Lebanon, conducted their own cross-border raids into Israel, killing three Israeli soldiers and kidnapping two more, who were later confirmed dead. Israel blamed the Lebanese government for failing to disarm Hezbollah and engaged in a military campaign lasting thirty-four days parallel to its Gaza action. A UN-backed cease-fire ended the Lebanon war in August, and an Egyptian-mediated truce ended the Gaza war in November, but not before the Israelis had inflicted extensive damage and the increase in rocket launches had eroded Israeli support for the withdrawals.

Despite the truce, the PA and Hamas continued to fight one another throughout the West Bank and Gaza. The Israelis were impressed by the PA's seriousness of purpose in combating Hamas, but the crisis of governance was disconcerting and deeply unpopular with Palestinians, who perceived the PA as undermining their struggle for national independence. Especially after the Gaza war, the outcry and pressure on the PA grew considerably. Neither Hamas nor Fatah wanted to be seen as obstacles to Palestinian unity, so in March 2007, in a move strongly opposed by Israel, the United States, and others troubled by Hamas's participation in the Palestinian government, they agreed to another truce and the formation of a national unity government.

The unity government was anything but unified. In June, three months after their truce, a short but brutal civil war erupted between Hamas and Fatah forces in Gaza. Hamas fighters overwhelmed the PA's, deposed them, and imposed their own organization's rule over Gaza. Abbas consolidated the PA's control over the West Bank, arrested Hamas leaders there, and dissolved the unity government. The Palestinians in the West Bank and Gaza were now not just physically separated; they were governed by two separate authorities claiming legitimacy: the PA and Fatah in the West Bank and Hamas in Gaza.

Long before the formation of the national unity government, Secretary of State Condoleezza Rice had pressed Olmert and Abbas to engage in negotiations. Olmert and his advisors were not enthusiastic with this departure from the Roadmap; Hamas violence persisted, undermining Phase I, and negotiations for final status were not called for until Phase III. Abbas and the PA, Rice told the Israelis, needed to show the Palestinian people that nonviolence and diplomacy produce results, that Abbas's peaceful efforts would more reliably lead to Palestinian statehood than Hamas's violence. In other words, Abbas needed a near political horizon to legitimize his moderate approach. For that reason, when the Palestinian national unity government broke down, Olmert agreed to relaunch direct negotiations with the Palestinians at an international peace conference in Annapolis, Maryland, on November 27, 2007. These were the first substantive negotiations since the collapse of Camp David in 2000. Perhaps most striking was the presence of Arab leaders from Morocco to Syria.

A secondary goal of Annapolis was to show the Israelis that the Arabs genuinely desired peace. In 2002, when the Arab League had issued its Peace Initiative, promising normalization of relations with Israel in exchange for an agreement with the Palestinians, the Israelis had minimized the gesture as a public relations tactic arguing that it was conditioned on their acquiescence to

Palestinian final status positions, such as on the right of return for Palestinian refugees to Israel. The Arabs' attendance at Annapolis was therefore meant to reinforce their sincerity.

President Bush had a year and a half left in office to help the parties push through to agreement, and they seemed genuinely interested in achieving that goal. Unfortunately the region soon descended into chaos once more, and negotiations again collapsed.

5

ANNAPOLIS

A s Barack Obama took office in January 2009, Israeli tanks were just beginning to roll out of the Gaza Strip. They were there as part of a three-week-long military operation to end the daily barrage of rocket and mortar fire by Hamas at cities and towns in Israel's south. The war effectively ensured that the conflict would be an early foreign policy test for the new president. Television news shows broadcast images of Hamas rockets fired from Gaza and of Israeli airstrikes and the ground invasion alongside classic scenes of a U.S. presidential transition.

Obama appointed me as his and Secretary of State Clinton's special envoy for Middle East peace on January 22, the second full day of his presidency. Some analysts had faulted President Bush for having been too slow to engage the Israelis and Palestinians, leaving the conflict to fester and worsen. I thought the criticism was unfair, especially given that the Second Intifada was escalating as Bush took office and because of the seriousness and genuine effort he made in his Roadmap and at Annapolis. In any case Obama was determined to move quickly, and I traveled to the Middle East within days of my appointment.

Israelis and Palestinians were still grieving for their dead from the latest round of fighting. Gazans were sorting through mounds of rubble to secure basic necessities, and Israelis were readjusting to life outside of bomb shelters, as thousands of IDF reserve soldiers, mobilized for the Gaza operation, were returning to civilian life. Israel was in the midst of an election campaign, for Prime Minister Olmert had resigned following charges of corruption.[1] I knew it would take a long time to persuade the parties to return to the negotiating table.

On that first trip my focus was on ensuring that the cease-fires declared by Israel and Hamas were observed and on working with the UN officials providing emergency humanitarian assistance to Gaza. I also wanted to learn more about the Annapolis negotiations: How far had they gotten? Where had they left off? The final meetings of those negotiations had occurred just two months earlier, but war and the U.S. presidential transition made them seem more distant. I already had been briefed on the Annapolis Process by members of my staff, several of whom had been deeply involved in those discussions. But I wanted to hear from Prime Minister Olmert and President Abbas themselves how they felt about those negotiations.

More important than what I was hoping to achieve on my first trip to the Middle East was what I was trying to avoid. I did not want to say or do anything that could be perceived as interference with the ongoing election campaign in Israel. Israeli parliamentary elections are much more like U.S. primary elections than like our general elections: dozens of candidates try to distinguish themselves from each other, each appealing to the most ideological voters in their base, trying to inspire the highest turnout. I knew that once in office political leaders can be more realistic and flexible in their positions, but until then it was best that I refrain from saying or asking for anything that would require potentially unhelpful reactions. Especially so soon after the Gaza conflict, supporting territorial or any other key concessions to Palestinians would be a liability for any Israeli leader, as would concessions to Israel by a Palestinian leader. I was careful to describe my trip as consultative, and I made no substantive remarks in public or to the press.

Olmert and I had a long and very instructive lunch at his residence in Jerusalem on January 28, 2009. I had met him before, when he was the mayor of Jerusalem and again when he was a minister in Sharon's government. I liked him and found him to be remarkably candid. Making no effort to hide his frustration he told me that in the Annapolis negotiations he had offered a peace deal to Abbas that accepted important Palestinian demands, especially on territory. He felt that his proposal would allow Abbas to claim he had gotten the equivalent of 100 percent of the West Bank and Gaza for the state of Palestine. But Abbas, he complained, never responded to his offer.

In their joint statement at the launch of negotiations on November 27, 2007, in Annapolis, Israelis and Palestinians established their goal: "to conclude a peace treaty, resolving all outstanding issues."[2] In that and other respects, the objective and structure of the Annapolis negotiations differed markedly from the Camp David talks in 2000, the most recent real effort at negotiations. Then, under President Clinton, the goal was agreement on the framework of a peace accord, with the details to be negotiated later.

his legacy to be about more than accusations of political corruption, and he may have concluded that since his political career seemed to be over he could withstand the criticism that any Israeli leader could expect for making concessions to Palestinians. Whatever the reason, Olmert wanted to make a bold move, so he chose to bypass the negotiations that Livni and Qurei had been conducting.

Those negotiations were painstaking. Mistrust and doubt about each other's intentions and willingness to be flexible on the core issues plagued the discussions for months. Still, after nearly a year, Livni and Qurei had made progress. Their teams identified nineteen sections of a comprehensive peace accord that would need to be drafted, agreed on, and signed: a preamble, general provisions, borders, settlements, security issues, refugees, Jerusalem, water, passage arrangements, environment, economic relations, state-to-state and infrastructure arrangements, legal relations, people-to-people issues, implementation of an agreement, coordination and dispute resolution, end of conflict and finality of claims, prisoners, and final clauses. The parties had written drafts for several of those sections, with language bracketed to show where there were still gaps.

Although these negotiations were slow, there was one important breakthrough. The Palestinians had long demanded that the basis for any boundary discussions be the 1967 lines; everything to the east of those lines would presumptively be Palestinian. Israel would therefore need to compensate Palestinians for any changes to the 1967 lines to accommodate settlements or other needs, such as security. Israel had always publicly opposed an explicit reference to the 1967 lines, believing that agreeing to them would effectively cede their claims to any of the West Bank and weaken their position in negotiations. From Israel's perspective, the establishment of a Palestinian state was enough of a concession. And accommodation for settlements and security was not up for negotiation; it was the only way a peace agreement would be possible.

Despite the obvious difficulties in these negotiations, Livni and Qurei found common ground. They agreed to define "the area under discussion" as territories Israel captured in 1967—Gaza, the West Bank, and East Jerusalem—as Livni knew that the Palestinians viewed reference to the 1967 lines as a litmus test of sincerity. Livni also agreed in principle to land swaps to compensate the Palestinians for Israeli adjustments to those lines. But the nature of those swaps—the ratio, quality, and location—remained a point of contention. What made these discussions feasible was the guiding principle, "Nothing is agreed until everything is agreed."

By the time Livni called on Olmert to step down, she and Qurei were still closer to the beginning than to the end of negotiations. On refugees and security, little progress had been made. Not surprisingly Livni would accept neither liability for Palestinian refugees nor their resettlement within Israel, while the Palestinians were demanding just that. On security the parties generally accepted that Palestine would not have a military force. But the timeline for Israel's withdrawal and the level of arms permitted for Palestine were sources of disagreement, especially given the tension between the dual goals of ensuring that the Palestinian government be able to provide for internal security but not be strong enough to threaten Israel. Jerusalem was barely discussed.

Olmert and Abbas had been meeting regularly, usually to review the progress made by their negotiators. By the end of the summer of 2008, however, Olmert decided he could no longer wait for Livni and Qurei to inch toward an agreement. The two leaders met on August 6, a little more than a month before the

Kadima Party election to replace Olmert. They spoke in English, the only language they shared in common. Olmert's English is impeccable. Abbas's is just enough to get by; he understands it much better than he can speak it. Olmert spoke boldly and presented the framework for an agreement. He wanted Abbas's immediate approval, but Abbas wanted his advisors to review the proposal.

The Bush administration learned of the proposal when Abbas complained to Secretary Rice that he was being pressured to sign off on a deal he did not fully understand. Just before the Kadima elections, at Rice's urging, Abbas submitted a list of twenty-five questions to Olmert, seeking to clarify his August proposal. In the document Abbas wrote, "Regardless of what happens in Israel, you are my partner until your last hour in office. I hope that we will remain in touch afterwards. We have come a long way since Annapolis—I reassure you that the negotiations will continue between us uninterrupted. I have carefully considered the proposals you made to me in our last meeting. Despite the fact that I was not given the map you showed me, I have several questions to help me understand what you have in mind."[3] Abbas presented his questions at their next meeting, on September 16, and Olmert again displayed his map showing a border between Palestine and Israel that most Israelis would regard as generous; he also reiterated his proposals for resolving some of the other key permanent status issues. Olmert knew he had little time to waste. The Kadima elections were the next day and, potentially within weeks, he would be replaced. He therefore urged Abbas to sign the map and agree to the proposal on the spot. Abbas declined. He wanted to take the map and proposal with him to review with his advisors and members of his cabinet, and he wanted answers to his questions. But Olmert feared premature media leaks; anything in writing would be a huge liability for him and for Abbas, risking the entire effort.

Abbas had to resort to tracing a copy of the proposed borders on a paper napkin.

U.S. officials, and perhaps Livni, knew only what they could piece together from the Palestinians and the little Olmert was willing to relay to lower-level officials. And each time the proposal was recounted, some elements varied slightly. What is now referred to as the Olmert Offer is a compilation of the various proposals as well as accounts Olmert gave to the press in his final days as prime minister.

On the issue of territory Olmert offered to draw the border along the 1967 lines with modifications to account for major Israeli settlements. Those modifications would cede to Israel 6.3 percent of Palestinian territories (though by some accounts, that percentage is 6.5 or even 6.7 percent). In return Olmert would compensate the Palestinian state with an equivalent amount of land within Israel, including a safe-passage corridor between the West Bank and Gaza that would remain under Israeli sovereignty but with Palestinian control and would count toward the swaps. In effect Olmert was offering a one-for-one land swap, conceding to a longtime Palestinian demand for territory. Olmert also told Abbas a meaningful settlement freeze was possible in those areas of the West Bank that Israel would hand over for a Palestinian state.

On Jerusalem Olmert's offer tracked a key element of the Clinton Parameters: Arab neighborhoods would be part of Palestine, and Jewish neighborhoods would be part of Israel. Regarding the Old City and the historic Holy Basin around it, however, Olmert apparently was less precise. Some contemporary accounts suggest that he was silent on the issue, while others suggest that he proposed a form of joint or international administration of the Holy Basin. But by all accounts the question of sovereignty, perhaps the most difficult question of all, was left open. On security Olmert insisted that Palestine be demilitarized but accepted the eventual presence of an international force along the Jordan Valley. Finally, on the issue of Palestinian refugees, he proposed the admission of between 5,000 and 15,000 to Israel over a five-year period on humanitarian grounds.

Two of the major concerns for Abbas were territory and refugees. The Palestinians had long insisted that the land swaps not exceed 1.9 percent to account for some, but not all, of the major Israeli settlements in the West Bank and to minimize the amount of territory Israel would retain. Yet Olmert's offer was for 6.3 percent, over three times larger. His aim was to include most of the largest Israeli population centers in the West Bank to minimize the number of settlers who would need to relocate into Israel. Furthermore it was not clear to the Palestinians on what basis Olmert calculated his percentages. Livni's maps looked similar to Olmert's, although she suggested the percentage of territory annexed to Israel was larger, closer to 8 or 10 percent.[4] As to Palestinian refugees, the basis of admission—humanitarian grounds—was unclear and in any case the numbers were not acceptable to Abbas. Abbas also questioned some of the other specifics of the Olmert proposal: What would be the status of the Old City and Holy Basin in Jerusalem? Who would be the sovereign? Would there be one municipality in Jerusalem or two? Why propose only a freeze of settlements in what would become Palestine? Would Israel also commit to full withdrawal of its civilian settlements and military from the territory that would become the Palestinian state?

It was clear that Olmert wanted the framework of an agreement, which would leave many of Abbas's questions to be resolved later, not a comprehensive agreement that resolved all issues at once or even established an agreed process for resolving them.

Livni easily won the Kadima primary elections, and Olmert officially became a lame duck. She would be given five weeks to form a new coalition government. If that failed, other political parties would be given three weeks to form a coalition. And if that failed, elections would be held again, in February of the following year. But Israelis and Palestinians alike considered Olmert the caretaker prime minister for a limited amount of time.

As the Israeli political clock ticked on, Abbas was pulled in different directions. Olmert pleaded with him that time was running out. The future is unknown, he said. Palestinians should take advantage of his offer while he was still the prime minister. Several weeks after Livni took over the leadership of Kadima, it was becoming clear that neither she nor any political party in Israel would be able to organize a new coalition government. Israel was headed for elections once again.

Abbas knew of course that elements of the territorial offer were the best an Israeli prime minister had ever offered to a Palestinian leader, despite the number of gaps on other critical issues. But he felt he couldn't persuade the Palestinian people to accept the agreement without being able to tell them that he had secured something meaningful on refugees, on sovereignty over part of the Old City of Jerusalem, and on an eventual and full Israeli withdrawal. In presenting the agreement to the people of Israel, the prime minister would inevitably emphasize the vague nature of their commitments on Jerusalem and refugees. But the vagueness that would be necessary for Olmert would be a liability for Abbas. That is why Abbas wanted to study the precise contours of the borders and why he wanted clarity on the other points.

In October 2008 Livni was fully embroiled in futile coalition negotiations to avoid new elections. Meanwhile Olmert began preparing for life after politics. It was also the last month of relative quiet under the six-month Egyptian-brokered Israel-Hamas truce. Although there had been a handful of rocket and mortar attacks on Israel between July and October, Olmert had been restrained in his response. But in November nearly 100 rocket and mortar attacks hit Israel, damaging infrastructure and wounding over a dozen people.

With so little time left in Bush's tenure, Secretary Rice saw the Annapolis effort slipping away. She believed that Olmert and Abbas wanted to accomplish something historic, but she was concerned about the constraints on both. So Rice asked President Bush to invite Olmert and Abbas to Washington, separately, for one last push.

The press described Olmert's visit in late November as a farewell tour, but his intention was to look forward, not back: like Rice, he desperately wanted a peace agreement. He explained his proposal to President Bush and his advisors; it likely was the first time a U.S. official heard the full proposal, and his representations differed in some key respects from how the Palestinians had described the proposal and indeed how Olmert subsequently described it publicly after leaving office. Olmert told Bush and Rice that he wanted the agreement signed by the time they left office, less than two months away. He urged them to deliver President Abbas. They promised to make their best effort and suggested it would help if he responded to the Palestinian questions—which Abbas had resubmitted before Olmert left Israel—before Abbas visited Washington in December. Olmert declined. Olmert also was consumed by the political turmoil in Israel over the charges against him and by the increasing focus on security as Hamas resumed rocket attacks from the Gaza Strip. But although he wasn't willing to give Abbas a proposal in writing, Olmert agreed that one of his top advisors, along with a map expert, could sit down with one of Abbas's closest advisors, Saeb Erekat, to discuss the proposal in greater detail.

When Olmert returned to Israel he was met with calls for a serious military operation in Gaza to end the rocket and mortar attacks. Sirens warning of attacks howled several times a day across southern Israel; several rockets had hit residential buildings and landed near schools. The tension in the region rose.

The meeting between Olmert's advisor and Erekat to discuss the details of the proposal was scheduled for December 4, just a few weeks after Olmert's meeting with Bush. But the meeting never took place. The reason why remains in dispute.

Abbas arrived in Washington on December 17. As they sat alone in the Oval Office, Bush pressed him to accept Olmert's proposals. But Abbas insisted that his questions be answered first. He wanted to continue to negotiate the terms of Olmert's offer, but he was reluctant to sign on to an agreement that was not fully clear on all of the core issues. He likely assumed that Livni would become prime minister, in which case negotiations could continue at a pace and with a clarity that he was more comfortable with. Livni was in fact urging Abbas to wait to resume negotiations with her and her team after the elections.[5] Whatever the reason, Abbas left Washington with no agreement.

President Bush and Secretary of State Rice devoted enormous time and effort in pursuit of an agreement between Israelis and Palestinians, and for this they deserve great credit. That they did not succeed should not reflect adversely on them. The time had come to hand over the portfolio to the next president in as good a shape as possible.

Secretary Rice was hopeful that Livni would win the election.

It was important that negotiations not start back at square one following transition periods in both the Israeli and U.S. governments.
Secretary Rice urged the parties to put their various proposals in
writing so that President-elect Obama could pick up where they
left off. But both declined. The Americans also floated the idea
of a presidential statement on the four core issues. But the parties
objected to that as well.

Rice decided to pursue a Security Council resolution to sym-
bolically lock in progress and to support a peaceful resolution of
the conflict. Olmert and Livni initially opposed a new UN resolution for the same reason the Palestinians supported it. Anything
that could pass through the veto-wielding members of the Security Council, especially countries with a pro-Palestinian bias like
Russia, would be one-sided and contrary to Israel's interests. The
Israelis also worried that the language of the resolution would
bind them to positions they took in negotiations only under the
principle "Nothing is agreed until everything is agreed."

But when it came time to vote on Security Council Resolution
1850, on the same day as Abbas's final meeting in the Oval Office
with President Bush, Secretary Rice joined the others at the table
as she raised her hand to vote affirmatively. "The United States has
a national interest in the conclusion of a final treaty," she said after
the vote. "And it is in the long-term interest of Israel to provide a
more hopeful society for Palestinians. The establishment of the
state of Palestine is long overdue, and there should be an end to
the occupation that began in 1967."[6]

The resolution reiterated the world's commitment to the two-
state solution. But it went further. It called on the parties to "fulfill
their obligations under the Performance-Based Roadmap . . . and
refrain from any steps that could undermine confidence or prejudice the outcome of negotiations." That phrase has long been used

as code for the Palestinians to continue institutional and security reforms and to end all forms of official incitement to violence. For Israel the phrase is a euphemism for ending settlement-related activity. The resolution also declared international "support for the negotiations initiated at Annapolis, Maryland, on 27 November 2007 and its commitment to the irreversibility of the bilateral negotiations."

But UN resolutions and statements did not avert the impending chaos. On December 18, the day after Abbas's meeting in the Oval Office and the vote on Resolution 1850, Hamas declared an end to the truce with Israel. Three days later Hamas fired fifty rockets and mortars at Israel; sixty more were fired three days after that. The Hamas leader Mahmoud al-Zahar was defiant in calling off the cease-fire, as if the barrage of rockets was not enough of a signal. "We've been hearing talk of a possible Israeli invasion for the past three years," he told the press. "Israel is like a teenager that starts to smoke, and then stops when he chokes. If they want to enter—they're welcome to do so."[7] That is exactly what Israel did.

On December 27 Israel initiated Operation Cast Lead. "After enduring an eight-year-long barrage of 12,000 rockets and having exhausted all other options," the Israeli Foreign Ministry explained that Israel launched the operation to reduce the military capabilities of Hamas and other militant groups in the Gaza and to end ongoing attacks and prevent future ones.[8]

Operation Cast Lead began with a heavy dose of airstrikes targeting Hamas installations, including rocket launchers, weapons caches, political institutions, and police stations. But Hamas rocket launches did not end; they intensified. Hamas had amassed and scattered thousands of rockets throughout Gaza, many hidden among civilians, in mosques, hospitals, and homes. The organization had created an underground network of tunnels to move people and weapons. Buildings were booby-trapped and rocket launchers were buried underground or placed on the backs of vehicles to avoid easy detection. As the IDF began calling up reservists in preparation for a ground invasion of the Gaza Strip, it became clear that the Annapolis peace process, both the Livni-Qurei and Olmert-Abbas tracks, was effectively dead. Secretary Rice shifted from working to secure a peace agreement to scrambling to secure a cease-fire.

Israel moved in with ground forces, and grueling urban warfare ensued. Well over 1,100 Palestinians were killed; many were militants, but the high number of civilian casualties caused alarm. Billions of dollars of damage was inflicted on Gaza's infrastructure. According to press reports and human rights organizations, four thousand buildings were destroyed, hospitals ran out of medical supplies, tens of thousands were left homeless, and hundreds of thousands were without running water.[9] On the other side of the border thirteen Israelis were killed by Hamas's rockets, hundreds were injured. According to Israel's government 1,500 claims were filed by Israeli citizens for damages to their homes, buildings, and other property.[10] Life in southern Israel grounded to a halt as a million Israelis were within reach of the rockets; hundreds of thousands fled their homes while others feared to venture out of bomb shelters.

Operation Cast Lead was not Israel's first war in Gaza since it evacuated the Strip in 2005, but it was the most destructive. And by all accounts it was messy, as were the subsequent debates over whether or not Israel was actually achieving its stated objectives. Hamas's rocket attacks persisted through the entirety of the war.

On January 18 Israel ended its military operations in the Gaza Strip and declared a unilateral cease-fire. Hamas responded twelve hours later by announcing its own one-week cease-fire. With that the war was over.

At lunch with Olmert during my first visit as special envoy I could see that he was dispirited. From his perspective, he had gone far out on a limb, and he was deeply disappointed that Abbas wouldn't agree to his proposal and that the United States was unable to convince Abbas otherwise.

After I left Olmert's residence, he met with Israeli reporters and told them essentially the same story he had told me. As a result, the next day, before I could meet with Abbas, I was confronted with the very media commotion I had hoped to avoid. *Yediot Ahronot*, a leading Israeli newspaper, carried a front-page story detailing Olmert's discussions with Abbas. It noted that Olmert offered to divide Jerusalem and "withdraw to the '67 borders as part of a final status agreement, with border corrections that will keep the big settlement blocs in the territories intact. In return for the annexation of settlement blocs, Israel will hand over land in Israel's south to the Palestinians, on a 1-1 km ratio."[11] The account was reprinted and broadcast in other Israeli media and in the international press.

Netanyahu was highly critical, calling Olmert's concessions "invalid and unimportant."[12] He pledged to put an end to any advances made in the peace process under Annapolis. The results of the February election were very close. Out of 120 parliamentary seats, Livni's Kadima Party edged out Netanyahu's Likud by one seat, 28 to 27. Customarily the party with the largest plurality of seats is selected by Israel's president to form a coalition government. But although Likud won one fewer seat than Kadima, right-leaning parties as a whole surged. Livni had had a considerable lead in the polls before the elections, but constant rocket attacks and the war in Gaza had shifted the electorate to the right, and she had not been able to form a coalition government. To the deep disappointment of Palestinians, Netanyahu again became Israel's prime minister.

Olmert's courage in the negotiations is admirable, but his decision to make public an account of the proposal just before the election is difficult to understand. He must have known that in the midst of a fierce campaign Netanyahu's reaction would be very negative and that Livni would be placed in a difficult position.

Many analysts in Israel and elsewhere have seen parallels in Olmert's 2008 offer to Abbas and Barak's 2000 offer to Arafat at Camp David: in both cases the Israeli prime minister offered, and the Palestinian leader rejected, a sweeping peace proposal more generous than any that had come before. One logical conclusion is that Abbas, like Arafat, was unable or unwilling to make peace with Israel. But the story of Annapolis and the Olmert offer is more nuanced than that, and the conclusions less clear.

No reasonable observer can question Olmert's seriousness and the breadth of his proposal. He offered more than any previous Israeli leader ever had, particularly on the issue of territory. At the same time Abbas's insistence on studying the text and map of Olmert's proposal was not unreasonable. He was being asked to sign an agreement that would have determined the future of his nation and the boundaries of his state, yet key elements of the proposal were unclear to Abbas at the time or altogether deferred, particularly on the sensitive issues of sovereignty in Jerusalem, refugees, and the precise location of the borders. Abbas may also have concluded that Olmert's lame-duck status reduced the likelihood that he could gain the support of the people of Israel for an agreement. Livni, by contrast, was ahead in the polls, and had she become prime minister an agreement would have had more legitimacy and therefore a greater likelihood of implementation.

But in a remarkable turn of events, twelve years after he first became prime minister, Netanyahu returned to that office. Netanyahu viewed Olmert's discussions with Abbas as dangerous for Israel, just as he did Rabin's agreements with Arafat in Oslo. But during his earlier term in office Netanyahu had been able to maneuver through a difficult relationship with President Clinton and conclude an agreement relinquishing control to Palestinians over additional territories in the West Bank. So while we recognized the difficulties, we still hoped that progress could be made.

6

CONTESTED TERRITORY

Netanyahu formed his coalition government in late March 2009, two months after Obama took office. I met with him both before his election and after, as he was negotiating with other political parties to organize a coalition government. After he had done so Obama invited him to Washington. At his request his visit was scheduled for mid-May, giving him time to conduct a thorough policy review. He told me of his desire for immediate and direct negotiations with the Palestinians to shore up the Palestinian economy and improve daily life in the West Bank, an approach consistent with U.S. policy and squarely on the international community's agenda. The difficult question was whether his focus on the economy would foreclose the political agenda of negotiations to achieve a two-state solution. At least during the campaign that led to his election, Netanyahu had opposed that outcome.[1]

The Second Intifada had wreaked havoc on the Palestinian economy. Under President Bush's Roadmap, the PA had agreed to reform its governing institutions, combat corruption, enforce the rule of law, and enhance security cooperation with Israel. In 2007 President Abbas appointed Salam Fayyad as prime minister to oversee those reforms. Fayyad was an experienced, able, and widely admired economist, educated in the United States, with a solid record of service at the World Bank and the International Monetary Fund; he had also managed the main Palestinian bank and had served as finance minister. His appointment, and his subsequent effective performance, led to billions of dollars in international investment in the West Bank. Gaza, though, was another story.

Gaza had been largely cut off from the international community since the victory of Hamas in the legislative elections of 2006. In the aftermath, Hamas had violently driven out the PA and its security forces, taking over control of all governmental services like security, education, and taxation. Hamas saw its control of Gaza as a way to demonstrate its ability to govern, and thereby gain international recognition and legitimacy. But the economic and living conditions of the people of Gaza had deteriorated under Hamas. Especially after Operation Cast Lead, many of the people there were even more reliant on humanitarian aid than they had been in prior decades. Many Palestinians there blamed Israel and the West for this more than they did Hamas.

Economic and humanitarian assistance prevented a full-blown humanitarian crisis, but the United States and others in the donor community required that all aid bypass Hamas. The PA also wanted some control over how the money was spent, both to prevent Hamas from benefiting politically from reconstruction efforts and to reassert its own control in Gaza. Israel's concern was that some of the materials needed for civil reconstruction in Gaza, such as concrete, steel, and piping, would be used by Hamas to build weapons or refortify their positions. Hamas wanted to be involved in aid distribution for the very reasons that Israel, the donor community, and the PA wanted to exclude them.

One of my early trips to the Middle East included a stop in Sharm El Sheikh, a Red Sea resort town on Egypt's Sinai Peninsula. There Secretary of State Hillary Clinton and I joined representatives of over seventy countries gathered to pledge funds for reconstruction of the Gaza Strip and to figure out how to distribute that aid.

I first met Hillary in 1992 when her husband was a candidate for president and I was serving as Senate Majority Leader. After his election she and I worked closely together for over a year on the president's unsuccessful effort to reform our health care system. After I left the Senate in 1995 I spent five years working on the Northern Ireland peace process; both President and Mrs. Clinton were personally interested and deeply involved in that process, and I again found myself working closely with her.

In the Middle East, as in Northern Ireland and on health care, Hillary was studious, well-informed, and effective. She carefully read and reread the briefing books prepared for her, she asked a lot of questions, and she was well prepared on both the people and the issues she dealt with.

Fayyad made an impressive presentation in Sharm El Sheikh, but the conference highlighted the deep divide between Hamas and the PA, as well as the approach to both by other countries. For some in the international community, reconciliation between the rival Palestinian groups was essential to any kind of political process with Israel. But for Israel and the United States and a handful of other Western countries, inclusion of Hamas in any

Palestinian government would cripple future peace efforts—that is, unless Hamas accepted the conditions demanded by the Quartet (the United States, the European Union, the UN, and Russia): renouncing the use of terrorism to achieve political goals, accepting previous agreements between Israel and the Palestinians, and acknowledging Israel's right to exist. Until then donor assistance would be distributed through UN agencies and independent local nongovernment organizations, subject to strict auditing and oversight.

For Fatah and the PA, reconciliation would mean relinquishing exclusive control of the Palestinian political entities and government agencies they had been accustomed to holding exclusively. They also knew that a government under even partial Hamas control could trigger U.S. and Israeli sanctions and risk withdrawal of other Western financial assistance. Especially at a time when daily life in the West Bank was improving, the entire project of reform and professionalization that Prime Minister Fayyad had undertaken, with near universal international support, would be at risk.[2]

But after the Israel-Hamas war anger was widespread among the Palestinian people over the continued political divide. Neither Hamas nor Fatah wanted to appear to be getting in the way of unity. President Abbas had been subjected to harsh criticism in the local and regional press during the war; neighboring state-controlled media condemned him for a lack of outrage over the destruction in Gaza and for using his security forces in the West Bank to block rallies and protests against Israel. Reconciliation talks with Hamas, Abbas and his advisors believed, were critical to improving their domestic image and to regaining a foothold in Gaza.[3]

I shuttled between Ramallah and Cairo to warn Abbas and the Egyptian officials who were serving as mediators between the PA and Hamas that unless Hamas accepted the Quartet's conditions, an agreement that resulted in the inclusion of Hamas in the PA government would alter the U.S. relationship with the Palestinians in a way detrimental to both. The Egyptians were emphatic that their goal in any reconciliation agreement was to weaken Hamas's grip in Gaza by either limiting their power within any national unity government or by ensuring that Hamas was blamed if reconciliation talks failed. But I was concerned. My warning wasn't just a political judgment; it was a matter of U.S. law. Congress had placed tight restrictions on providing assistance to a PA that included Hamas.[4] Hundreds of millions of dollars of direct budget assistance to the PA would be jeopardized.

The reconciliation talks did not go anywhere. There was deep mutual distrust between Hamas and the PA, and each was vested in its own status quo: the PA in the West Bank and Hamas in Gaza. Predictably they blamed one another for the lack of unity. But in the post–Gaza war atmosphere, Abbas found himself in an intensifying political competition with Hamas. When Netanyahu told me that he wanted to negotiate with the Palestinians and shore up the Palestinian economy, he suggested that he wanted to help Abbas. But Abbas didn't see that as help. He believed that Netanyahu only wanted to discuss how to make the status quo more comfortable, not to allow for the emergence of an independent Palestine. Despite my efforts to convince them otherwise, the Palestinian team concluded that if Abbas entered talks with an Israeli prime minister who had campaigned against a two-state solution and who thought that Operation Cast Lead did not go far enough, whatever credibility Abbas had would vanish. To Abbas, Netanyahu's public rejection of Olmert's proposals in the Annapolis talks as "invalid and unimportant" confirmed his assessment.

After four months of shuttling back and forth to the Middle

East, it was clear to me that accomplishing anything at all, let alone resuming negotiations, would be extremely difficult, perhaps impossible. I was struck by the extent to which the Israelis and the Palestinians held completely opposite views: Netanyahu rejected the substance of the Annapolis negotiations and, in fact, the goal of the two-state solution, but he said he favored resuming negotiations; Abbas accepted the substance of Annapolis and wanted two states, but he distrusted Netanyahu and was unwilling to negotiate directly with him.

With no possibility of resuming the Annapolis negotiations, we considered other courses of action. One was to avoid any overt proposals or initiatives. I could keep shuttling to the Middle East and focus either on Netanyahu's plan to improve the Palestinian economy or on the Wye River precedent of incrementally expanding areas in the West Bank under Palestinian control, hoping that one or both of the parties might alter their position to permit entry into negotiations. As the conflict in Gaza receded in time and memory Netanyahu might change his position on Palestinian statehood or Abbas might agree to negotiate without preconditions. But the prospect of a change of position by either leader seemed remote. In any event Abbas rejected further interim agreements. He suspected that Netanyahu would just drag out those talks to avoid negotiations on Palestinian statehood.

In my initial round of meetings in the Middle East, Arab leaders without exception strongly insisted on a settlement freeze and expressed enormous frustration with the peace process; most of them pressed for a firm U.S. timeline for concluding an agreement. Some, including the Jordanians and the Saudis, went further, urging President Obama to lay down U.S. principles on the final status issues, similar to the Clinton Parameters, and then push the parties to negotiate on that basis. Several former U.S. and Israeli negotiators and other former U.S. government officials agreed; they saw no reason to believe the current players could work together constructively. Because Obama was at the pinnacle of his political popularity at home and abroad, they argued, a detailed set of U.S. principles could command an international consensus on the issue, provide something for the Israeli and Palestinian supporters of peace to rally around, and set a marker for future negotiations.

But the Arab leaders who urged the president to make a proposal simultaneously opposed the inclusion of anything that might be difficult for the Palestinians to accept, as on the right of return of refugees. And the government of Israel, from Netanyahu on down, was strenuously opposed to any U.S. proposal at all. As a result, and given the still high hostility aroused by the war in Gaza, I thought this approach at this time would do more harm than good. I was certain that Netanyahu's government would immediately and categorically reject any such effort, and we would find ourselves in a major U.S.-Israel confrontation from which there was no apparent exit. If and when we could get the parties to resume negotiations, we would have ample opportunity to make proposals in a context that offered some chance of success. To just drop a public proposal on them now, so early in the new administration, in the absence of negotiations or even initial discussions, and over vehement Israeli (and potentially Palestinian) opposition, would almost guarantee failure.

The approach ultimately approved by Obama was to focus on putting together a package of reciprocal Arab, Israeli, and Palestinian confidence-building measures that might create an atmosphere conducive to negotiations. This was not a new concept. Bush's Roadmap was offered to help the parties move past the violence and political stalemate of the Second Intifada. Prior to the Second Intifada, and to some extent immediately prior to the Gaza war, Israel had had quasi-diplomatic economic interest offices in some Arab countries, and Israelis and Arabs had even cooperated on some regional issues, such as the environment and water. The Israelis wanted to deepen those ties, but the Arab governments preferred to keep Israel at arm's length to avoid being seen as losing interest in the Palestinian cause. Normalization between Israel and the Arab and Muslim world is also considered a bargaining chip for Palestinians in their negotiations with Israel. But we wanted Arab governments to restore some lower-level links to give Israelis a sense that regional peace and cooperation were possible. Netanyahu told me several times that a public meeting between him and a prominent Arab leader in the Gulf could lead to a real breakthrough in how Israelis saw their place in the region.

We proposed that the Palestinians halt incitement to violence against Israel, clamp down on threats against Israel, and improve security coordination with Israel. The PA had made significant progress since the Roadmap, but there was still much work to be done, especially with respect to disarming militants. Fayyad's good governance reforms were popular abroad, but in Palestinian society he faced intense opposition. For years the PA had been poorly run and corrupt; reform meant tackling the cronyism and taking on some politically powerful Palestinians.

We also asked Israel to end settlement activity.

No issue has generated more controversy and hostility toward Israel than the construction of settlements, and no grievance came up more consistently in my discussions with Palestinians and other Arabs. Most of the initial rush to construct settlements focused on the Jordan Valley and the hills surrounding Jerusalem. A presence there, Israeli governments believed, could block an Arab invasion from the east and could reinforce Israel's position in areas that had seen heavy fighting in previous Arab-Israeli wars. Today it is almost impossible to drive through any part of the West Bank without seeing Israeli settlements. Every Israeli prime minister from every political party in Israel has permitted or actively encouraged settlement activity.

Settlements are an obstacle to peace because they are constructed on land that the Palestinians and the international community, including the United States, believe should be reserved for a Palestinian state. Each neighborhood expansion, or increased security buffer, represents land unavailable to Palestinians. As of 2014, there were more than 580,000 Israeli settlers, nearly 10 percent of Jewish Israelis, living in hundreds of settlements in areas Israeli captured in the Six-Day War in 1967. Some reports based on Israeli government data suggest that close to one-third of all land controlled by settlements is the private property of Palestinians.[5]

Many Israelis cannot envision ever handing back the entirety of the West Bank. The majority of Israel's population lives in the central plains, where the country is most narrow. Had Israel not stopped them, the Jordanian and Iraqi armies would have been able to cut across from the hills of the West Bank down to the Mediterranean Sea, through the center of Israel, in a matter of hours. After the Arab League met in Khartoum, Sudan, after the 1967 War and issued its infamous Three No's—"No peace with Israel, no recognition of Israel, no negotiations with it"—the question wasn't whether to settle, but where and how.

From the beginning U.S. leaders unequivocally opposed Israel's settlement activities. Following the 1967 War, President Johnson did not pressure Israel to unilaterally withdraw from territories, as President Eisenhower had following the 1956 Suez War. Instead

ISRAELI SETTLEMENTS

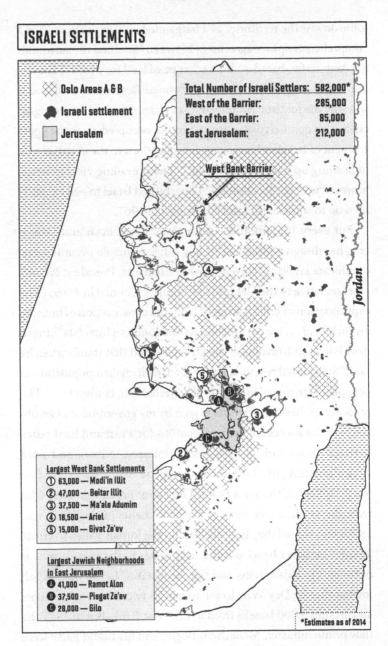

Oslo Areas A & B

Israeli settlement

Jerusalem

Total Number of Israeli Settlers:	582,000*
West of the Barrier:	285,000
East of the Barrier:	85,000
East Jerusalem:	212,000

West Bank Barrier

Jordan

Largest West Bank Settlements
① 63,000 — Modi'in Illit
② 47,000 — Beitar Illit
③ 37,500 — Ma'ale Adumim
④ 18,500 — Ariel
⑤ 15,000 — Givat Ze'ev

Largest Jewish Neighborhoods in East Jerusalem
Ⓐ 41,000 — Ramot Alon
Ⓑ 37,500 — Pisgat Ze'ev
Ⓒ 28,000 — Gilo

*Estimates as of 2014

Johnson saw the territories as a bargaining chip in the pursuit of a comprehensive peace agreement between Israel and the surrounding Arab states, based on the exchange of land for peace. That was the foundation for UN Security Council Resolution 242, and it was why the Johnson Administration warned Israel, "By setting up civilian or quasi-civilian outposts in the occupied areas the [government of Israel] adds serious complications to the eventual task of drawing up a peace settlement."[6] The prevailing view in Israel, however, was that Resolution 242 permitted Israel to permanently hold on to some of the land it captured in 1967.

But every U.S. president since then, Republican and Democrat, has disagreed that 242 or any other principle permits Israel to relocate civilians to West Bank settlements. President Nixon's representative to the UN told the Security Council in 1969, "The expropriation or confiscation of land, the construction of housing on such land . . . are detrimental to our common interests."[7] President Ford's ambassador to the UN reiterated that stance when he said, "Substantial resettlement of the Israeli civilian population in occupied territories, including East Jerusalem, is illegal. . . . The presence of these settlements is seen by my government as an obstacle to the success of the negotiations for a just and final peace between Israel and its neighbors."[8] Johnson, Nixon, and Ford were all reacting to a settlement enterprise that largely stayed on the periphery of the West Bank. The Labor prime ministers who were the original architects of the settlements in the 1960s and 1970s envisioned they be placed along the Jordan Valley to create a buffer between Israel and the Arab states to the east, as well as between the Palestinians and the Arab states. In the decade following the Six-Day War, Israel approved two dozen settlements and around 5,000 Israelis lived in the West Bank. But in 1977 the new prime minister, Menachem Begin, and his Likud Party were unwilling to relinquish even nominal control over any of the West Bank. They considered the land to be sacred to the Jewish people and inseparable from Israel. Although in 1948 the government, led by David Ben-Gurion, had accepted the 1947 UN Partition Plan, which divided up the British Mandate of Palestine, Begin himself had vigorously opposed it. Following his election Begin and his likeminded compatriots had an opportunity to undo that decision. His administration approved and fast-tracked dozens of settlements deep in the West Bank, adjacent to, in between, and around Palestinian population centers. Most settlers, however, lived in areas that hugged the pre-1967 lines. Settlements offered a housing option that was cheap and convenient for average Israeli families, and by the end of Begin's tenure, in 1983, nearly 30,000 Israelis were living in 106 settlements in the West Bank and Gaza.

The marked change in Israel's attitude toward settlements worried President Reagan, who insisted, "The immediate adoption of a settlements freeze by Israel, more than any other action, could create the confidence needed for wider participation in [peace] talks. Further settlement activity is in no way necessary for the security of Israel and only diminishes the confidence of the Arabs that a final outcome can be free and fairly negotiated."[9]

As the George H. W. Bush administration engaged in the Madrid peace talks in 1991, Secretary of State James Baker became increasingly frustrated with Israel's settlement policies. "Every time I have gone to Israel in connection with the peace process," he said, "on each of my trips I have been met with the announcement of new settlement activity. This does violate United States policy. It is the first thing that Arabs, Arab governments—the first thing that Palestinians in the territories—whose situation is really quite desperate—the first thing they raise when we talk to them.

I don't think there is any greater obstacle to peace than settlement activity that continues not only unabated but at an advanced pace."[10] When some Americans criticized Baker for his stance against settlements, President Bush stood by his side: "Secretary Baker was speaking for this administration, and I strongly support what he said. . . . It would make a big contribution to peace if these settlements would stop. That's what the secretary was trying to say . . . and I'm one hundred percent for him."[11] In reaction to Israel's continuing settlement construction, Bush and Baker refused to support Israel's request for additional billions of dollars in loan guarantees.

Some analysts and historians believe Likud lost reelection in 1992 because of this contentious relationship with the Bush administration.[12] Whatever the reason, within a month of taking office Labor prime minister Yitzhak Rabin initiated a change in Israel's settlement policy. Rabin pledged that Israel would no longer establish new settlements and would end government subsidies to those that existed, but would allow the existing settlements to expand to meet the needs and natural growth of the communities. Every prime minister since, including Netanyahu during his first term in 1996, has at least rhetorically committed himself to those principles.

The 1992 Rabin pledge was a major shift in Israel's settlement policy. Prior to that the Israeli government took the initiative to identify, plan, and construct settlements, and after settlements were constructed, it created financial incentives for the relocation of Israelis to those settlements. Rabin's commitment was to end that process. Whatever construction might take place to meet the needs of natural growth within existing settlements would be private; construction would require approval by the government, but the government would not sponsor new construction. At the time of the Rabin pledge over 100,000 Israelis lived in 130 individual settlements established in the West Bank alone.

But the commitment to build only in existing settlements has never led to restraint on settlement construction in the West Bank. That is because the phrase "existing settlements" has two meanings. "Exiting settlements" is used to describe only the built-up areas of existing settlements and their immediate vicinity. It also is used to describe the total amount of land already allocated by Israel to settlements in the West Bank, which is some twenty times larger in size than the built-up areas. As a result Israel could easily double or triple the number of Israelis in the West Bank by building only in "existing settlements," or establish entirely new neighborhoods deeper into the West Bank. Indeed, Israel has done both.

After the 1992 Oslo Accords, as negotiations between Israelis and Palestinians seemed to be advancing toward a two-state goal, a new phenomenon appeared. Feeling threatened, rightist political leaders took a page out of Begin's handbook and encouraged settlers to establish new enclaves throughout the West Bank without the government's approval. "Let everyone get a move on and take some hilltops!" Ariel Sharon proclaimed in 1998. "Whatever we take, will be ours, and whatever we don't take, will not be ours!"[13] Sharon was speaking to the most motivated of the settlers, a constituency he would later battle during his unilateral withdrawals from Gaza and parts of the West Bank. But when he spoke in 1998, they listened. Over one hundred outposts have sprung up across the West Bank, housing roughly 10,000 Israelis as of 2011. Some consist of a few shacks or campers housing a few individuals or families; others contain fully built homes housing several hundred. All are illegal under Israeli law, though recently the Israeli government has taken steps to retroactively legalize several of them, violating even the Rabin pledge of not approving new settlements in the West Bank.

In a 2005 report commissioned by Sharon, Israel's lead prosecutor exposed widespread support within key ministries in the Israeli government for unauthorized construction within existing settlements and new settlement outposts. Talya Sason, the report's author, wrote that despite the commitment from the highest levels of the Israeli government to the contrary, several key ministries continued to assist in the establishment of outposts with funding and resources. The Ministry of Construction and Housing, for instance, owned residential campers that it transferred to outpost settlers. The West Bank's Civil Administration, an arm of the Ministry of Defense, then permitted the transfer of campers through the West Bank, as well as their connection to water and electricity. Sason explained further:

> The outposts are mostly established by bypassing procedure and violating the law, displaying false pretense towards some of the State authorities, and enjoying the cooperation of other authorities in harsh violation of the law.
>
> One way to establish an outpost is . . . by "expansions" and "neighborhoods" in disguise, within an existing [and legal] outpost. The new outpost is named as the old one, as though it were just a neighborhood, even when it is sometimes kilometers away as the crow flies. . . . This enables financing the new outpost by the different authorities: the money supposedly goes to the old settlement, as known to the authorities. In fact, it goes to the new outpost. After a while, when the outpost stands still, it is no longer convenient for its inhabitants to be considered just as a neighborhood of an existing settlement.[14]

Sason's report was strongly disputed and harshly criticized by settlers and others on the Israeli Right; to this day she and her report are reviled by them. But Sharon himself had commissioned the Sason Report in 2001, after he promised Bush he would prevent new outposts and remove those established after he became prime minister. In March 2005 Sharon's cabinet voted 18 to 1 to approve recommendations in the Sason Report for ministerial-level reforms and committed to removing the two dozen outposts erected after his election. The commitment was invoked by Bush in Phase I of his 2002 Roadmap, in addition to his call on Israel to freeze settlement activity more broadly.

The commitments by Sharon and his cabinet were never kept; almost all outposts remain to this day. On the rare occasion that the government removed one, settlers have generally returned to rebuild it.

Not only did the proliferation of outposts contradict the commitments of several Israeli prime ministers; so too did the rapid growth within established settlements themselves. Rabin's pledge included a carve-out for natural growth, but the settler population in the West Bank grew many times faster than the population within Israel proper. Since Oslo, Israel's population has grown roughly 2.3 percent on average per year, yet the settler population has increased by roughly 6 percent. In 1992 over 100,000 Israelis lived in West Bank settlements; when Obama took office in 2009 that number was close to 300,000. In mid-2016 it was estimated at over 400,000.

Most of these settlers live in territories that Israel is likely to keep in a final peace agreement. For that reason some Israelis and Americans do not consider them a serious obstacle to peace. However, the population in settlements deep in the West Bank— east of the separation barrier—continues to grow, some years at even a faster rate than those closer to the Green Line. At the time of the failed 2000 Camp David peace summit, 45,000 Israelis lived east of the separation barrier. That number has since doubled. As a result the number of Israelis who will likely need to be relocated in the context of a peace agreement continues to increase, complicating the conflict's resolution both practically and psychologically. The political constituency within Israel fiercely opposed to any withdrawal increases alongside settlement expansion.

The first meeting between President Obama and Prime Minister Netanyahu was scheduled for May 18, 2009, three months after the election in Israel. Arabs and Israelis seemed to have lost faith in the peace process. After Israel's 2005 withdrawal, the rocket launches from Gaza, internal Palestinian political division, and the 2009 War, pessimism ran deep on all sides. That is why the president decided to ask for Israeli, Palestinian, and Arab gestures. His aim was to rebuild confidence in the peace process and to lay a solid foundation for negotiations.

At the meeting Obama discussed this confidence-building approach with the prime minister. We knew that ending settlement activity was a lot to ask of any Israeli government. But we believed that nothing short of a significant gesture by Israel on settlements would induce the Arab states to take steps toward the normalization of relations with Israel or convince the Palestinians to enter negotiations with Netanyahu.

Netanyahu agreed on the need to rebuild trust and confidence. He declared, "I want to make it clear that we don't want to govern the Palestinians. We want to live in peace with them. . . . We're prepared to move with the President and with others in the Arab world if they're prepared to move, as well. And I think the important thing that we discussed, among other things, is how to buttress the Israeli-Palestinian peace tracks, which we want to resume right away, with participation from others in the Arab world; how we give confidence to each other that would—changes the reality, it changes the reality on the ground, changing political realities top-down, as well, while we work to broaden the circle of peace."[15]

Netanyahu said he had "had two excellent meetings with President Obama": "He was very much interested in the ideas that I put forward to him on advancing a new path for peace."[16] Even Netanyahu's new, strongly nationalist foreign minister, Avigdor Lieberman, weighed in, telling the press, "On the Palestinian issue, there is agreement as to the final destination. . . . Everyone wants to see security, economic prosperity, and stability. . . . There is much more in common and much more positive points."[17]

Maybe—finally—some good would come.

7

OVERCOMING THE TRUST DEFICIT

After he met with Obama, Netanyahu visited the State Department, where Secretary Clinton hosted a small dinner for him and other Israeli officials. The mood was pleasant and upbeat. The discussion focused on the president's request that the Arab nations take steps toward normalization of relations with Israel as part of his confidence-building measures. Netanyahu spoke at length about the importance of getting some movement from the Saudis, and he asked that the president discuss this issue directly with the king of Saudi Arabia.[1] There was no discussion of the president's request for an Israeli settlement freeze; everyone seemed to assume that the next step would be an initial rejection by Israel, to be followed by intense negotiations.

The rejection came quickly. After returning to Jerusalem, Netanyahu declared, "The demand for a total stop to building is not something that can be justified and I don't think that anyone here at this table accepts it."[2] Later his spokesman Mark Regev told the press that Israel would not stop settlement activity and would continue to build, but only in existing settlements, a nod to Rabin's pledge. "We have to allow normal life in those communities to continue," Regev said.[3] Netanyahu's government "does not accept limitations on building."[4]

The press understandably highlighted the negative comments and reported that Netanyahu had publicly "defied" Obama, "setting the stage for friction."[5] The reports created the unfortunate impression that Obama had given Netanyahu an ultimatum. I knew the Israelis would take issue with Obama's request, and I got a clear indication of the difficulty ahead when Netanyahu's new minister for strategic affairs, Moshe Ya'alon, said that Israel would not allow the United States to dictate policy: "We won't let them threaten us."[6] But no one had threatened or intended to threaten Israel. Six years earlier President George W. Bush had made the identical request for a settlement freeze, then went further and assembled a worldwide coalition and a UN Security Council resolution in support of his position. Yet this had not been taken as a threat. Why should the identical request by Obama be interpreted differently?

Within days of Netanyahu's return to Israel the IDF moved to evacuate an illegal outpost in the West Bank known as Maoz Esther, which consisted of a few shacks on a hilltop. Settlement leaders and the Israeli Right were outraged. The timing created the impression that Netanyahu was responding to a demand from Obama, although that was not the case. Ehud Barak, whom Netanyahu had appointed defense minister, publicly insisted that the timing of the outpost's removal was coincidental and unrelated to the Obama-Netanyahu meeting. In fact for weeks Barak had been warning of pending outpost removals, explaining that removal was a matter of enforcing Israeli law. But that explanation did not satisfy the settlers and their supporters.

"The Israeli electorate set a clear line for this government," warned Dani Dayan, head of the Yesha Council.[7] Yesha, a Hebrew acronym for Judea, Samaria, and Gaza, represents settlement communities. Dayan not so subtly threatened to topple Netanyahu's newly formed government: "We have strong support in the new Knesset and the things we hear among politicians certainly encourage us that if Netanyahu [halts settlement building] the Knesset will stand at our side."[8] The Israeli Right already felt betrayed by Netanyahu's concessions in the 1998 Wye River negotiations with President Clinton; some analysts suggest they contributed to the loss of his premiership in 1999.[9] So after the Maoz Esther removal and the reaction by the Israeli settlers, Netanyahu adopted their defiant tone. He would not be outflanked on the right again.

Shortly before the prime minister's meeting with the president I had talked with Israeli officials. Their principal concern was the press speculation that Obama would lay out detailed American U.S. principles for negotiations; to that they expressed very strong objections. I assured them that the president had no such plan, and explained our hope to launch negotiations after a series of confidence-building measures were taken by all the parties: the Palestinians, the Israelis, and the other Arab states.

In late May I met with Yitzhak Molcho, Netanyahu's personal lawyer and close confidant, and an Israeli negotiating team in London. I expressed discomfort with the frantic and confrontational tone of the media reports and asked that our conversations remain private. These were discussions between friends; a public disagreement between the United States and Israel served neither of our interests, even if there were some differences in our policies. Our goal was not to engage in a dispute with Israel or to condition negotiations on a freeze. In the aftermath of the Israeli-Hamas war of late 2008, our goal was to build trust by presenting to Israel, the Palestinians, and the Arab states a package of mutual actions credible enough to create an atmosphere within which meaningful negotiation could take place. Everyone was being asked to contribute something.

The Israeli negotiators also regretted the atmosphere created in the media. Dan Meridor, Netanyahu's deputy and the senior member of the Israeli negotiating team, was a seasoned and effective public official. Also present was Mike Herzog, a retired general and experienced diplomat. I knew, liked, and trusted them. Meridor calmly explained that it was hard to control the many members of the Israeli cabinet. Indeed to secure a coalition Netanyahu had set up the largest government in Israel's history, appointing thirty ministers and nine deputy ministers and ministers without portfolio. As a result over a quarter of the members of the Knesset were also part of the executive.

Given the openness and vigor, indeed the bluntness of Israeli politics, Netanyahu governed in constant fear that others in his coalition were trying to undercut him from the right. His abandonment by the Israeli right during his first tenure as Prime Minister in the 1990s likely affected his thinking. For that reason, and because of the inflated size of his cabinet, he also had set up a so-called security cabinet. This was essentially a subcabinet within the cabinet. It included eight of the most politically powerful or strategic members of the various parties in his coalition. The prime minister submitted all major decisions to this security cabinet. Politically this helped reinforce the governing coalition and kept it from collapsing. But substantively Netanyahu now had to gain the approval of the most right-wing parties in Israel for any major action taken by his government. I understood the pressure from Netanyahu's right and appreciated Meridor's candid assessment of the situation.

I asked that both sides not engage in leaks to the press. Unfortunately, less than a day after the meeting one of the Israelis leaked details of our conversations and called our requests "unfair."[10]

The media commentary that had begun after the prime minister's meeting with Obama intensified. The request for a settlement freeze was described as an "ultimatum," not as part of a request for confidence-building measures from all sides. It was also described as "Obama's idea," suggesting a new and different approach rather than one similar to Phase I of President Bush's Roadmap, proposed just a few years earlier.[11] Every U.S. president since 1967 has publicly opposed Israel's settlement policy and actions, and every Israeli administration has continued to build.

Unfortunately we did not get a definitive statement from the Palestinians or the Arab states. They were unwilling to take any steps toward normalization as long as the Israelis refused to freeze settlement construction. President Abbas claimed he had no choice but to insist on that precondition, and he blamed Obama for raising the bar so high. The *Washington Post* reported, "Mahmoud Abbas says there is nothing for him to do."[12] Yet describing Israeli compliance with our requests on settlements as a precondition to negotiations was an inaccurate description of the policy we set out to pursue. Furthermore, continued construction in the West Bank had never in the past prevented the Palestinians from negotiating with Israel. There was no freeze when Arafat negotiated with Rabin in Oslo and with Barak at Camp David. Abbas personally had negotiated with Livni and Olmert in 2008 while construction continued. So Abbas ignored his own actions, and those of other Palestinian leaders, when he blamed Obama. Indeed, Abbas and his aides had for years called for a full freeze before then agreeing to conduct negotiations while construction continued.

This time around, Abbas had actually refused direct negotiations with Netanyahu before the issue of settlements took center stage. But the renewed media focus on Netanyahu and settlements served to reduce criticism of Abbas for refusing to negotiate. While Netanyahu's refusal to freeze settlements was critically important to his political constituency, outside of Israel and the United States he was seen as obstructing progress.

To this day I regret that I and others in the Obama administration did not do a good job of clarifying that our request for Israeli action on settlements was not intended to be a precondition for negotiations. That clarification might have helped us move past or at least mitigate the impasse exacerbated by the media firestorm. In all likelihood, though, if settlements had not become the dominant issue, something else would have. The controversy over settlements was the result, not the cause, of the deep distrust, low expectations, and wide policy differences that foreclosed early negotiations.

Over the summer months I continued to meet with the Israelis in London, New York, Washington, and Jerusalem. Initially they were adamant about rejecting a total freeze and excluding Jerusalem from our discussions, but they gradually moved from publicly rejecting any limitation on settlement construction to privately considering some limitations.

In late June Barak told me that Israel might consider freezing all new housing construction starts in settlements for three months but that buildings already under construction had to be completed. Any limitation represented some progress, but three months plainly was not long enough to solicit significant Arab steps toward normalization. I could not credibly ask them to re-open trade offices indefinitely as long as Israel would commit to only a three-month moratorium. That also was not enough time to build a minimum level of trust between Israelis and Palestinians and begin meaningful negotiations, which of course was the point of the mutual confidence-building measures. In addition, ongoing construction meant there would be little indication on the ground that a freeze had been initiated.

By the summer Israel had lengthened its proposal to six months. Barak and Herzog gave me a list of just over 700 buildings under construction in the West Bank and insisted that progress on those buildings had to continue. I asked if there was a way to stop ongoing construction in the deepest parts of the West Bank. Twenty percent of the 700 buildings were located east of the barrier. Though Israel has always described the barrier as purely for security, its path is the most tangible image of what constitutes "the blocs." The largest settlements are on Israel's side of the barrier, which had been located for that purpose. Settlements to the east are far less likely to be incorporated into Israel. But Barak and Netanyahu insisted there was no way they could freeze any construction that had already begun, anywhere. Since Rabin's tenure as prime minister most settlement construction had been undertaken by private individuals and companies, not by the government. Barak argued that the government would be financially liable for damages in lawsuits brought by those individuals and companies because of delays in construction.

Roughly one-third of all Israeli settlers live in East Jerusalem. Those neighborhoods are constructed on land that was not part of Jerusalem prior to 1967; it was part of the West Bank. Following the war of that year Israel expanded the borders of Jerusalem into the West Bank, doubling the land area of the city and incorporated neighboring Palestinian towns within Jerusalem's limits. Most countries in the world, including the United States, have never recognized these annexations, but the vast majority of Israelis, both secular and religious, do not consider those neighborhoods to be settlements and do not regard the Israelis living there as settlers.

Although we were making progress on West Bank settlements, Netanyahu would not permit East Jerusalem to be a part of our negotiations on a settlement freeze. Nonetheless, I urged that controversial actions in East Jerusalem be avoided, such as major construction announcements and the demolition of Palestinian homes built without the required permitting. Some Palestinians reject that Israel's municipality has any legitimate authority over them while others note the futility of trying to obtain legitimate permits. Several dozen homes are typically demolished by the municipality each year. But the Israelis made clear that refraining from enforcing their laws or avoiding construction anywhere in their capital was too much to ask.

Still, even without East Jerusalem, I felt that freezing new housing starts on the West Bank for several months could be a significant action. I also hoped that if we could get serious negotiations under way, the construction moratorium might be extended. If there was an extended period of no new housing starts, then, as ongoing construction was completed, settlement activity in the West Bank would decline and eventually dry up. Better yet, the issue might lose significance altogether if the parties could negotiate seriously on borders.

Though largely overshadowed by the media's focus on settlements, our confidence-building approach called for gestures toward normalization from the Arabs in return for Israel's construction moratorium. In my early trips to the Middle East there was genuine interest on the part of some Arab states to take steps in that direction. From Morocco to Bahrain some leaders understood our approach and wanted to help. Most likely wanted to start off on the right footing with the new American president. By the end of July 2009 we had made modest progress in some of those discussions: Morocco indicated it might allow Israeli commercial planes to fly over its territory; the United Arab Emirates was considering an increase in commercial ties and other links, including transportation and mail; Oman and Qatar considered opening trade offices. Although no one step was major, in totality, we hoped, reestablishing some ties between Israel and the Arab world would be a political plus for Israel and, as Netanyahu put it to Secretary Clinton, would show the Israeli public that peace is possible.

I recognized that the Arabs were not finally or firmly committed and worried that when the details of the moratorium were made public, especially the exclusion of East Jerusalem, they were likely to back away from whatever steps they were considering taking. Indeed, when the moratorium was announced that is what happened. By that time, there was broad recognition in the administration, among many Europeans, and even by some Arab states that the settlement issue had become too much of a distraction, an end in itself rather than a means to negotiations. Ending Israeli settlement activity is the right policy to pursue, but the moratorium we were discussing had become much more about the United States and Israel than about Israel and the Palestinians and other Arabs. I was determined to put the dispute behind us.

The UN General Assembly's annual meeting in New York was scheduled for late September, and the administration decided to use the occasion as a deadline to bring the settlement discussions to an end. We also hoped to launch direct negotiations between Israel and the Palestinians, with the support of the international community. Throughout the month of August my staff and I worked on a document to provide terms of reference for negotiations; the Palestinians insisted that without such an outline they would not meet with the Israelis. "We can't keep going back to square one," Saeb Erekat, the lead Palestinian negotiator, repeated. For Erekat and Abbas, not going back to square one meant that Israel had to accept the 1967 lines as a basis for the negotiations. But Erekat also wanted to constrain territorial negotiations beyond that. With respect to the amount of Palestinian territory that Israel would retain in a final status agreement, he told me several times that, "Olmert offered 6.5 percent and we offered 1.9 percent; those should be the upper and lower limits of what is acceptable."

But the Israelis were adamant in their opposition to the Palestinian demand. And their position was justified. Had Livni become prime minister she no doubt would have resumed negotiations with the Palestinians, but it is unlikely she would have agreed to be bound in advance by all elements of Olmert's incomplete discussions with Abbas. Livni, too, had refused any reference to the 1967 lines until after Annapolis and months of negotiations. Under the mutually accepted rules of that negotiation, since everything hadn't been agreed to by the end of Annapolis, nothing had been agreed to. From Israel's perspective the Palestinians sought to make Israeli concessions in previous negotiations the starting point for the next round.

From the Palestinians' perspective, however, the 1967 lines have been a reference point as far back as 2000. When President Clinton proposed and Barak agreed to a Palestinian state on 95 percent of the territories, and when Olmert in 2008 proposed a solution he described as giving the Palestinians 100 percent of the territory, both were implicitly using the 1967 lines as the basis for their calculations.

The Israelis would agree only to terms of reference that underscored the parties' commitment to the goal of peace, mutual respect, and two states. More than once Molcho told me, "If what they want is for us to agree in advance to their maximalist positions, we will be happy to provide you draft terms with our maximalist positions as well."

Netanyahu refused to even broach the topic of borders. On a large sheet of paper spread out on a table in his residence he drew a series of figures. "When we get this"—he pointed to a circle in which he had written the word *security*—"then they'll get this," and he pointed to a circle in which he had written *borders*.

Obama appointed a team of civilian and military experts to talk directly with their Israeli counterparts to address the prime minister's specific concern: the Jordan Valley. The Jordan River forms a boundary between Jordan to the east and Israel and the Palestinian territories to the west. Israel and Jordan have a common interest and a close and effective relationship in securing that border, so there is a substantial Israeli military presence in the West Bank, along the west side of the river. Netanyahu feared that if the river became the border between Jordan and an independent Palestinian state it could become much less secure, thus posing a direct military threat to Israel. Netanyahu constantly invoked Olmert's omission of security arrangements in this area as a major reason for his refusal to consider resuming the Annapolis discussions. Instead Netanyahu wanted an iron-clad agreement with the United States that would assure Israel's security on that border; in his view that could be achieved only if Israel's military forces were stationed along the border for a period he defined as "many decades." Then, and only then, would he agree to even begin discussions with either the United States or the Palestinians on the issue of territory and borders.

The commitment of the United States to Israel's safety and security is not and never has been in doubt; to back it up the United States has provided Israel with over \$120 billion of military and economic aid over several decades to guarantee that Israel will maintain a qualitative military edge over its neighbors. But a corollary U.S. policy has been to devise an effective alternative to a permanent or even decades long Israeli military presence within the borders of a Palestinian state. And no Palestinian leader has ever given any indication of a willingness to consent to a long-term Israeli military presence. Indeed, when Netanyahu later made that proposal directly to Abbas, Abbas strongly and categorically rejected it.

In a speech in June 2009 Netanyahu reversed his prior position and accepted the general concept of a two-state solution for the first time. "In my vision of peace there are two free peoples living side by side in this small land, with good neighborly relations and mutual respect, each with its flag, anthem and government, with neither one threatening its neighbor's security and existence. . . . We are ready to agree to a real peace agreement, a demilitarized Palestinian state side by side with the Jewish state."[13]

We were hopeful, but the Palestinians were not persuaded. Their fears had been heightened when, after the June speech, Netanyahu's father said in an interview that his son "does not support [a Palestinian state]. He supports such conditions that they (the Arabs) will never accept it. That is what I heard from him. I didn't propose these conditions, he did. They will never accept these conditions. Not one of them."[14]

The Palestinians pointed to what they regarded as hedges and

conditions in Netanyahu's speech. They suspected that the state
he envisioned was a symbolic entity that would be the result of
limited Israeli withdrawals or territorial concessions, aside from
what had already been transferred to the Palestinians under the
Oslo Accords. Their concerns were heightened by talk of a "provisional" state.

The concept of a provisional state is simple: Israel would permit the emergence of an independent Palestinian state over some
60 percent of the territory in the West Bank. This would include
Oslo Areas A and B (largely urban areas) as well as some additional lands and connecting roads. The Jordan Valley, East Jerusalem, and those parts of the West Bank where there are many Israeli
settlements would remain under Israeli control. A provisional
Palestinian state, proponents argued, would give Palestinians their
independence, Israel its security, and leave open for future negotiations the question of final borders.

In parallel with our negotiation over settlements, Israeli negotiators had in fact suggested a Palestinian state with provisional
borders. They believed it would have a better chance of being accepted by the Palestinians if the United States proposed it and,
with support from some within our administration, urged that we
pursue the idea. We did not. From the start of the Administration,
the Palestinians had made clear that such a proposal was totally
unacceptable. They have deep suspicions that any provisional
borders would become permanent, and they insisted they cannot
agree to a Palestinian state with no sovereignty over East Jerusalem and on just over half of the West Bank.

Throughout these long and seemingly irreconcilable discussions I came to believe that Netanyahu's desire for provisional
borders and the accommodation of Israel's security needs in the
Jordan Valley were not ultimately incompatible with Abbas's

demand to negotiate the final borders of a Palestinian state. If the parties were ever to agree to a peace accord, Israel almost certainly would withdraw from the territories in phases, over an agreed length of time, with benchmarks to measure progress. Could Netanyahu's concept of provisional statehood be the first phase of Israeli withdrawal, with the last phase being Abbas's goal of full Israeli withdrawal to final borders? An early focus on territory and security in negotiations might help flesh out and clarify these scenarios and would allow us to determine whether gaps could be bridged. Israel could present its plan for provisional borders, and the Palestinians could present their plan for final borders. There would be plenty of room for creativity in how to then negotiate between those positions.

In August I traveled to Israel to try to conclude the negotiations on a building moratorium in Israeli settlements in the West Bank. The UN General Assembly meeting was a month away. Our goal remained a trilateral meeting in New York at which we could announce the launch of direct negotiations between the parties and the start on October 1 of Israel's moratorium, following the Jewish High Holidays of Rosh Hashanah and Yom Kippur. President Obama agreed to support a moratorium in which the 700 or so buildings under construction would continue to be built, but continued to believe that six months was not sufficient. We decided to ask for twelve months and accept no fewer than ten.

When I asked the Israelis to agree to twelve months, they didn't dismiss it out of hand, but they responded with a request of their own: in addition to completing the 700 buildings already under construction, they wanted 200 new buildings to be started during the moratorium. I was astonished. If new buildings were started during a moratorium, it wouldn't be a moratorium. And because not many more than 200 buildings were started in any normal six-month period, there would effectively be no change and the result could not possibly be described as a moratorium.

Molcho was blunt about why the additional new starts were necessary: Netanyahu had to ensure that key settler constituencies and their leadership would not revolt against his government. He needed to buy support, one opponent and one building at a time. Having served for six years as Senate majority leader I understood his predicament and his proposed solution, but I told Molcho I didn't think it was possible; they were asking for too much.

The following week I again met with Molcho and Herzog, this time in New York. They presented a scaled-down plan under which Israel would initiate construction on only 100 to 150 new buildings. Molcho emphasized that these were needed to prevent what he called "a tsunami of opposition." "But," I asked, "how can the prime minister tell us and the world that he is placing a moratorium on new housing starts, and at the same time tell the settlers they can have new housing starts?" Any number of new housing starts during the moratorium would undermine the very concept of a moratorium.

President Abbas continued to refuse to enter into direct negotiations. He made clear his displeasure when I told him to expect something significant on settlements, though not a full freeze. Erekat spoke for Abbas and himself when he shouted, "That's worse than nothing!" Abbas was convinced that Netanyahu wanted direct negotiations only to relieve the pressure on him from the United States and the international community. Abbas feared the talks would fail and Netanyahu would pin the blame for that failure on the Palestinians.

"But whether you like him or not," I told Abbas, "you have to deal with Netanyahu to have any chance of making progress on the ground." Direct negotiations might not lead immediately to agreement on the core issues, but they made forward movement possible. But Abbas would not budge.

Then came a surprise, a headline from an Israeli newspaper: "Netanyahu to Okay New West Bank Homes Before Freeze."[15] The article stated further that "Netanyahu informed U.S. officials of his decision to authorize the construction a few weeks ago." Were the Israelis acting unilaterally, circumventing our negotiations? Molcho was quick to assuage my concerns, claiming that this announcement had nothing to do with the additional 100 to 150 buildings he had previously discussed with me. The approvals leaked to the press were for units that would not be started before or during the moratorium. Netanyahu was under a lot of pressure from his party and coalition members; promising to keep building after the moratorium ended was one way to release some of that pressure.

Of course the announcement alienated the international community, the Palestinians, and the other Arabs for the same reason it helped Netanyahu with the Israeli Right. I had regularly briefed our partners in the international community on the status of our moratorium discussions with Israel. Although I did not share all of the details, I emphasized that a moratorium meant that, for the first time in history, and for a substantial period of time, there would be no new housing construction starts. But the latest headline threatened to undermine or at least greatly devalue the promise of a moratorium. And the General Assembly meeting was just weeks away.

8

MUCH PROCESS,
NO PROGRESS

As September approached, I prepared for the possibility that there would be no trilateral meeting at the UN General Assembly, no Arab gestures toward normalization of relations with Israel, no Israeli moratorium on building in the settlements, and no negotiations. We would be back to where we were in January.

Obama was frustrated by Abbas's continuing refusal to meet with Netanyahu. Obama firmly supported Israel's security and Palestinian independence; as George W. Bush had put it, neither could obtain its objective by denying to the other side its objective. We understood Abbas's hesitation over Netanyahu's intentions; we too were uncertain about the strength of his support for a two-state solution. But we also knew that, in the absence of negotiations, we would be unable to bridge gaps between their positions or exert any influence in moving them toward agreement.

As the date of the General Assembly neared, the Arabs began to share our frustration. Several Arab leaders agreed to help persuade Abbas to at least meet with Obama and Netanyahu in a trilateral meeting in New York. President Mubarak of Egypt, King Abdullah of Jordan, and Sheikh Mohammed Bin Zayed, the Crown Prince of the United Arab Emirates, were especially helpful. We welcomed their efforts, but our task was complicated by the fact that they echoed the Palestinian argument that any Israeli construction moratorium would not be meaningful if it did not include limitations on construction in East Jerusalem; no Arab leader wanted to be seen as rewarding what they believed to be Israeli intransigence. Still they supported talks because they believed Obama genuinely wanted peace and because they too feared the consequences of another failed effort. They also realized that delay was not helping the Palestinians. For decades Abbas had opposed violence against Israel; his political career has been based on trying to make progress through diplomacy and negotiations. While there could be no guarantee of success in another round of negotiations, the absence of negotiations meant continuing failure, for Abbas and for his policy of nonviolence.

Just two weeks before Obama was scheduled to arrive in New York for the General Assembly, I met Abbas in Ramallah to deliver a stern message: The president cannot help you if you will not help yourselves. The president expects your attendance at a trilateral meeting with Prime Minister Netanyahu and will not understand your not showing up.

Just as I left that meeting with Abbas to travel to Jerusalem to meet with Netanyahu, a new and unexpected threat appeared. On September 15 the UN Human Rights Council released a report by their Fact Finding Mission on the Gaza Conflict, also known as the Goldstone Report; it had been commissioned by the Council following Israel's Operation Cast Lead, which had ended just days before Obama took office. Judge Richard Goldstone and his team concluded that both Israel and Hamas had committed war crimes.

The accusations against Israel were severe. The report accused the IDF of disproportionate force, using human shields, and intentionally targeting Palestinian civilians and civilian institutions. Netanyahu was livid. Rockets had rained down on Israel in the months leading up to the war. Several times a day civilians had to drop everything to take cover at a moment's notice. Hamas and other Palestinian militants strategically stored ammunition caches in and launched rockets from crowded civilian neighborhoods, in close proximity to schools, hospitals, and mosques. Netanyahu saw the report as a direct attack on Israel's right to defend itself, handcuffing future Israeli governments. Acceptance of the Goldstone Report, he told me, would mean the end of the peace process.

After an internal review of the report the United States agreed that it was biased and inaccurate and promptly issued a public statement to that effect. The war had been destructive and tragic, especially for Gazans, and there had been some serious missteps by the IDF during its operations. And Goldstone, himself a Jew and a former judge of the South African Supreme Court, was a reputable and credible figure. But we rejected the report for many reasons. We emphasized two of them. First, the report gave insufficient consideration to the actions by Hamas and other militant groups in Gaza. While accusations of Israeli crimes were elaborated in great detail (and were based primarily on Palestinian accounts), where the report did criticize Hamas, it did so largely in general terms. I was troubled by Goldstone's failure to sufficiently acknowledge the extreme difficulty of conducting military operations in densely crowded urban areas. I had some familiarity with the problems encountered by U.S. troops in Iraq and Afghanistan and other Western armies in such situations.

It became clear that the mandate given to Goldstone by the Human Rights Council was politically motivated. Many members of the Council were flagrant violators of human rights in their own countries. Yet roughly half of all resolutions passed through the council focus on Israel. The council's transparent bias against and unrelenting focus on Israel was not only hypocritical but also a way of deflecting any inquiry into the abuses of those Council members.

The second reason we opposed the report was that Israel was already in the process of investigating allegations of misconduct in its actions during Gaza. Many of Israel's critics suspected that its investigation was not serious, but we felt that no action by the international community should be considered until that process was completed. Indeed international norms require as much and the U.S. government would expect no less for itself.

Judge Goldstone has since confirmed the validity of our initial response of bias in the report, and in a 2011 op-ed in the *Washington Post* he recanted some of his conclusions:[1] "If I had known then what I know now, the Goldstone Report would have been a different document." He wrote that a follow-on document to his report indicated that "Israel has dedicated significant resources to investigate over 400 allegations of operational misconduct in Gaza," while "the de facto authorities (i.e., Hamas) have not conducted any investigations into the launching of rocket and mortar attacks against Israel." Information obtained from those investigations now led him to the conclusion that "civilians were not intentionally targeted [by Israel] as a matter of policy."[2] At the time of the report's release, of course, Israel faced intense international criticism and condemnation on the basis of that charge.

On my return to Washington following the release of the Gold-stone Report, I received word from U.S. diplomats in the region that Abbas would accept Obama's invitation for a trilateral meeting. I was not sure what had changed his mind. He may have feared los-ing the support of the president, or he may have felt pressure from Arab and European leaders; perhaps his concerns were alleviated by the international and regional focus on the conclusions of the Goldstone Report. Whatever the reason, I was relieved that Abbas agreed to attend the meeting. But faced with considerable domes-tic criticism for his decision to do so, Abbas clarified publicly and privately that the meeting would be a one-time event, not an offi-cial resumption of negotiations. While not ideal, and certainly not what we had in mind, it was important for the two leaders to sit down face-to-face; for both to hear the same, unfiltered message from Obama about the need for peace; for each leader to have the opportunity to signal a sincere willingness to move forward.

On September 22, 2009, Obama, Netanyahu, and Abbas finally met in New York, at a table surrounded by U.S., Israeli, and Pales-tinian flags. Although many words were spoken, the position of each can be summarized briefly: Obama spoke calmly but force-fully, urging the two leaders to begin direct negotiations; Netan-yahu said he was ready to do so; Abbas insisted on a full settlement freeze.

When the meeting ended, Obama struck a hopeful but un-satisfied tone in his public comments. "Simply put," he said, "it is past time to talk about starting negotiations—it is time to move forward. It is time to show the flexibility and common sense and sense of compromise that's necessary to achieve our goals. Perma-nent status negotiations must begin and begin soon. And more importantly, we must give those negotiations the opportunity to succeed."[3]

By early October, two weeks after the trilateral meeting, the Human Rights Council was scheduled to vote on a resolution to officially adopt the findings of the Goldstone Report. The resolution was a kick in the groin of peace, Netanyahu told me. He secretly sent a small delegation of senior Israeli officials who were respected by Abbas to meet with the Palestinian leader. As the vote drew closer, U.S. representatives to the Council worked around the clock to negotiate changes to the resolution; they tried to insert some balance and address our concerns with the report. But suddenly, just before the vote was to take place, the Palestinians withdrew their support for the resolution.

President Abbas's public rationale for his reversal was that it lacked enough votes to pass and that a failed resolution was worse than no resolution at all. He said he needed time to secure additional support from member states of the Human Rights Council before moving forward. But that explanation was widely disbelieved, and Hamas took the opportunity of the resolution's withdrawal to launch attacks on Abbas's credibility as a leader. Ismail Haniyeh, the leader of Hamas in Gaza, called the decision "shameful and irresponsible" and charged that it "traffics in the blood of our women and children in Gaza."[4] Hamas even called for stripping Abbas of his Palestinian citizenship and accused him of high treason.[5]

The volume and ferocity of criticism was echoed by the traditional Arab allies of Abbas, Palestinians themselves, and even members of Abbas's own Fatah Party. Demonstrations erupted in Ramallah and the Gaza Strip. Some PA officials resigned in protest. Even officials from Egypt and Jordan, countries on which Abbas relied for legitimacy and political cover, criticized his move.

Abbas was portrayed as having caved in to Western pressure and of collusion with Israel. One press account claimed he withdrew his support from the resolution after Israeli officials threatened to expose his active encouragement of Operation Cast Lead. The report alleged that Israel had threatened to release recordings of Abbas urging that the IDF be tougher on Hamas, suggesting targets, and disregarding civilian casualties.[6] Abbas forcefully denied the reports and said they were contrived. The news agency behind the report was based in the Hamas-controlled Gaza Strip; there had been reports originating in Israel that had become public through Palestinian agencies, but we did not know if that was the case in this instance. The allegations about Abbas have never been corroborated, but they were distributed as fact by news sources in Israel and the Arab world, where conspiracy theories often find willing patrons.

I met with Abbas in Amman. He was introspective and visibly angry; he spoke of his isolation from his traditional Arab allies, and he worried that he might not be able to rely on their support in the future, especially during negotiations with Israel. He was convinced that Netanyahu's government had leaked the allegations that were most personally damaging to him. He regretted having attended the trilateral meeting with Obama and Netanyahu. He worried that Netanyahu was conspiring with Hamas to bring down his moderate government.

Abbas also was angry over an agreement Netanyahu had just struck with Hamas to release twenty female Palestinian prisoners in exchange for a video and a sign of life from Gilad Shalit, the Israeli soldier held hostage by Hamas.[7] That deal was announced after the trilateral meeting and before the Goldstone debacle, and it was widely publicized. Shalit had not been seen or heard from since his kidnapping in a 2006 cross-border raid. His well-being had become a national preoccupation and rallying cry for Israelis. The issue of prisoners runs just as deep for Palestinians; many thousands have cycled through Israeli prisons over many years. A prisoner release to Hamas made Abbas look ineffective and served to promote Hamas's narrative that their use of violence worked and deserved more Arab support than did Abbas's commitment to nonviolence and diplomacy. When I suggested to Netanyahu that he release some low-level prisoners to Abbas my suggestion was rejected outright. As an alternative Israel considered some modest economic measures to help boost Abbas's political standing.

There could be doubt that Israel's actions conveyed to Palestinians and other Arabs that Hamas's refusal to recognize Israel and its use of violence and kidnapping paid off, but a commitment by Abbas and the Palestinian Authority to recognize Israel, to renounce violence, and to rely on peaceful negotiation did not. All the more reason, I argued in vain to Abbas, to begin direct negotiations with Israel. But in the intense political atmosphere Abbas worried that minor Israeli economic concessions would play into Hamas's narrative that he and the PA were weak and ineffective; that would do him more harm than good.

Feeling dangerously weakened and backed into a corner by Hamas, Netanyahu, the Arab states, and the United States, Abbas announced his resignation and called for new Palestinian elections. This was not the first time he had threatened to resign and throw the PA, and consequently the West Bank, into disarray. We knew the odds were low of elections being held in the Palestinian territories within a few months because Hamas refused to allow them to be held in Gaza. They never took place. Still, at the time, we could not be sure that Abbas was bluffing. "I think he is realizing that he came all this way with the peace process in order to create a Palestinian state, but he sees no state coming," Erekat said. "So he really doesn't think there is a need to be president or to have an Authority. This is not about who is going to replace him. This is about our leaving our posts."[8] If Abbas resigned, the peace process would be set back indefinitely. The ensuing political vacuum would lead to an intra-Palestinian struggle for power and undo much of the economic development, institution building, and other reforms in the West Bank. Israeli-Palestinian security cooperation could end, with terrible consequences for both.

The professionalization of the Palestinian security services and their cooperative relationship with their Israeli counterparts, under Abbas' leadership, had given Prime Minister Olmert the confidence to loosen the IDF's West Bank security regime, enabling greater Palestinian freedom of movement. Netanyahu continued the trend. By the time of the trilateral meeting, many major checkpoints in the West Bank had been removed. The UN agency monitoring the situation reported, "Israeli authorities continued implementing measures that increased the freedom of movement of Palestinians between most urban centers in the West Bank." Those measures "resulted in a significant reduction in travel time between the main Palestinian urban centers (excluding East Jerusalem), as well as in the level of friction between Palestinians and Israeli forces at checkpoints."[9] While many serious restrictions remained, "large segments of the Palestinian population enjoy[ed] better access to services, places of work and markets."[10]

That progress would be jeopardized if Abbas resigned. We could not be certain that the new leader would continue to support the path of diplomacy, international engagement, and non-violence. We could not be certain that a successor to Abbas would have the legitimacy and legacy needed to keep the PA intact or come to a political agreement with Israel, as far off as that seemed.

Immediately after my meeting with Abbas in Amman, I met

with King Abdullah of Jordan, who shared my concerns about Abbas and the future of the PA and the West Bank. Jordan shares a border with the West Bank and remains fully invested in Abbas and in peace and stability. The king therefore committed to helping rehabilitate Abbas's image in the Arab world, and he joined me in asking Egypt and other Arab governments to do the same. Within days the front pages of major Egyptian and Jordanian papers ran large photographs of Abbas with Mubarak and Abdullah, respectively, a clear public signal of their continued confidence in his leadership. Other Arab leaders called Abbas to reassure him of their backing and support. The UAE transferred millions of dollars in budget support to his government. Demonstrators took to the streets in several Palestinian cities demanding that he stay in power.

Over time Abbas recovered, personally and politically. But his belief that Netanyahu was responsible for the highly personal leaks to the press hardened his resolve. His distrust of Netanyahu, already deep, became absolute. His hesitation to expose himself politically became more pronounced.

Once again we were faced with a stalemate. On my first visit to the region as the U.S. envoy, Netanyahu was opposed to the creation of a Palestinian state but said he wanted direct negotiations; Abbas's goal was a Palestinian state, but he had no interest in negotiating with Netanyahu. Ten months later we were still unable to engage the parties in negotiations.

By early November, a month after Abbas withdrew his support for the Goldstone resolution, Secretary Clinton flew to the Middle East to meet with Israeli and Palestinian and other Arab leaders to underscore the administration's desire for and commitment to move forward on negotiations. That same month, the Israelis were finally ready to announce their moratorium on new housing starts in the West Bank settlements. When Netanyahu had said he needed to initiate building in the West Bank settlements during the moratorium, his solution, obvious in retrospect but not at the time, was for builders to expedite housing starts in August and September and delay the onset of the moratorium until November.

In response, the Arab states made it finally and totally clear that absent a full settlement freeze there would be no steps toward normalization with Israel; there would be no quid pro quo for a moratorium, especially one that did not include East Jerusalem. As is often the case in the Middle East, irony abounded. When I conveyed their decision to Netanyahu he shrugged and said he would proceed with the moratorium, which had become more valuable to him politically than to the Palestinians or Arabs. He believed that Israel was being criticized unfairly and inaccurately in the international press for rejecting serious negotiations, when he had been calling for direct negotiations with Abbas from the day he took office. He hoped the moratorium would demonstrate his sincerity and show critics within Israel who felt he had been harming relations with the United States and Europe that he ultimately cooperated with the U.S. administration. If the moratorium led to direct negotiations it would be worth the price he paid, and the last-minute surge in new construction helped him to defuse other internal critics.

It was, of course, a highly imperfect political compromise, vulnerable to the avalanche of criticism that began immediately following its announcement. The Palestinians angrily condemned it as "worse than useless." Other Arabs too were opposed, albeit with varying degrees of intensity; their criticism focused on the exclusion of East Jerusalem. The settler supporters in Israel and elsewhere criticized Netanyahu. Many American supporters of Israel criticized Obama.

Even though I shared some of these misgivings, especially as they related to the last-minute surge of new construction, I understood the very difficult political context within which Netanyahu and his aides had been forced to negotiate. And I believed strongly that, despite its limitations, the agreed moratorium could at least help us move past the issue of settlements.

I announced the moratorium at a State Department press conference on November 25, 2009, with three goals in mind. The first was to credit Israel for meaningful action:

> While they fall short of a full freeze, we believe the steps announced by the prime minister are significant and could have substantial impact on the ground. For the first time ever, an Israeli Government will stop housing approvals and all new construction of housing units and related infrastructure in West Bank settlements. That's a positive development.... Under the moratorium, those buildings already under construction will be completed. But the number of buildings under construction will decline since, as each new building is completed, there will not be a new building started. So implementation of the moratorium could mean much less settlement construction than would occur if there is no moratorium.[11]

Two days earlier I received word that the Jerusalem Municipality would imminently announce a new project to construct 884 housing units in the East Jerusalem neighborhood of Gilo. We asked that the prime minister prevent the announcement because it would undermine the goodwill we were trying to build with the moratorium. Netanyahu said he had not been aware in advance of the announcement, but he refused to stop it. The political backlash would be too great.

With the omission of East Jerusalem from the moratorium in renewed focus, my second goal was to address Palestinian and other Arab criticism. "The United States," I said, "also disagrees with some Israeli actions in Jerusalem affecting Palestinians in areas such as housing, including the continuing pattern of evictions and demolitions of Palestinian homes."

I still held out some hope for my third goal, that the moratorium could help with the resumption of negotiations. For that reason, I also expressed America's view that through good-faith negotiations, the parties can mutually agree on an outcome which ends the conflict and reconciles the Palestinian goal of an independent and viable state, based on the 1967 lines, with agreed swaps, and the Israeli goal of a Jewish state with secure and recognized borders that reflect subsequent developments and meet Israeli security requirements. "Let me say to all the people of the region and world: Our commitment to achieving a solution with two states living side by side in peace and security is unwavering."[12] We wanted to make clear to both parties that we respected and understood their goals. Palestinians needed to know that the United States recognized the need to include provisions critical to Israel's security, which includes ensuring the ethnic Jewish character of the state. And Israel needed to know that we viewed the Palestinian objective of a state based on the 1967 lines, with agreed swaps, as reasonable and appropriate.

I was relieved to have the construction moratorium begin but knew that even more difficult issues remained. The Palestinians saw no value in the moratorium and were opposed to negotiations with Netanyahu in the absence of a full settlement freeze; Abbas was no doubt influenced by strong opposition to talks from his own Fatah Party and from other elements of the PLO.

I accepted the reality that there would not be direct negotiations between Israelis and Palestinians at this point. Netanyahu was not happy when I informed him of my conclusion; he believed the Palestinians were trying to squeeze more concessions out of him.

In January 2010 I raised the possibility of indirect negotiations, or proximity talks, with Netanyahu and Abbas. I asked them to provide the details of their positions on the core issues so that I could gain a better understanding of their underlying needs and interests. Perhaps, despite the hostility, there existed some substantive overlap or creative work-arounds that could lay the foundation for direct negotiations in the future. I assured them that our discussions would be in total confidence. I promised to convey their respective positions to the other side only with their express permission and when I thought doing so would be helpful. Indirect negotiation was an admittedly underwhelming concept, but the purpose was to use such talks as a way to ease the parties into direct negotiation.

Netanyahu was disappointed; he wanted to talk with Abbas directly. The ten-month moratorium would expire in eight months, and he wanted direct talks before that happened. Still, indirect talks were preferable to the Israelis than what was coming out of Europe.

Just weeks before I proposed indirect talks, the EU adopted, for the first time, language on final status consistent with what the Palestinians had been seeking: "The European Union will not recognize any changes to the pre-1967 borders including with regard to Jerusalem, other than those agreed by the parties. . . . If there is to be a genuine peace, a way must be found through negotiations to resolve the status of Jerusalem as the future capital of two states."[13] Netanyahu was unable to alter the

reality that while it was the Palestinians who refused direct negotiations, he was so widely distrusted that many in the international community viewed his actions and substantive positions
as the major obstacle to progress.

Though consistent in his desire for direct negotiations, Netanyahu was simultaneously unwilling to discuss territory and
borders—despite the fact that the Palestinian position on direct
negotiations was unchanged, and unchangeable, until Abbas received some reassurance on the issue of territory. Netanyahu continued to insist on being fully satisfied by the United States on
security issues before he would discuss territory, with us or with
the Palestinians. Yet after Obama appointed U.S. military and civilian officials to begin those security discussions, Israel delayed
meetings between the IDF and our officials for eight months.
Through the summer and fall meeting after meeting was scheduled, then canceled. Finally, when one cancelation came at the last
minute, I telephoned Defense Minister Barak, reminded him that
these meetings were to be held at the request of Israel, and bluntly
demanded that the Israelis end the delay in getting them started.
He agreed, but the excuses and delays continued.

Netanyahu next proposed the alternative of secret back-channel
negotiations. He wanted the indirect talks to serve as a cover for
undisclosed negotiations, somewhere in Europe, between Israeli
and Palestinian representatives. Both sides would have total deni-
ability. Netanyahu knew that my efforts to convince Abbas to accept our proposal and to restrain various European countries from
proposing their own were complicated by continuing reminders
that Israeli actions in East Jerusalem were unrestrained by the
moratorium. Through the end of 2009 local authorities repeatedly
publicized progress on new Israeli housing projects in East Jerusalem and demolished Palestinian homes built without the required

Israeli permits. "How can I agree to negotiate in the middle of all of these actions?" Abbas asked me over and over again.

"Refusal to negotiate means more construction and more demolitions, not less," I reminded him. "An agreement is the only way to ensure they stop permanently!" But Abbas would not consent to negotiate directly with Netanyahu.

Meanwhile, even during the moratorium, settlement construction continued to raise tensions. Even given the well-known competitiveness of the internal politics of Israel, it was difficult to accept cabinet ministers repeatedly making announcements on settlements without the prime minister's knowledge or consent. But that is what Netanyahu claimed and we were not aware of any evidence to the contrary. And even if Abbas wanted to enter negotiations, politically he could not do so in the context of high negative emotions aroused by constant announcements of construction in East Jerusalem. These emotions were multiplied by the fact that, under Israel's complex process, every project was announced at each of several stages of planning, approval, and construction. But the announcements were irregular, and fortuitously there appeared to be a slowdown in the solicitation of construction bids for new housing projects in late February 2010. That's when Abbas agreed to indirect negotiations. The recent relative quiet in East Jerusalem certainly helped, and I hoped it would continue as long as possible. I told Abbas that restraint was more likely during negotiations than in their absence.

The idea of a secret channel for negotiations was much more difficult for Abbas to accept. Would Israel disclose the back channel as a way of embarrassing him? He was still very angry about the embarrassing leaks following the Goldstone Report, which he firmly believed were orchestrated by Netanyahu.

Around the time of the moratorium announcement in

November, Israeli president Shimon Peres had secretly reached out to Abbas. Though the presidency is largely symbolic, Palestinian leaders admire Peres and believe him to be sincere in his desire for reconciliation. But the Peres talks went nowhere. After five meetings he called off the effort because he had been unable to secure any commitment or guiding principle from Netanyahu on territory, the issue that remained Abbas's central concern. From Abbas's perspective, if even the president of Israel was unable to get anything from Netanyahu, why run the risk of another back channel?

But Peres had acted on his own—and had been a leader of Israel's Labor Party and an architect of the Oslo Accords, both opposed by Netanyahu. For the private channel now under consideration Netanyahu would send one of his most trusted advisors, Molcho, who could genuinely speak on his behalf. Who Abbas would appoint, though, was potentially a problem. Netanyahu and Molcho made clear their distrust of Erekat; they thought him overly emotional and too revealing in discussions with the press. There had been routine leaks from Israelis as well, but often these were from members of the government other than Netanyahu or Molcho. Netanyahu regularly briefed his inner cabinet members on our discussions, several of whom strongly and publicly opposed the two-state solution. Israeli leaks, then, were at times as much about constraining Netanyahu as they were to embarrass us or the Palestinians.

I announced the launch of proximity talks in the first week of March 2010 with significantly less fanfare than the trilateral meeting in September. We hoped that with the passage of time Netanyahu would be forthcoming on territory and that the negotiations would not be the political liability that Abbas feared. These talks were minimal; no one had high expectations.

Abbas conditioned his participation on the approval of the

Arab League, a strategy meant to shield him from critics and to prevent the uproar he had faced over his actions on the Goldstone resolution. Arab approval was also a way for Abbas to deflect some of the pressure we and the Israelis placed on him for public and direct negotiations. Just as Netanyahu used his conservative backers and inner cabinet as justification for his unwillingness to discuss territory and borders, so too would Abbas shroud himself in the Arab League.

"Despite not being convinced about the sincerity of the Israeli side to achieve a just peace," said Amr Moussa, chief of the Arab League, on March 3, "the committee sees . . . indirect negotiations as a last initiative." The Palestinians knew that we and the Israelis wanted to pivot quickly to direct negotiations. Moussa, though, made it clear that the Arab League would not be so easily persuaded. "The indirect talks should not be automatically translated into direct talks," he said.[14]

Time was not on our side. The construction moratorium would end in September and the Arab League planned to make a reassessment in July. To keep alive any kind of diplomatic process, we would have to convince Netanyahu to extend the moratorium or agree to discuss the issue of territory in a way serious enough to persuade Abbas that he could achieve more with negotiations than without them.

For months Abbas had been considering once again unilaterally declaring a Palestinian state in Gaza and on all of the West Bank and East Jerusalem. When Arafat and the PLO first unilaterally declared statehood in 1988, roughly one hundred countries—Arab and Muslim states, much of the developing world, and Soviet-aligned states—supported the move and recognized Palestine. That was before the emphasis on negotiations that began in Madrid and Oslo in the early 1990s. Since then, unilateralism had been discouraged. Now, as we struggled to resume negotiations, unilateralism was creeping back. Palestinian representatives abroad were successfully convincing a handful of states, primarily in Latin America, to confer statehood status by upgrading their diplomatic missions to full-fledged embassies. Abbas also considered the idea of taking that effort a step further by seeking Palestine's admission to the United Nations. I cautioned him against such a move; it would only be symbolic, would push away the Israelis, and would do little to advance the cause of Palestinian statehood. "What progress are we making now?" he asked me. "I need something." He didn't go through with it, but his threat to do so was obvious to Israel and to us. And he had growing support among the major powers of Europe.

On March 16, the day on which I announced proximity talks, Vice President Biden landed in Israel to underscore the administration's commitment to the U.S.-Israeli relationship. He was the most senior U.S. official to visit Israel since the start of the Obama administration. The president faced continuing criticism for not having visited Israel since assuming office; he should have done so. But Biden was a well-known and well-liked figure in Israel; he could help us move past both real and imagined tensions with Netanyahu. I briefed him on the day's events and on the status of our discussions with Israelis and Palestinians. I then left the hotel and was driven to the airport, where I boarded a flight to return to the United States.

As if on cue, just before the vice president began his meetings with Israeli officials, the Jerusalem Municipality announced plans to expand the neighborhood of Ramat Shlomo by 1,600 housing units. I learned of it while I was in the air over Europe. It was a direct and astonishing insult. Just days earlier Molcho had assured me there would be no surprises. How could this have happened? Once again we were told that the prime minister did not know about it in advance.

The plans for Ramat Shlomo would have little impact on the future border of Jerusalem. The neighborhood is located just outside the Green Line and the new units would fill in a strip of land between it and pre-1967 Israel. The announcement delayed the proximity talks. Several countries suggested that the UN Security Council condemn the Israeli action. But President Obama opposed UN action;[15] instead we convinced those countries to support a strong statement by the Quartet condemning the announcement.

Netanyahu was offended by the Quartet's statement. "Jerusalem is our capital," he told me. "How is it that we're condemned in the international community for building in our own capital when our oppressive, undemocratic neighbors receive no condemnation for their behavior!" But no country recognizes East Jerusalem as part of Israel, though almost all Israelis view it as part of their capital. I understood his frustration and later explained that it was the only way we could keep the Europeans and Russians from even harsher words against Israel. This was the best and least we could do. "You've got to get these settlement announcements under control," I urged him.

The diplomatic incident ended when Netanyahu promised to implement greater oversight over the municipality's actions in East Jerusalem. He couldn't prevent everything, he said, but we would not be surprised again. We had received the same promise many times before, so we gave it little weight. But Netanyahu promised additionally that construction on the Ramat Shlomo expansion would not take place for at least two years. It was enough to allow the proximity talks to go ahead.

.   .   .

The proximity talks finally began in early May, one year after the first Obama-Netanyahu meeting. The Palestinians presented detailed position papers on each of the core issues: territory, security, refugees, Jerusalem. These were virtually identical to the proposals they had made years earlier during the Annapolis Process, so the Israelis already had them in their possession. Netanyahu recommended starting with less difficult issues: infrastructure, the economy, water, and the environment. I had urged that Netanyahu commit to real discussions about territory and other core issues during the proximity talks, that they not be used solely as a cover for a private channel. But when I asked the Israelis to discuss territory, I again was told that the U.S.-Israeli security dialogue had to be concluded first.

As we considered ways to breathe life into the proximity talks, a new challenge arose. For years Israel and Egypt had maintained a tight security perimeter, controlling the flow of goods and people into and out of Gaza; especially since Operation Cast Lead, many Gazans lived in squalor and poverty, dependent on goods allowed in by Israel or smuggled in by Hamas. Now, in late May a flotilla of six ships filled with civilian activists sailed from southern Europe with the intention of breaking Israel's blockade of the Gaza Strip. They ignored Israel's demand that it be allowed to inspect and then transfer their cargo to Gaza, so Israel intercepted the flotilla on May 31. The operation began peacefully, but on one of the ships, the *Mavi Marmara*, a fierce battle ensued. By the end of it Israeli commandoes had killed nine activists, eight of them Turkish nationals.

Israel felt justified in its blockade and its actions to prevent the flotilla from reaching Gaza, but Israeli-Turkish relations collapsed.[16] Abbas believed his status declined further amid accusations that he was complicit in Gaza's impoverishment. Like the Egyptians, he was stuck between demanding an "end to the siege" on humanitarian grounds and an aversion to any action that could strengthen Hamas. In an unsuccessful effort to justify the blockade publicly, some Israeli cabinet ministers said that it was done in part to help Abbas's standing relative to Hamas's, which further hurt his reputation. Palestinians and other Arabs considered Hamas and Turkey the political victors in the episode.

The flotilla incident marked the end of the Arab League's full cooperation with us, and some Arab countries that had worked to prevent the Arab League from obstructing U.S. initiatives now moved away. Notwithstanding their reaction, we stood by Israel, agreeing that it had the right to prevent the ships from reaching Hamas in the Gaza Strip, even if we disagreed with the full breadth of their restrictions. The Israelis, faced with tremendous international pressure did realize they had to do something to reduce criticism of their policies toward Gaza. Their solution, the result of negotiations with us, the UN, and others, was to create a list of items prohibited from importation into Gaza to replace the list of approved items. This enabled a much wider array of items to enter Gaza and with greater ease. Prior to the flotilla we had repeatedly and unsuccessfully asked Israel to ease their restrictions on goods into Gaza, both on humanitarian grounds and as a way to boost the stature of President Abbas. What we couldn't accomplish with diplomacy and persuasion, the flotilla activists had accomplished, at a cost of nine lives, except that the easing of restrictions didn't accrue to Abbas's credit.

I met with Abbas to review the status of the proximity talks, but he wanted to discuss the secret channel. He had designated Hussein Agha, a longtime confidant and unofficial advisor, as his representative.[17] But despite my many assurances to him of total secrecy and the promise that the secret channel would involve only Molcho and Agha, Molcho had asked a U.S. official to join the secret discussions in London. Even more worrisome, Abbas then told me that shortly after he learned of this breach in confidentiality, he was visited by two private citizens, one an American. To Abbas's surprise, both began to openly discuss with him the private channel. Angry and upset, feeling betrayed by the United States, he effectively ended the secret talks. He had been worried about Israeli leaks; he didn't anticipate that leaks would come from the Americans. The channel had accomplished nothing.[18]

As the proximity talks faded away Prime Minister Netanyahu asked President Obama to make one final attempt at direct talks. Israel's construction moratorium was soon to expire. The window of opportunity to have anything positive come of the moratorium and of our efforts to date was quickly closing.

To our surprise President Abbas did not immediately reject the idea of direct negotiations, but he insisted that Israel had to first extend the moratorium. What had been "worse than useless" a few months earlier had now become "indispensable." This confirmed our belief that if Abbas was unsatisfied with the direct negotiations, he would use the moratorium's expiration as justification for calling them off.

On July 6 in Washington, Netanyahu again strongly urged Obama to push for direct talks. He reassured the president of his commitment to peace and, more important, told him that he knew what the Palestinians needed on territory and promised to send the right signals. He seemed to have come around. His reassurance was enough for the president to agree to press for direct talks. Based on that meeting, we told Abbas that if he agreed to direct talks, Netanyahu would discuss the issue of territory, put forth his own positions, as well as seriously consider the Palesttinian positions. Abbas accepted the proposal.

When the direct talks began on September 2 I tempered my expectations but hoped that the tensions of the past twenty months would subside. We hoped Abbas and Netanyahu would gain traction from and for the talks and we urged them to overcome their reluctance to compromise. Regrettably, however, it took only four meetings to validate their long-held suspicions of and negative feelings toward each other.

The first three meetings—one in Washington and two in Egypt—were general in nature. Serious discussion began in the fourth meeting, held at the prime minister's residence in Jerusalem. It was devoted entirely to a lengthy statement by Netanyahu on Israel's security demands. He forcefully insisted that there would have to be an Israeli military force within any Palestinian state along the border with Jordan "for many decades"; he repeated the phrase several times. Abbas immediately and categorically rejected the demand. But he said that he could accept such a presence for a "transition" period of one to three years; he also offered to accept "for an indefinite period" an international force around all of the borders of a Palestinian state.

I had planned to urge the two leaders to discuss territory and borders at their next meeting, which I hoped we could schedule in the next few days. But there was no fifth meeting. When the construction moratorium expired on September 26—it had not been extended, despite our wishes—so did the direct talks.

.   .   .

For months after the talks ended, I shuttled between Washington and Jerusalem to try to get the parties back together. But they were entrenched in their positions and blamed one another for the impasse. Though both parties have rhetorically committed themselves to the goal of two states, they had different beliefs about what that meant and how they would get there.

In December 2010 one man's protest against the Tunisian government turned into a popular revolution. By mid-January the Tunisian president fled his country. For the first time in the modern era, the Arab world saw a dictator peacefully deposed. Inspired by those events, protests broke out in capitals across the Middle East and North Africa. By mid-March President Mubarak of Egypt had resigned under public pressure, civil wars broke out in Libya and Syria, and Saudi Arabian forces entered Bahrain to help the government restore order. The Middle East fell into a disarray unseen in decades.

In April 2011 President Obama delivered a major speech on the Middle East focused on turmoil and transition. He expressed America's opposition to the violent suppression of popular protest in the Arab world, pledged to support political and economic reform throughout the region, and underscored that change in the Middle East "cannot be denied." The sentiments were sound and consistent with American values. But there frequently is tension between our values and immediate political interests. Several of these embattled Arab governments, especially in Egypt and the Gulf, were pillars of stability in the region. We believe in representative government, even as we recognize that it may result in more opposition to American policies in the region.

President Obama did not believe the United States could undo or prevent the revolutions. He was concerned about the consequences to long-term American interests if we were seen as attempting to thwart the most profound expression of desire by Arab peoples in recent history.

Israel's neighbors were experiencing unprecedented unrest; Netanyahu believed that Israel should not make major decisions until the storm passed and the regional outlook cleared.

Abbas had lost his most reliable Arab backer when Mubarak stepped down. Additionally, the West Bank was not immune from the kind of protest and revolt that had taken hold in the rest of the Arab world.

In addition to the "Arab Spring," Obama in his April speech briefly addressed the Israeli-Palestinian conflict. On territory, he said that negotiations "should be based on the 1967 lines with mutually agreed swaps." On security, he said that "Israel must be able to defend itself—by itself—against any threat," that Palestine should be a nonmilitarized Palestinian state, and that Israel's withdrawal should be in agreed phases and that "the effectiveness of security arrangements must be demonstrated."[19]

The Palestinian reaction to the speech was muted. Prime Minister Netanyahu reacted negatively to the President's language on the 1967 lines. He had consistently opposed any reference to the lines, or to any discussion of borders.

When President Obama and Secretary Clinton appointed me as their Special Envoy in January 2009, I told them that, having spent five years on Northern Ireland, I could not commit to four years in the Middle East. We agreed on two years. That period expired months before the president's April speech. Had we been making progress, I likely would have stayed longer. But there had been none, and there was no prospect of any in the near future. In May 2011 I returned to private life.

9

ISRATINE

The day after Barack Obama's first inauguration Muammar Gaddafi, then the undisputed leader of Libya, published an op-ed in the *New York Times* denigrating years of "desperate diplomacy" to solve the conflict between Israel and the Palestinians. "A just and lasting peace," he wrote, "is possible but it lies in the history of the people of this conflicted land, and not in the tired rhetoric of partition and two-state solutions. . . . The compromise is one state for all."[1] Though Gaddafi has long since been disgraced, the idea for a state he called "Isratine" is no joke. Indeed talk of a one-state solution has become more common on both ends of the political spectrum.

Growing extremism, failed negotiations, Israeli settlement expansion, Palestinian disunity—many have become disillusioned with the conflict's entrenchment. Carlo Strenger, an editorialist for the left-leaning Israeli periodical *Haaretz*, wrote in 2012, "There are moments when the truth flies into your face and you realize your political program is no longer viable. But while I have no alternative to offer, I know one thing is sure: the two-state solution is dead."[2] We believe Strenger's requiem was premature, but the death of the two-state solution is exactly what its supporters warn Israel of.

Their argument is grounded in part in demographics. Today in the territory of the former British Mandate for Palestine (Israel, the West Bank, and Gaza) there are an almost equal number of Jews and Arabs—about 6.2 million each.[3] Because of demographics, Israel cannot permanently hold on to the Palestinian territories without either denying the Palestinians full citizenship and repudiating Israel's democracy, or granting the Palestinians the right to vote and surrendering Jewish self-determination. But this is a false paradigm in that it presents territorial maximalism—a binational or undemocratic one-state solution—as a viable alternative, which it is not.

We need not look beyond these very lands to foresee the likely result of ethnic competition under one government: it was the incompatibility of Jewish and Arab national, cultural, and political aspirations in the British Mandate for Palestine that led to Israeli-Palestinian partition in the first place. Violent attacks and retributions were constant; tragedy spared few. And the consequences of ethnic and political tensions in Israel today are worrying.

The Israeli Right, including the sitting Justice Minister, have regularly attacked the structure and independence of Israel's Supreme Court. The Knesset has passed bills that have been criticized by the political left as veiled attempts to discourage political activism and NGO activities. In late 2014 and early 2015, the Knesset seriously considered what has been labeled the Jewish

Nation State bill, which aimed to more explicitly anchor Israel's
Jewish identity in the state's laws by, for example, removing Arabic, the native tongue of twenty percent of Israel's population, as
one of the state's official languages. The bill has been shelved for
the time being, though many expect that it will resurface in the
coming years.

In the March 2015 Israeli elections, in a last-ditch effort to
persuade his base to vote, Prime Minister Netanyahu warned of
Arab voters "heading to the polling station in droves."[4] In May
2016 all of Israel's major university presidents released a statement "to warn about the gradual and continuous erosion of the
foundations of Israeli democracy, which is manifested in hurt-
ful discourse, verbal violence, and lack of tolerance toward the
other and the different."[5] For two peoples with a long history of
conflict and competing identities, severe internal conflict would
be all but guaranteed. Any iteration of the one-state solution en-
sures continuing hostility.

The tensions of binationalism are most apparent today in Jerusalem, where most Palestinians hold residency cards but not Israeli citizenship. They have the right to seek Israeli citizenship, but
of the city's 350,000 Palestinian residents, fewer than 10 percent
have done so.[6] Even fewer, less than 2 percent, vote in Jerusalem
municipal elections.[7] Since 1967, when Israel unified the city
under one municipality, the state has accelerated its development
of new Jewish neighborhoods in East Jerusalem. Yet in 1967, Palestinians accounted for 25 percent of the city's population, while
today they are 38 percent. Haim Ramon, the Vice Prime Minister under Olmert, has warned that if Palestinians choose participation in Jerusalem's politics, "Jerusalem's next mayor won't be
[Jewish]—he will be a Palestinian."[8]

Today, as a result of their electoral boycott, Palestinian East

Jerusalemites have little influence in the municipality and receive but a fraction of the services and investment their Israeli neighbors enjoy. The result is a clear division between Israelis and Palestinians in Jerusalem geographically, economically, and psychologically. Tension, crime, and strife have increased, particularly in East Jerusalem but also spilling over into West Jerusalem. For several months in 2015 and 2016 the level of attacks on Israelis led some to conclude that a third Palestinian intifada—a "knife intifada"—was under way. Hundreds of reprehensible lone wolf attacks involving stabbings, vehicle ramming, and other individual and random attacks proved difficult to prevent. As of this writing the spike in violence seems to have subsided, but it is clear that Jerusalem is a city on edge.

A few voices suggest that a nondemocratic version of the one-state solution has already come about but we have not yet realized it. They compare Israel's government to that in South Africa under apartheid. That comparison is wrong on a number of counts; for one, the Israeli-Palestinian conflict is about nationalism, occupation, and independence, not civil rights and equal citizenship. The equality the Palestinians seek is in having their own state, not participating in Israel's. But that Israel's democracy would erode in a one-state scenario is not unthinkable, especially if the Palestinian national movement shifts goals and pursues equal voting rights within Israel rather than independence from it. Israelis will staunchly oppose including the Palestinian national movement within their own; they will likely pass the Jewish Nation State bill and others like it aimed at ensuring Jewish national control of the government.

At the same time there are many influential Israelis who believe that demographics are no cause for alarm. They suggest that because it withdrew from Gaza in 2005, the most Israel would ever consider annexing is the West Bank; that would bring the Jewish-Arab ratio to 60-40. Palestinian and Israeli birth rates are stabilizing, the argument continues, and so Israel's democracy can be preserved alongside a Jewish-majority future.

A vocal minority takes this argument one step further, alleging that both official Israeli and Palestinian population counts in the West Bank are misleading and inflated.[9] By their count Israel's Jewish population would retain a two-thirds majority even with full annexation of the West Bank.

Israelis do not need to become a minority in order for the perils of the one-state scenario to materialize. In that kind of zero-sum environment, actions taken by one group will be perceived and reacted to as a direct threat to the other. In the hypothetical scenario in which Israel extends its sovereignty over the Palestinians, their conflict will only escalate. The premise of the two-state solution is that Israelis and Palestinians will be able to exercise their national aspirations separately, alongside one another. If the Palestinians are deprived of their own government in which to express their identity, they will naturally look to do that within Israel. The outcome will be entrenchment, civil strife, intercommunal violence, and fatigue. While it could take decades of violence to realize, the result of a one-state scenario will inevitably be what was proposed in 1947: partition into a Jewish and an Arab state. The one-state option is really no option at all.

All roads eventually lead to partition, but not all partitions are the same. An Israeli-Palestinian peace accord is what the United States and the international community have been pursuing for decades. But in light of the stalemate in negotiations, it is becoming increasingly popular for some of Israel's leaders to revive calls for unilateral withdrawal from Palestinian territories. They know that a one-state solution will eventually lead to partition and do not want to wait until isolation or civil strife become unbearable. "Until now, everybody who wanted to see some progress believed in direct negotiations," said Ami Ayalon, the former head of Israel's internal security service and commander of its navy. A group he helped found, Blue and White Future, is calling on Israel to take unilateral steps to begin to withdraw from the West Bank. "We need a new paradigm."[10]

Unilateral withdrawal is not a new concept, of course. But for most Israelis the idea was discredited because of what happened in Gaza in 2005. During the withdrawal itself even those who supported the operation found it difficult to watch their fellow citizens being forcibly dragged out of their homes. Following withdrawal Hamas took over the Strip and rocket attacks intensified. Israelis resurrecting the idea today argue that withdrawal is the right choice but that its execution in Gaza was flawed. Lessons were learned: a withdrawal of civilian populations from most of the West Bank should happen over years instead of a matter of days; the military should remain in place during the interim rather than withdraw alongside civilian populations, leaving a power vacuum for extremists to fill; and permanent resettlement locations should be planned and constructed in advance rather than subjecting evacuees to the instability of temporary and indefinite housing arrangements.

The resurgence of interest in unilateral withdrawal has been slow, but proponents see how untenable Israel's continued presence is in the West Bank. Advocates can now be found on Israel's political Left, Center, and Right. Prime Minister Netanyahu's former ambassador to the United States, Michael Oren, has come to the conclusion "that the only alternative Israel has to save itself as a Jewish state—and let's be frank about that, the Jewish state is predicated on having a Jewish majority—the only way we can do that is by unilaterally withdrawing [sic] our border and withdrawing our settlements in the West Bank."[11]

Even on Israel's Left, Isaac Herzog, head of the political bloc opposing Netanyahu in the Knesset, has said, "I wish to separate from as many Palestinians as possible, as quickly as possible. . . . They over there and we over here; we'll erect a big wall between us. That is the kind of co-existence that's possible now." Herzog was speaking in January 2016, amid the resurgence of violence, particularly in Jerusalem. "Then," he said, "we'll re-unite the true Jerusalem without hundreds of thousands of Palestinians."[12] In other words, in addition to separating from the West Bank, Herzog wants to divide Jerusalem to the extent possible along ethnic lines. Of course if Israel unilaterally withdraws, Israelis will decide its borders.

Withdrawal from the West Bank, even in the context of a peace agreement, will come at a high cost to Israeli society, both financially and socially. At least 80,000 settlers, ten times the number in Gaza in 2005, will need to be relocated to Israel. Especially if a plan for redrawing the borders of Jerusalem accompanies a unilateral withdrawal from the West Bank, Israel will have borne most of the costs of a peace agreement without getting reciprocal concessions from the Palestinians or the Arabs countries.

Many disagree that Israel's options are so stark. "The story of Israel is unique," says Dani Dayan. He is right of course. That a scattered population could regather itself after centuries of exile and establish a modern and prosperous state was without precedent. "That's why," Dayan concludes, "the solution to the conflict will have to be unique as well."[13] Between 2007 and 2013 Dayan chaired the Yesha Council, the umbrella organization for Israeli settlement municipalities. He was the leader of Israeli settlement leaders, although he doesn't fit the stereotype of an Israeli settler. He is a secular and successful businessman in Israel's booming tech sector. From his perspective, settlements are less about the fulfillment of biblical promises and more about Israel's security. They ensure Israel's permanent presence and control in the West Bank and thereby provide strategic depth for the Jewish state.

Dayan immigrated to Israel from Argentina in 1971. "I came from a staunch Likud family," he said. "Begin types." Begin was Israel's first right-wing prime minister and received the Nobel Peace Prize for concluding a peace treaty with Egypt. But Israelis who say they are "Begin types" are referring to Begin the territorial maximalist. Dayan created a stir when he wrote a *New York Times* op-ed referring to the two-state solution as "a manifestly immoral outcome" and concluding that "the settlements of Judea and Samaria are not the problem—they are part of the solution."[14]

With respect to Israeli-Palestinian negotiations, Dayan says, "There is no point which reconciles Israel's security requirements, even the most modest ones, for the most modest Palestinian demands."[15] Dayan, though, has no illusions about the consequences of Israel annexing the West Bank and absorbing the Palestinian population there, as other Israelis on the Right propose. "That would be catastrophic. And it won't happen because Israelis, although we have a lot of difference of opinions, agree on one thing—the importance of a Jewish state. Israeli society is not suicidal, it will not grant citizenship to the Arabs in Judea and Samaria."

What's left is the "modus vivendi": "Fine tuning this status quo is the only solution for the mid-range future. This includes

understanding that (a) there will be no other sovereignty but Israel west of the Jordan River; (b) security must remain in Israel's
hands from the Mediterranean to the Jordan River; and (c) the
Palestinian Authority should continue to rule the life of Palestinians as much as possible in Area A and B." Dayan is referring to the
zones of control agreed to in the Oslo Accords. Area A, roughly
20 percent of the West Bank, is under full Palestinian security and
civil control. Area B, also about 20 percent of the West Bank, is
divided between Palestinian civil control and Israeli security control. Area C is the rest of the West Bank and is under full Israeli
control.

"I'm going to surprise you with this one," Dayan adds: "[There
also needs to be] (d) a sharp change of attitude towards Palestinian
dignity and human rights. Every checkpoint that can be removed
is a benefit. The ideal is complete freedom of movement for everyone. And, at the risk of sounding too optimistic, we should dis-
mantle the security barrier."

Put another way, Dayan's proposal is for a one-state solution
with some regional autonomy, but not citizenship, for Palestinians
within that state. But he believes Israel does not need to choose
between democracy and Jewish self-determination. Instead he
imagines the current conflict is like a mathematical equation with
no solution. "So, to solve the problem, a variable must change,"
and that variable is Jordan.

The Israeli Right has a slogan: "Jordan is Palestine." Because
Palestinians are estimated to make up half of Jordan's population,
Israeli believers in that slogan advocate that Palestinians express
their national aspirations there, east of the Jordan River. Dayan
views democratic changes in Jordan, or at least the erosion of
Hashemite rule, as an inevitability that will present real challenges
as well as some new opportunities to resolve the conflict.

"If you ask me, 'What can be the outcome?,' I say two states with joint rule over the Palestinians. The River Jordan is the limit of each state, as it is today. One is Israel. The other is Jordan-Palestine. Israel will grant Jordan-Palestine responsibility over the Palestinian lives in the West Bank; Israel will be responsible for security." That arrangement would allow Israel to avoid having to choose between its Jewish character, its democracy, and full territorial control. It would get all three. Dayan calls this "a functional compromise." Needless to say, Palestinians, Jordanians, and all other Arabs disagree. They call it capitulation, not compromise.

Dayan's long-term vision of an association between the Palestinians and Jordan should sound familiar because it is close to the approach suggested by President Reagan in 1982. The United States, Reagan said, would "not support the establishment of an independent Palestinian state in the West Bank and Gaza" but would push for Palestinian self-rule in association with Jordan—the Jordanian option.[16] Begin—Dayan's hero—immediately and in the strongest terms rejected Reagan's proposal.

If Palestinians do acquire more control over the Jordanian government, as Dayan anticipates, Palestinian influence and power will grow. As a result their positions are likely to harden, not soften.

Palestinian self-rule, of course, does not require an official connection with Jordan. Dayan's Jordan proposal is only theoretical and aspirational. It is what he said about "fine-tuning" the status quo that is far more relevant because there is no other strategy that both legitimizes continued settlement expansion and responds to claims that Israel risks losing its Jewish and democratic character. And fine-tuning the status quo is the so-called solution that many in Israel believe it is pursuing today.

Essential to this fine tuning is that the PA will indefinitely continue to serve as the outlet for Palestinian national expression and democratic participation. Some proponents of this approach do not mind that the Palestinians have declared their state, have their own flag, or carry Palestinian passports. The more symbols of independence they have, the less real independence they will need.

Dayan and a significant constituency in Israel believe that improving the economy and quality of life in the West Bank will secure Palestinian support. Their goal is for West Bank Palestinians to be able to travel from their cities and towns seeing as few Israelis as possible. For years, in fact, Israel has steadily invested in new roads, tunnels, and other infrastructure aimed at ensuring just that. As Dayan says, "Every checkpoint that can be removed is a benefit."[17]

The Palestinian economy in the West Bank is improving: GDP has more than doubled in the past decade, and investment in Palestinian economic development projects continues. Abbas's internal reforms and commitment to nonviolence have attracted record levels of direct foreign budget assistance, which allows the PA to continue governing and to also serve as the West Bank's largest employer.

Remarkably the Israeli-Palestinian security relationship has also deepened and matured. Under Abbas's rule Palestinian security services were restructured and professionalized and have become increasingly responsive to Israel's needs. The PA has shown it is capable of subduing militancy and conducting antiterror operations. It has suppressed dozens of large protests and demonstrations, even amid Israel's wars with Hamas in Gaza and during the Arab Spring. Israelis are not yet confident that the PA can operate effectively without their support and intelligence sharing, but most are impressed nevertheless. In 2015 Israel's military governor of the West Bank praised the Palestinian security apparatus, saying that the "West Bank is the only region with stability and calm amid a region that is full of security risks such as Jordan, Syria, Lebanon, Egypt and Gaza."[18]

Supporters of status-quo permanence take comfort in the improving economic conditions in the West Bank and in the PA's current approach. The soundness of their long-term vision depends on it. But the hope that economic prosperity will subdue Palestinian desires for national independence is not new. When Israel first captured the West Bank and Gaza, it invested heavily in improving the Palestinian economy and infrastructure. Between 1967 and 1973 alone the Palestinian GDP in the West Bank grew by 80 percent and continued to grow for years thereafter. In Gaza Israel allocated millions to construct new sewage systems, erect street lights, extend credit for new housing, and establish public transportation links with Israel and the West Bank. Palestinian unemployment was at record lows, and their GDP was climbing faster than any of their Arab neighbors'. Palestinian life expectancy rose by ten years; infant mortality was cut in half; and the number of homes with access to clean drinking water and refrigeration skyrocketed. Aside from isolated incidents, Israelis saw the West Bank and Gaza flourishing under their administration. Of course that was all prior to the First Intifada, which, despite heavy casualties and ruinous economic effects, persisted for five years.

Doing nothing is all that is required to test whether economic prosperity will subdue Palestinian desires for national independence this time around, whether they will accept being able to express their national and cultural identity only within limited autonomous zones under Israel's permanent military control. Over and over the Palestinians have demonstrated their willingness to sacrifice their comfort and material well-being for the cause of national independence. That intense commitment should come as no surprise to Israelis; their will to achieve the dignity of Jewish self-determination was no less fierce.

As Oren and Herzog make the case for unilateral withdrawal, and Dayan makes the case for status quo permanence, both positions have substantial support in Israel. But so does the view that a negotiated two-state solution remains the best option. That position was articulated by Tzipi Livni in an interview published in *Foreign Affairs* in the summer of 2016:[19]

QUESTION: You've spoken in the past about the dangers of not doing anything to address the situation. But given the disarray on the Palestinian side, and the fact that Abu Mazen's [Mahmoud Abbas'] days are numbered, what can be done?

LIVNI: Israel needs to decide which road we want to take; we need to decide on our destination. If the destination is Greater Israel [permanent Israel retention of the West Bank], it doesn't matter whether there's a partner on the other side. But if your destination is a secure Israel that is Jewish and democratic, then it can't be on the entire land. That is our GPS setting. To get there, we'd prefer to have an agreement with the Palestinians, because that is the way to create a secure border, a demilitarized Palestinian state, and an end to the conflict. Because you cannot end the conflict without their consent. And if we cannot end the conflict tomorrow morning, let's at least start moving toward our goal. That means not doing things that take you in the opposite direction. Netanyahu says his destination is two states for two peoples. But he's going in the opposite direction.

QUESTION: So what do you propose?

LIVNI: First, we need to win the trust of the international community and the Palestinians by saying this is where we want to go. Not for you, not as a favor to the United States. But because it's in our own interests. Second, we should stop doing things for the different vision of Israel.

QUESTION: Such as?

LIVNI: Stop expanding settlements, especially those outside the fence that are not going to be part of Israel. Then let's change the atmosphere. Let's show we're serious. Let's give the Palestinians the right to build in Area C. Let's see whether these and other confidence-building measures can create enough trust to relaunch negotiations. And then in the negotiations we need to find out what they really want. Are they willing to end the conflict and take steps that would serve their interests as well? And we need to work completely differently with the international community. We have lost their trust by speaking about two states but then acting in ways that serve the vision of a Greater Israel. There are certain things that nobody in Israel would give up. Security: a Palestinian state should be demilitarized. And the major settlement blocs would become part of Israel.

Livni's concerns are widely shared among Israel's military and intelligence leaders. Fourteen former and living IDF chiefs of staff, directors of the Shin Bet (internal security, FBI equivalent), and heads of the Mossad (intelligence agency, CIA equivalent) publicly decried the current stalemate and urged progress toward a two-state solution.[20]

In the absence of a state, Palestinians increasingly perceive the PA as serving Israel's territorial interests more than Palestine's independence. Instead of preparing to take over from Israel's rule, the PA is seen as behaving like a security subcontractor easing the burden for Israel of the occupation.

Abbas is not deaf to those accusations. His approach is meant not only to assert authority over Hamas and others but also to show to the PA's Western donors, and to Israel, that it can be a responsible government in the region. Abbas has therefore said that Israeli-Palestinian security cooperation is "sacred and that it will continue, whether Israelis and Palestinians agree or disagree in politics."[21] He wants to undermine any argument against Israeli withdrawal grounded in instability and insecurity while also increasing internal and external pressure on Israel's government for a peace agreement that he and the Palestinian people can accept. From his perspective that is a more assured path to achieve Palestinian independence than the violence of Hamas or intifadas.

Today Abbas bridges his internal credibility gap with achievements in the diplomatic and foreign policy arena, such as securing Palestine's nonmember observer-state status at the UN, encouraging the settlement products boycott in Europe, and similar wins on the international stage. But while many Palestinians accept this approach as credible, the more distant Palestine's independence appears, the less legitimate that approach will seem. Palestinians already blame Abbas and the PA as least as much as they do Hamas for the rift between the West Bank and Gaza.

The Palestinian legislature has been nonfunctioning since Hamas's electoral victory in 2006. Since then, Abbas has ruled by decree and, as opposition to his governance grows, so has his consolidation of power. In 2013 Prime Minister Fayyad resigned in dismay over Abbas's lack of support for political and fiscal reforms unpopular among Fatah party leaders.

The political crisis within the PA is weakening its connection with the Palestinian people. The disconnect should be concerning not only for those who wish to see democratic and peaceful Palestinian leaders, but also for those who wish to soon see a negotiated agreement and Israeli-Palestinian cooperation. In March 2015, for example, the PLO Central Committee, an elected body that makes decisions when the full National Council is not in session, called for the suspension of "all forms of security coordination given Israel's systematic and ongoing non-compliance with its obligations under signed agreements."[22] Abbas ignored their calls, but it remains unclear how long he will be able to do so with impunity.

Absent any progress toward independence, there is little doubt that the PA will either move away from cooperation with Israel or collapse altogether. The pool of potential moves in the diplomatic arena is not endless. At some point those victories will seem hollow and lose their appeal; popular backlash against Abbas's governance, not least of which includes his close working relationship with Israel's security establishment, is a real possibility.

And international aid could easily dry up or be redirected if the PA's resolve weakens. This is the dilemma facing Israel. On one side are those who believe the risk is too great that an agreed Palestinian state will fail and the West Bank will be taken over by Hamas or more radical groups. On the other side are those who believe that the risk of the PA failing and a West Bank takeover by Hamas or others is much greater in the absence of a peace agreement.

The IDF has recently begun conducting extensive drills to prepare for this eventuality. One IDF leader in that effort said, "Looking at Judea and Samaria [the West Bank], we have to recognize that the scenarios [we practiced] are not unrealistic. They represent the nature of things here."[23]

The PA has relieved Israel of the enormous and expensive burden of administering the day-to-day affairs of the Palestinian people in the West Bank. If for any reason the PA ceases to play that role, especially with respect to security, Israel may have no choice but to fill the void and reoccupy the towns and cities of the West Bank. They may be able to maintain that posture for a limited period of time, but the administrative and financial burdens on Israeli society would be enormous and draining. The IDF would be stretched thin, perhaps too thin to effectively deal with potentially bigger threats.

This dynamic of Israel's dependence on the PA for stability has provided the Palestinians with leverage in the relationship. In 2015, for example, Netanyahu withheld $127 million in tax revenues that Israel collected on behalf of the PA, in retaliation for a formal Palestinian bid to join the International Criminal Court, where it intends to sue Israel for war crimes. The resulting fiscal deficit forced the PA to stop paying the salaries of tens of thousands of its civil servants. Israel's president promptly criticized the move. "Freezing the transfer of Palestinian tax funds," he said, "does not benefit us and does not benefit them. Using these funds, the Palestinians sustain themselves and [keep] the Palestinian Authority functioning. Israel's interest is a functioning PA."[24] So great was the fear of a backlash and an erosion of the PA's effectiveness and credibility that Israel's defense minister, as well as its military and internal security leaders, successfully pushed Netanyahu to unfreeze the funds with no strings attached.

Abbas regularly threatens to turn the keys of the West Bank over to Israel. It is doubtful he would ever go that far, but the risk increases the anxiety of Israel's defense establishment.

Over the decades the political and territorial compromises offered by Israel have looked more and more like long-standing Palestinian demands than their own. That Israel's leverage has decreased over time seems counterintuitive. Israel has what is widely considered to be the most advanced economy and powerful military force in the region. It controls all entrances to the Palestinian territories, except one crossing between Gaza and Egypt. In the West Bank, Israel is able to act as it pleases and Palestinians have little recourse on the ground. But the progression of negotiations is unmistakable.

In the 1980s Begin and Shamir strongly opposed "land for peace" and engagement of the PLO. Yet what was unacceptable to them soon became the foundation of the 1993 Oslo Accords. By the late 1990s Netanyahu, Shamir's successor in the Likud, even sat down with the PLO and agreed to expand the amount of territory under the PA's control by some 50 percent. Soon after, in 2000, Israel's labor prime minister indicated agreement with President Clinton's proposal of withdrawing from 95 percent of the West Bank and dividing Jerusalem along ethnic lines. Then Ariel Sharon, a father of Israel's settlement movement, accepted the two-state solution and withdrew unilaterally from the Gaza Strip. His hand-picked successor, Ehud Olmert, discussed proposals for Palestine's independence in an area equivalent to 100 percent of the territory that Israel had occupied in 1967.

More than decreasing Israel's leverage in negotiations, delay has foreclosed potential avenues for an agreement. Take, for example, the Jordanian option in Reagan's 1982 plan: many believe that Reagan could not have implemented his plan because of Palestinian and other Arab opposition. We will never know. But Jordan and Israel had actually made considerable progress toward implementing Reagan's ideas. With the help of the Reagan administration, Prime Minister Shimon Peres pursued secret discussions with King Hussein for over two years. Peres proposed a three-year temporary power-sharing arrangement in which Jordan would begin to take over swaths of the West Bank. The year Peres became prime minister, 1984, Jordan and the PLO reconciled their differences and agreed to jointly work to pursue a peace agreement with Israel based on Jordanian-Palestinian confederation in the occupied territories.[25] But negotiating with Arafat, even in conjunction with Jordan, was a step too far and too soon for Israel.

Peres continued to push his proposals even after Shamir replaced him as prime minister. Peres's persistence paid off in April 1987, when, after secret and marathon meetings in London, he and Hussein agreed on a formula for negotiations in pursuit of the Jordanian option. But when Peres presented the proposal to Shamir and the Likud Party, they rejected it, as they had the Reagan plan five years earlier. Now it is essentially the objective of many of their political successors.

But the moment of opportunity for that plan has long since passed. In 1988, less than a year after his meetings with Peres in London, King Hussein relinquished his claims and severed all of Jordan's legal and governmental ties to the West Bank. The move took Israel by surprise, especially Peres. Hussein justified his actions as a way to bolster Palestinian rights and independence. But in reality, he was deeply discouraged that Peres was unable to deliver his government. In the wake of the First Intifada, Hussein decided that Jordan was better off leaving Israel to deal with the chaos in the West Bank.[26]

Herein lies Israel's ultimate challenge. Absent progress in negotiations with the Palestinians, Dayan's "fine tuning" of the status quo is Israel's default solution, though it may be described in other words. Supporters of making the status quo permanent do not deny that Abbas and the PA may be imperiled. What they believe, as they must, is that Israel will always be able to pick up the pieces and find new and suitable Palestinian partners willing to fill a void in governance; when Abbas is no longer president, there will be another leader to take the helm, and then another after that, and if the PA fails, something else will rise in its place. Meanwhile the Palestinian people and their leaders will permanently accept relative economic comfort in exchange for limited autonomy under Israeli military rule. Israelis who support this approach may be right for a while, perhaps even decades. But that is not enough. They have to be right for the rest of Israel's future.

If they are wrong, the consequence is not, as many suggest, a one-state solution in which Israel has to choose between its democracy and its Jewish character. The consequence is that the path back to partition from a one-state reality will be long and destructive. And the longer it takes Israel to realize, the more complicated the solution will be to negotiate; options will continue to worsen; Israel will receive less in exchange for conceding more; and implementation of an agreement will steadily rise in cost. Unilateral withdrawal, for instance, forecloses the possibility that some Israeli settlers can remain in Palestine, or that when Israel withdraws it will have a partner on the other side willing to be as cooperative as the PA is today on the issue of non-violence.

Prime Minister Netanyahu's most recent position is support for a two-state solution but not now, because the time is not right. That position has much support within Israel and the United States. But when in the sixty-eight years of Israel's history has the time been "right"? Certainly it was not in 1979 and 1994, when Israel reached peace agreements with Egypt and Jordan; Israel now places a high value on maintaining those agreements, as we believe it would an agreement with the Palestinians.

The right time may never come given the turbulence and upheaval that now exist in the region and is likely to continue for decades. Unlike the circumstances that existed during most of early

Israel's history, the principal threat does not come from a land invasion from neighboring armies, but from the uncertain situation in the West Bank, from Iran's quest for regional hegemony, and from terrorist organizations operating just outside Israel's borders. Any one of those threats should be enough to keep Israel's security establishment awake at night; the combination of all three is daunting.

Some of the nonstate actors in the region are supported by Iran; others are deeply hostile to it; all view Israel as an enemy. As the United States has learned in its own counterterrorism efforts, the most effective way to counter nonstate actors, the proliferation of contraband, and terror financing is through broad and close intelligence and security coordination across the region. Many Arab governments, particularly in the Gulf, fear nonstate actors and Iran's backing of those actors, as much as the Israelis do. In this respect, their interests are aligned with Israel's.

In 2002 the Arab League endorsed the Arab Peace Initiative, initially proposed by the late King Abdullah of Saudi Arabia. It offered Israel the normalization of relations with the Arab and Muslim world in exchange for its withdrawal from territories it occupied in 1967 and a "just solution" to the Palestinian refugee issue. Israelis believed it was insincere and inflexible on final status issues, a take-it-or-leave-it proposal. Fifteen years later, the initiative remains on the table. In the interim, some Arab leaders have disagreed with the Israeli characterization of the initiative and have indicated some flexibility in their position.[27]

The absence of a peace agreement—or waiting for "the right time"—makes less likely that Arab countries will be willing to normalize relations with the Jewish State. Israelis fear that the Arab states will endlessly condition normalization to extract more concession; that the stability of Arab governments, and therefore the value of their commitments, is uncertain. One important lesson from the

Arab Spring, however, is that Israel's peace treaty with Egypt—long a foundation of security and stability for Israel—survived the Muslim Brotherhood presidency of Muhammad Morsi. Even though the treaty remains unpopular among the Egyptian people, and even though Hamas is an offshoot and ally of the Muslim Brotherhood, Morsi never challenged the treaty. Today, under the new Egyptian government, military relations with Israel remain close.[28]

Absent an Israeli-Palestinian peace agreement, Israel risks a deterioration of stability in the West Bank and effective cooperation with the PA on security. It also misses an opportunity to shape favorable regional coalitions and to establish deeper and more comprehensive regional cooperation to combat Iran, nonstate actors, and other mutual threats; agreements and relationships that may be able to withstand, or even help mitigate, the consequences of the Middle East's unpredictability.

The trajectory of negotiations seems to favor Palestinian interests and positions, measured in terms of the contours of their state. That is at least part of the reason they do not appear desperate to negotiate or to agree to just any state. But that does not mean it is in their benefit to stall. I have unsuccessfully tried to convince the Palestinians of the perils of delay since at least the collapse of Camp David in 2000.

In the spring of 2001 I met with Arafat at his office in Gaza. My colleagues and I were there as members of what became known as the International Fact-Finding Commission on Violence in the Middle East, appointed by President Clinton, Prime Minister Barak, and Arafat, following the outbreak of the Second Intifada.[29]

Like the man, his office was not ostentatious. He was wearing the same slightly scruffy military-style uniform he always had on, and his face had a stubble of beard. One notable change was the evident quiver in his lower lip, a result of the extent to which he suffered from Parkinson's disease. He sat at his desk, and we sat across from him. Aides from both sides formed half-circles around us. As with all of my discussions with Arafat, the tone was serious and civil. There were disagreements, and we all made our points emphatically but without anger or hostility. His English was imperfect; he understood it better than he spoke it, but he rarely relied on the interpreter by his side.

At one point he suddenly announced he had a request. That evening a large group of civic leaders from all over the Gaza Strip were meeting at a nearby conference center. Would I and my colleagues go there after dinner to talk with them and answer questions? "There may be some difficulty," he said, "because some are from Hamas and they will be critical of America. But"—he paused, laughed, and waved at Warren Rudman and me—"you senators can take care of them."

"Well," I answered, "we will go, and we'll try to take care of them."

The time seemed right, and I then said to Arafat, "You have to figure out a way to meet again with the Israelis and negotiate an agreement." It had been less than a year since the failed effort at Camp David in 2000; that was very much on my mind. "You and every other Arab leader would now gladly accept the terms of the proposal for partition that was made by the United Nations in 1947." That proposal had been accepted by Israel but rejected by the Arab nations. "It was turned down because the Arabs then thought they could easily defeat the Israelis. They couldn't, and Israel is much stronger now. The only way you can get what you want is to negotiate with them and get a state. You won't get all you want, you may think it unfair, but the important thing is to get a state so your people can govern themselves. The perfect solution is never going to be available. You've got to get back into negotiations and stay there until you get an agreement." He smiled and said he wanted an agreement, but it had to be one he and his people could accept. The discussion ended inconclusively, as did most of my meetings with Arafat.

Around a large oval-shaped table at the conference center were about three dozen men. As we walked toward the head of the table, where three empty chairs waited, Rudman whispered to me, "Remember, if you call on me, I'm Senator O'Malley from Massachusetts." I smiled and assured him I wouldn't call on him.

There was a lively discussion, with familiar questions and equally familiar answers. A few Hamas officials were pointed but not rude in their comments and questions. I answered in the same way. The meeting lasted about two hours. Our team felt it had been useful; we had heard directly from a wide range of community leaders, businessmen, clergy, and government officials; most supported Arafat, but some did not; most were favorably inclined toward the United States, but some were not. As we left the building and walked to our car I said to Rudman, "I've never before seen you sit through a meeting without saying anything." He laughed and replied, "There's a first time for everything, but that's probably the last time too." He was a close associate and a very dear friend whose blunt outspokenness sometimes masked an incisive mind. He proved to be a major contributor to the report that our commission delivered to President Bush a few months later.

Nearly a decade later, when I returned to the region as President Obama's special envoy, on several occasions I said essentially the same thing to President Abbas that I had said to Arafat. My discussions with Abbas were detailed and frequent. Always, inevitably, he expressed his concern about settlements, refusing to enter into direct and meaningful negotiations with Netanyahu until all construction was halted.

In vain I argued with Abbas that if he wanted to end settlement construction, he should negotiate as soon as possible and try to reach an agreement on borders; once that was settled the dispute over settlements would be resolved: Israelis could build whatever they wanted in areas designated as part of Israel, and Palestinians could build whatever they wanted within their borders. I thought my argument was persuasive, but Abbas did not. He continued to insist that there had to be a full settlement freeze before he could enter negotiations with Netanyahu.

I told him I thought he was wrong to do so, and I still do. Since I first urged Arafat to reach an agreement in 2001, the number of Israeli settlers in the West Bank alone has more than doubled, from 190,000 to 400,000. And since I had those discussions with Abbas in 2009 and 2010, the West Bank settlement population has grown by about 75,000. Abbas continues to insist on preconditions to negotiations. In 2015 he said he would resume negotiations only if Israel agreed to a settlement freeze, released some Palestinian prisoners, and accepted a tight timeline for "ending the occupation."

Instead of negotiations Abbas has focused on putting pressure on Israel in various international institutions. His hope appears to be that further isolation of Israel will either force it to accept preconditions for negotiations or convince the people of Israel to vote into office leaders with whom he can make peace. Neither of those outcomes appears likely. If anything, Israel's people and politics have moved to the right.

However, the Palestinians and their supporters have made some progress in the international community: raising their flag at the UN, securing recognition of statehood by a growing number of countries, even the settlements boycott. Boycotts and divestment movements continue to sprout across Europe and in the United States. Many Israelis are taken aback by these trends. But Israel's diplomatic relations and ties around the world are also deepening. In 2010 Israel joined the Organization for Economic Cooperation and Development. The EU included Israel as the only non-EU partner in Horizon 2012, an $80 billion funding scheme promoted as the "biggest EU Research and Innovation programme ever."[30] And in 2013 Israel was unanimously admitted as the first non-European member of the European Organization for Nuclear Research. These are only a few examples. Palestinian efforts to cripple Israel in the international community may succeed in the future, but current trends do not suggest that will happen soon.

In retrospect delays in negotiation may have served some Palestinian interests. Even if that is the case, though, the Palestinians risk overplaying their hand. The Palestinians have succeeded in convincing the people and governments of many countries that the reason for stalemate is the refusal of the government of Israel to negotiate seriously on the final status issues, not the unwillingness of the Palestinians to enter into direct negotiations.

Among Israelis there is uncertainty over whether Abbas, or any Palestinian leader, will ever be prepared to make the concessions necessary for agreement. That conclusion is evident in the Labor Party leadership's recent focus on unilateral withdrawal. And unilateral Israeli withdrawal could be a serious setback to the prospect of Palestinian independence and statehood. While it is true that Israel would pay a high price and receive little in return in Palestinian and Arab concessions, what Israel would receive is time and demographic security. The many pitfalls of the one-state solution would no longer drive the conflict or their decision-making process. As the leader of Israel's Labor Party said in frustration, "They over there and we over here." In the meantime Palestinians will continue to be stateless, refugees will receive no compensation, and Dayan's "functional compromise" for Israeli control, Jewish self-determination, and democracy may be attainable, albeit without many of the settlements.

Support for the two-state solution remains strong in the United States, Europe, and Asia. In a February 2016 report the Quartet (the U.S., the UN, the EU, and Russia) reiterated that a "negotiated two-state solution is the only way to achieve an enduring peace that meets Israeli security needs and Palestinian aspirations for statehood and sovereignty."[31] The report, however, stressed it was "seriously concerned that continuing on the current course will make this prospect increasingly more remote," and listed three trends that "severely undermine the hope for peace":

- "continuing violence, terrorist attacks against civilians, and incitement to violence;"
- "the continuing policy of settlement construction and expansion;" and
- "the illicit arms build-up and militant activity, continuing absence of Palestinian unity, and [the] dire humanitarian situation in Gaza."

The report also called on the parties to "independently demonstrate, through policies and actions, a genuine commitment to the two-state solution." This call to action reflects the growing sense of urgency felt by the international community.

The emergence of a Palestinian state will create clear winners and losers, and the losers will undoubtedly seek retribution. In abundance on both sides are groups that will violently oppose an agreement and actively seek to prevent its implementation. Their tactics may vary, but their intentions will be the same.

On the Palestinian side are the many militants in their midst. Several are so extreme they make Hamas appear moderate. Continued conflict serves as a useful recruiting tactic not just for their paramilitary objectives but for their Islamic agenda. They do not accept Israel's presence in the Middle East or the PA's leadership of the Palestinian people.

On the Israeli side are radical settlers and their organizations. The vast majority of settlers in the West Bank will respect agreements their government enters into, even if they disagree politically. A minority numbering in the tens of thousands will actively oppose withdrawal with civil disobedience. Some may even take up arms against the IDF and seek retribution on Palestinians. The Gaza withdrawal invigorated their movement; an Israeli withdrawal from the West Bank, whether unilaterally or in the context of a peace agreement, would unleash them. Even if there is an Israeli-Palestinian peace agreement, these groups and others will become more aggressive.

The question is not whether there will be partition or violence in the future. Both are likely. What the parties must ask themselves is which path to partition will better position them to deal with regional and domestic threats; which will be less difficult and less costly, especially in human lives; and whether there will ever be a "right time." We believe the answer is obvious. No one-state scenario is viable in the long run, including "fine-tuning" the status quo. Withdrawal is inevitable. What cannot be known is when that will be and how much instability and violence will precede it. Withdrawal can take place unilaterally by Israel or as the result of an Israeli-Palestinian peace agreement. An agreement will be very difficult to achieve and will have its own problems, but an agreement offers both Israelis and Palestinians much less pain and expense than they otherwise will endure.

10

A PATH TO PEACE

U.S. administrations come and go, but the Israeli-Palestinian conflict goes on. In the effort to negotiate with which we were deeply involved from 2009 to 2011 we learned that lesson the hard way. Shortly after becoming secretary of state in 2013, John Kerry invested countless hours and dozens of overseas trips encouraging Israelis and Palestinians to pursue an agreement in earnest. Ultimately his efforts, like all those before him, were unsuccessful.

For eight years the Obama administration encountered the same obstacles to progress that have always been present: the intense hostility on both sides, intensified by so much death and destruction; the absence of political will; the deep well of mistrust between the leaders and between the two peoples; the profound sense of victimization in both societies; the mismatch in interest and strength between them; the changing nature of their internal politics, especially growing hostility in both societies from those who vigorously oppose a two-state solution; and the complexity and unpredictability of external events and pressures. Now it is President Donald Trump's turn to do what prior presidents could not do.

The right wing in Israel was enthusiastic about the Trump presidency. As a candidate, Trump repeatedly promised to move the U.S. Embassy from Tel Aviv to Jerusalem, and many of the president's advisors were ideologically aligned with those in Israel who support settlements and oppose placing pressure on Israel for concessions. And unlike prior American presidents who were clear in their support for the two-state solution, President Trump has, to date, been less conclusive.

Those opposed to the two-state solution rejoiced when, following his first meeting with Prime Minister Netanyahu, President Trump said, "I'm looking at two states and one state, and I like the one both parties like."[1] The Israeli member of Parliament and minister Naftali Bennett, for example, called on his government to seize the opportunity to hasten Israeli settlement activity and assert Israel's sovereignty over the West Bank to end any prospect of a Palestinian state in the West Bank and Gaza. "The Palestinian flag," Bennett said after the meeting, was "lowered from the mast and replaced with the Israeli flag. The Palestinians already have two states: in Gaza and in Jordan. There is no need for a third one."[2]

But the enthusiasm of the Israeli Right has since been tempered. "There is limited land left," Trump said less than a month after taking office, "and every time you take land for settlements, there's less land left. I'm not someone who believes that advancing the settlements is good for peace."[3] Indeed Trump expressed a desire to strike the "ultimate deal" between the parties. Once in office he distanced himself from his campaign promises to quickly move the U.S. Embassy to Jerusalem. He invited President Abbas to the White House and spoke of a "positive ongoing partnership" with the Palestinians and a commitment to "working with Israel and the Palestinians to reach an agreement."[4] He traveled to Israel and the Palestinian territories on his first official overseas trip and has appointed a team of trusted advisors, including a special envoy, who have been shuttling between Jerusalem and Washington in pursuit of an agreement. What may come of these efforts is unclear. What is clear, though, is that the context in which these efforts are being pursued is markedly different than it was in prior administrations.

One difference is the absence of widespread violence, so far, between Israelis and Palestinians. Trump's predecessors had little choice but to prioritize the Israeli-Palestinian conflict and shape their diplomatic posture in the Middle East amid crisis. President Clinton took office as the First Palestinian Intifada raged, President Bush during the Second Intifada, and President Obama just as a destructive war between Israel and Hamas had ended. Of course moments of crisis and unrest have in the past been an impetus for cooperation and deal-making between the parties. None, however, has led to resolution of the conflict. But the relatively low level of Israeli-Palestinian violence at the moment provides the space for a more measured and thoughtful strategic approach.

The Israeli-Palestinian conflict also is less than ever a preoccupation of Arab governments. Arab governments traditionally capitalized and even promoted a focus on conflict with Israel. However, since the popular Arab uprisings—the overthrow of some long-standing regimes and the political and civil turmoil that has swept the region since 2011—many Arab governments are concentrating on their internal challenges. Indeed cooperative relations between Israel and the Arab states to combat jihadist groups, Iranian influence, and other subversive elements are growing.

This Arab-Israeli cooperation is a third reality that will shape the Trump administration's approach to peace. Today Israel and many key Arab states work together and more closely than ever before to fight the Islamic State and other extremist groups. Iran is viewed with disdain and as a common threat. Long conducted in secret, Israel's intelligence and security relationships with key Arab states in the Gulf and elsewhere are strengthening, given the apparent and growing realization that Israel's technical capabilities and Arab human intelligence assets could be a formidable combination.

How the Trump administration chooses to proceed given the current realities in the Middle East is uncertain. The president has not yet revealed any detailed plan or strategy. Others have discussed the so-called regional approach, in which Arab states take certain confidence-building steps simultaneously with Israeli gestures to the Palestinians. Press reports have indicated that several Arab states are considering allowing overflights of Israeli commercial aircraft, direct communications with Israel, and even Israeli access to their markets, in exchange for Israeli actions on settlements and the easing of restrictions on Palestinians.[5] This approach is not new: it closely resembles the package of confidence-building steps proposed by Obama shortly after he took office.

Like President Trump, one of President Obama's first trips abroad was to Saudi Arabia. He asked the Saudis to take confidence-building steps. We traveled across the Arab world to do the same. Ultimately the regional effort did not succeed. That effort was also not new. The logic of a regional initiative was behind President Bush's invitation to dozens of Arab and Muslim world leaders to launch negotiations in 2007, and it also was behind the Arab Peace Initiative proposed by Saudi Arabia in 2002.

Given recent events in the region, there may be reason for optimism that a regional approach may now work. But Arab-Israeli relationships are still limited and rarely discussed publicly. The Palestinian issue may no longer be the most pressing for Arab leaders, but it remains a source of anger and resentment on the Arab street. That's why Arab leaders have so far calculated that giving Israel a semblance of normalization in the absence of a peace accord, let alone the implementation of one, is a step too far. What the Obama and Bush administrations discovered, and what the Trump administration too may discover, is that hopes for Arab gestures are often not realized.

The Trump administration could pursue an interim Israeli-Palestinian agreement short of a full peace, similar to the one Prime Minister Netanyahu and Chairman Arafat agreed to in the 1999 Wye Agreement. At the time, and as a continuation of the Oslo Agreements of the early 1990s, President Clinton was able to convince Netanyahu to withdraw from additional West Bank territories, increasing the area under the civil control of the Palestinian Authority from 27 to 40 percent. Today the areas of control remain largely what they were in 1999. Palestinian-controlled areas, however, are not contiguous and lands that can be used for development and economic activity are difficult to access or off-limits altogether. The Trump administration could therefore try to increase, even modestly, the amount of territory under Palestinian Authority control above the current 40 percent.

During the Obama presidency, the Palestinians were clear in their opposition to an interim deal. However, they may be more amenable now given that serious and substantive negotiations have failed to materialize for close to a decade. Withdrawals will undoubtedly benefit average Palestinians and the economy of the West Bank. Also looming is Palestinian succession. Abbas, now in his mid-eighties, and the Israelis are considering what the future Palestinian leadership will look like. Hamas will undoubtedly try to use the opportunity to increase their influence in the West Bank. An interim arrangement has the potential to help reinforce the message of Palestinians advocating diplomacy and negotiations—as opposed to the violence of Hamas—as the best way to achieve Palestinian objectives. Limited Israeli withdrawals could also help reinforce and create incentives for additional Israeli-Palestinian security cooperation, at a time when Palestinian political uncertainty may serve to destabilize it.

An interim approach may be attractive given the heavy lift of negotiating final borders and other pressing issues. But securing additional Israeli withdrawals may prove to be as difficult to achieve as a full-fledged accord. Though Netanyahu ultimately signed it in 1999, the Wye Agreement angered some in his own party and contributed to the collapse of his government. Netanyahu's current coalition is opposed to any additional territorial concessions to Palestinians. In fact many remain opposed to those previously made. Additionally, to secure support in his coalition for further withdrawals, Netanyahu is likely to seek concessions on other issues, such as security or refugees, that Palestinians would consider only in the context of a final agreement.

However the Trump administration decides to proceed, the circumstances will be difficult and trying. But if the president is serious about achieving the "ultimate deal" as opposed to interim agreements—as we believe he is—he must realize that negotiations will not succeed until the parties are speaking the same language on peace and final status. No amount of skilled negotiation can overcome gaps between two parties whose end goals bear no resemblance to one another. Of course there must come a time when both parties are willing to take the painful and politically difficult steps that will be necessary to reach an agreement. But that time has not yet come.

While President Trump's early engagement is commendable, we believe it will soon become clear that there is no realistic alternative to the two-state solution. The United States should seek to resume negotiations only when we are assured that the parties are truly, not just rhetorically, ready to act.

On December 23, 2000, President Clinton convened a meeting in the White House of Israeli and Palestinian officials and members of his administration. It was the last gasp of negotiations that had begun with high hopes six months earlier at Camp David. But those talks had ended unsuccessfully, and the Middle East had been rocked by Israeli-Palestinian violence that began in Jerusalem in late September. In October, in a desperate effort to end the violence, Clinton and other heads of state gathered for a summit in Egypt. Besides Clinton the central figures were President Hosni Mubarak of Egypt and the leaders who had been with Clinton at Camp David: Prime Minister Ehud Barak of Israel and Chairman Yasser Arafat of the Palestine Liberation Organization. They created an international commission to make recommendations on how to end the violence and bring the parties back to the negotiating table. But even as that commission assembled to begin its work, Clinton, nearing the end of his presidency, continued his effort. At the White House meeting, using notes but without a prepared text, the president described what he believed would be a fair resolution of the differences between Israelis and Palestinians. But there was no further progress.

While he may have been disappointed, Clinton could not have

been surprised. He may have been surprised, however, by the extent to which his words were subsequently distributed, discussed, and considered, soon acquiring a title he had not used: the Clinton Parameters. That distribution was abetted by a speech he made at the Waldorf Astoria Hotel in New York two weeks later. There, on January 7, 2001, thirteen days before he left office, Clinton addressed a meeting of the members of the Israel Policy Forum. In a prepared speech he again set forth the parameters, this time accompanied by detailed comments.

What is most striking about the Clinton Parameters is their endurance. More than fifteen years later they remain an important part of any serious discussion of the Israeli-Palestinian conflict. They also may have established a precedent.

On January 10, 2008, President George W. Bush spoke to a group of Palestinian and Israeli leaders at the King David Hotel in Jerusalem. Six years earlier Bush had announced his Performance-Based Roadmap for Peace, a detailed major effort to achieve a permanent two-state solution to the Israeli-Palestinian conflict. In his address to the somber crowd at the King David Hotel, he concentrated on forcefully arguing that Israelis and Palestinians should be vested in each other's success because it was the only way each could achieve its objectives. He concisely described his goals:

> The point of departure for permanent status negotiations . . . is clear: There should be an end to the occupation that began in 1967. The agreement must establish Palestine as a homeland for the Palestinian people, just as Israel is a homeland for the Jewish people. These negotiations must ensure that Israel has secure, recognized and defensible borders. And they must ensure that the State of Palestine is viable, contiguous, sovereign, and independent. It is vital that each side understands

that satisfying the other's fundamental objectives is key to a successful agreement. Security for Israel and viability for the Palestinian state are in the mutual interest of both parties.[6]

But despite many meetings and much progress, time ran out. In late December 2008, as Bush prepared to leave the White House, conflict again erupted in Gaza between Israel and Hamas, and the Annapolis Process ended in failure and recrimination.

These and other efforts represent a small part of the many plans, statements, maps, and other proposals that have been made over the past several decades.[7] Governments, think tanks, and a host of individuals have expressed themselves in a wide variety of forums. When added to the many books and articles that have been written about the various negotiations, and efforts to negotiate, the volume is massive. But it has produced results that are simultaneously clarifying and confusing.

The clarification is in what the outcome is likely to be; the lack of clarity is in how to get there. While there no doubt are some who strongly disagree, it has become accepted by many who follow this issue closely that an agreement, if and when reached, will generally be based on the following principles, which themselves are based on elements of the Clinton Parameters and Bush's Roadmap and 2008 speech:

- **TERRITORY:** An agreement should be based on the 1967 lines, with agreed land swaps.

    Every negotiation since 2000 has implicitly been based on the 1967 lines. But every negotiation also included adjustments to those lines to permit the most densely populated settlements in the West Bank to remain in Israel. In 2011 President Obama said, "We believe the borders of

Israel and Palestine should be based on the 1967 lines with mutually agreed swaps, so that secure and recognized borders are established for both states."[8] President Bush in 2008 said that a peace agreement will require "mutually agreed adjustments to the armistice lines of 1949 [pre-1967 lines] to reflect current realities and to ensure that the Palestinian state is viable and contiguous."[9]

The goal of swaps should be to minimize both the number of Israeli settlers who must be relocated from their homes and the amount of territory annexed to Israel. In 2000 President Clinton suggested that Israel annex roughly 5 percent of the West Bank. In Annapolis Olmert wanted 6.3 percent of the Palestinian territories and Abbas countered with 1.9 percent. Roughly 9 percent of the Palestinian territories are on the western side of Israel's barrier. Somewhere within this range is a number serious parties can agree on in a good-faith negotiation.

- **REFUGEES:** A solution will inevitably consist of a combination of compensation, repatriation to the Palestinian state, and resettlement. Whatever the solution, it must be consistent with Israeli and Palestinian sovereignty and their respective national identities.

Anything less than complete acceptance of their demands on refugees will be difficult for Palestinians to agree to, given how central the issue is to their narrative as a people. But there is no chance that any Israeli leader will be able to accept the unrestricted right of return to Israel. During the Annapolis Process Abbas described as unacceptable Olmert's proposal to allow 5,000 to 15,000 refugees over five years, but since then Abbas has acknowledged that the 5 million refugees and their descendants will not all be able to move to Israel and that a creative solution needs to be found.[10]

The principle we suggest makes no mention of the right of return or of Israel's acknowledging that it played a role in creating the Palestinian diaspora. We believe the parties can find ways to address the Palestinian narrative without Israel's needing to accept it in its entirety. That should be left for the parties to negotiate. But Israelis undoubtedly will need to be reassured that the solution to the refugee issue is resolvable primarily outside its borders.

- **SECURITY:** "Provisions must also be robust enough to prevent a resurgence of terrorism; to stop the infiltration of weapons; and to provide effective border security. . . . The full and phased withdrawal of Israeli military forces should be coordinated with the assumption of Palestinian security responsibility in a sovereign, non-militarized state. And the duration of this transition period must be agreed, and the effectiveness of security arrangements must be demonstrated."[11]

These words, spoken by Obama in 2011, are consistent with the long-standing assumption that Palestine will be a nonmilitarized state. The goal is to provide security assurances to Israel, such as limitations on Palestinian arms, and benchmarks that would trigger Israel's withdrawal from the territories. This is a difficult issue for Israelis, who recall that in both Gaza and south Lebanon, hostile organizations flourish in the void filled by their withdrawal. The stability of the West Bank and the effectiveness and cooperation of the Palestinian security apparatus will always be a source of anxiety for Israel. But the risks inherent in a peace accord—of phased Israeli withdrawals coordinated with

the PA—pale in comparison to its absence and can be miti-
gated with support and assurances from the United States
and the international community.

At the same time the Palestinians must be reassured that
the final stages of implementation of a peace accord would
result in a complete end to Israel's occupation. That means
full withdrawal. What the benchmarks for withdrawal are
and how long it will take are necessarily a subject for negotiation.

- **JERUSALEM:** Jerusalem should serve as the capital of both
  states. While the Old City and Holy Basin may require special treatment, as a general matter Jewish areas should be
  under the sovereignty of Israel and Arab areas under the
  sovereignty of Palestine.[12]

Most Israelis object to the division of Jerusalem in
any way, so this will be a very difficult issue for them. Yet
every negotiation since 2000 has involved the division of
the city along ethnic lines, recognizing that the Palestinians will never accept an agreement that does not establish
their capital there.

Israel's Labor Party leader has already put forward ideas
about unilateral withdrawal from Arab neighborhoods in
Jerusalem. The status of the Old City and the Holy Basin
will be far more controversial. In 2000 Clinton recommended that sovereignty in the Old City also be divided
along ethnic lines, but that sovereignty over the Haram
al-Sharif/Temple Mount, holy to both Jews and Muslims,
should be split horizontally. The Temple Mount, he suggested, would be in Israel, but the Haram al-Sharif and the
Dome of the Rock that sit on top of the Temple Mount
would be in Palestine.

During the Annapolis discussions Olmert avoided the issue of sovereignty and suggested that the Holy Basin come under an international regime. He wrote in his memoirs, "Slowly, I began to feel that the slogans about Jerusalem as a unified city did not match the reality of life in the city, which I got to know as only a mayor can. The gap between the western and eastern parts of the city was intolerable. . . . I went through a long process of soul-searching. . . . But I could not continue to deceive myself."[13]

Both parties will have to make adjustments to their current position if agreement is to be reached. History has shown that real breakthroughs between Israelis and Arabs occur only when the parties themselves realize that the cost of continued conflict outweighs the risk of an agreement. The United States can and must, at the appropriate time, urge Israel and the Palestinians into negotiations, as we have from Madrid to Annapolis and briefly during the Obama administration. But even when we have succeeded in getting them into negotiations, the two parties have not been able to conclude them successfully. Only they can make the final decisions. Some therefore suggest that the United States should increase the cost of inaction by withholding aid to Israel and cutting it off completely to the Palestinians. But those views are based on misconceptions of U.S. influence and work against the result they hope to achieve.

If we cut aid to the Palestinian Authority, as some in the Congress unwisely suggest, we may precipitate at worst the collapse of the PA and the takeover by Hamas of the West Bank, or at best an end to security and civil cooperation between the PA and Israel. It would be a counterproductive course of action for the United States and for Israel. Similarly, halting aid to Israel, as regularly suggested by many Arabs and Europeans, would not serve U.S. or Palestinian interests. Israel spends roughly $18 billion a year on defense; its total national budget is over $80 billion, and its GDP will soon exceed $300 billion. The $3 billion in U.S. assistance therefore accounts for at most 4 percent of its budget and 1 percent of its GDP. So while U.S. aid is important, Israel could survive without it.

Of course U.S. assistance has meaning far beyond just dollars. To Palestinians our assistance signals support for eventual and responsible self-governance. To Israelis our assistance confirms our commitment to their security. The consequence of a retreat from those commitments is unlikely to be a softening of their views; rather their conflict will likely become even more entrenched. Palestinians will look elsewhere for support, and Israelis will feel yet more alone and insecure. Even good friends disagree from time to time, but there is no need or justification for acts that could rupture the relationship.

Instead the United States should seek to create strong incentives for the parties to reach agreement. Much of the effort in the international community and within multilateral institutions is focused on statements and resolutions that criticize and allocate blame. At times such statements and resolutions are warranted, but too often international bodies become just another venue for the expression of conflict, not its resolution. The United States should harness that energy into positive and productive action to help the parties enter negotiations and succeed in them. We suggest the following actions:

- **ESTABLISH AN INTERNATIONAL FUND FOR PALESTINIAN REFUGEES:** If the Palestinians are ever to accept that their right of return is limited, as we believe they must and will, it will be helpful for them to know what alternatives are going to be available to them. A successful outcome will need to address compensation, rehabilitation, and resettlement, a tremendous undertaking under any realistic peace agreement. How the parties ultimately choose to address the refugee issue politically is uncertain. What is certain, however, is the need for a large financial contribution by the United States and other countries for compensation of refugees and, potentially, their host states. The United States should therefore work with the Quartet and other partners to establish an international fund for Palestinian refugees that would grow over time and would be disbursed only to implement a peace agreement. There are, of course, many ongoing crisis requests competing for assistance; the international humanitarian system is under constant stress; and the Trump administration is looking to decrease international aid overall. But the reality that resources are limited is precisely why a fund should be established as soon as possible. When negotiations are more realistic, a preexisting and substantial refugee fund would create an incentive for political flexibility by the parties, and especially for the Palestinians on the refugee issue. It is likely that both Israel and the Arab states will eventually contribute to a refugee fund as one way of signaling responsibility for their role in Palestinian and Jewish displacement following the 1948 War. Arab and Israeli concessions on this point will likely come only as part of a peace agreement. An existing fund could accelerate that process. Establishment of a fund, though, is not without some risk. Too small a fund may have the opposite effect. The next administration should therefore first ensure the sufficiency of donor contributions before proceeding.

- **GUARANTEE ISRAEL'S SECURITY:** U.S. discussions with Israel about security are already intense. Israel also has close military relations with Europe, with India, and with other nations. Unique to the United States because of its status as the dominant power will be arrangements to take effect after a peace agreement is reached. The United States should initiate a dialogue with NATO and major European and Eurasian military powers on increasing the inclusion of Israel in multinational military alliances. This effort will be important not just for military security; it also would show the Israeli public that their security is taken seriously.

- **ESTABLISH HOUSING AND STATE-BUILDING FUNDS:** If and when an agreement is reached, both Israelis and Palestinians will need assistance in housing and public services for many thousands of their citizens—Israeli settlers in those parts of the West Bank that will be within the new state of Palestine, and Palestinians for the construction of new housing, infrastructure, and investment in education and the economy. The United States and other interested nations could create and hold in escrow a huge fund, in the billions of dollars, to enable the creation of new communities where Palestinians and Israelis could find new homes in their own countries.

These are examples of what the United States can do. Positive incentives are, in fact, what the United States does best. While some of our suggestions will impose significant costs, the resulting peace will be well worth the investment because, among other reasons, resolution of the Israeli-Palestinian conflict and the normalization of relations between Israel and the Arab world is important to U.S. security.

·   ·   ·

When the time comes for a major push to restart negotiations, what will be needed is a realistic path. For that the Bush Roadmap can serve as a guideline. That effort failed for many reasons, one of which is that it attempted to go all the way from the very beginning to a full and final agreement. As admirable as that objective is, it proved too much for the parties. Many steps were proposed; none were taken.

We believe an approach that is segmented and initially more limited may have a better chance of success. The initial phase would be a series of actions taken sequentially, some in words and others in deeds, many of which are included in the Roadmap. But in the process we suggest they would be designed exclusively to get the parties into serious direct negotiations, not to decide the outcome.

On July 15, 1999, more than a year after the Good Friday Agreement ended the conflict in Northern Ireland, I was at Buckingham Palace to be knighted by Queen Elizabeth. By a highly unfortunate coincidence, on that day the Northern Ireland Assembly, which had been established pursuant to the Agreement, collapsed. That evening, at the request of President Clinton and the prime ministers of the United Kingdom and Ireland, I agreed to return to Northern Ireland to try to put the process back together.

There, as in the Middle East, the most difficult obstacle was the deep distrust on both sides. As a result each was unwilling to take the first step. To compensate for this, in three intense months I negotiated with both sides a series of reciprocal steps they would take, sequentially, over the next few months. Before the first step was taken, all were spelled out in precise detail and agreed on. For example, the first two steps were to be statements by Gerry

Adams, the leader of Sinn Fein, one of the major nationalist parties, and David Trimble, the leader of the Ulster Unionist Party. We spent several difficult days negotiating every word of those statements, then we spent weeks negotiating in equally precise detail every later step to be taken by both sides. So when Adams began reading his statement at a press conference on a cold morning in late November 1999, Trimble knew exactly what he was going to say, as was the case with Adams when Trimble gave his response the following day. Neither man added or left out a single word from the statements that had previously been agreed. The same was true of every step taken over the next few months, at the end of which the process was back on track.

It was a very slow, difficult, and fragile process, but the detail was necessary to overcome the profound mistrust on both sides. Neither would accept the other's word; there had to be an act demonstrating good faith, based on a detailed script agreed in advance.

The Middle East is much more complex and difficult than was Northern Ireland two decades ago. The conflict is more entrenched, the hostility is deeper, the mistrust greater, the destruction more widespread, the deaths more frequent. But we believe that a process similar to the one that worked in Northern Ireland can work in the Middle East if the two sides want it to work. That last point is crucial: peace between Israelis and Palestinians cannot be externally imposed, by the United States or anyone else. The United States is indispensable, and others can help, but in the end the relationship between Israelis and Palestinians will be determined by Israelis and Palestinians.

We suggest that the United States propose direct negotiations only after it detects seriousness of purpose by both parties, such as public or private assurances that a U.S. framework is reasonable. Based on our experience this will be a formidable task, requiring ingenuity and perseverance by American negotiators. Reflecting the gap in how they perceive negotiations, the Israelis want brief and general terms of reference, while the Palestinians want them to be long and specific. Reaching a reasonable compromise on this issue will be an important early test of the seriousness of purpose of the two parties.

Once this requirement is satisfied, the United States should initiate parallel discussions with Israeli and Palestinian officials to urge that they agree on a series of procedural steps that would be intended to counter the paralyzing mistrust that has kept them out of negotiations. Although largely procedural, such steps necessarily implicate substantive issues; for that reason there must be a crystal-clear understanding by each party of each step, written and agreed in advance. A misunderstanding, even on a minor point, would be fatal to the effort. The precise steps to be agreed will, of course, depend upon the circumstances that exist at the time. But based on our experience in the region, the following examples suggest a possible approach.

Israel could agree to a six-month moratorium on new housing starts in the West Bank (without a pre-moratorium surge of new construction), to take effect only if and when the Palestinians enter direct negotiations. The Palestinians would do so, in turn, only on the Israeli assurance, agreed at the outset, that the first six months would be devoted to an intense effort to reach agreement on territory and borders, an issue of critical importance to the Palestinians. This assurance would in turn be given only on the Palestinian assurance, also given at the outset, that the second substantive issue to be taken up would be security, an issue of critical importance to the Israelis. This of course will be preceded by an intensive discussion by the United States and Israel on security measures in the context of a peace agreement.

In this introductory process the parties would need other as-surances as well. For example, in order to persuade the Israelis to take even a first, modest step, they will have to be assured that any agreement reached will be full and final, extinguishing all other claims. For their part the Palestinians have always insisted that any and all discussions be conducted under the principle "Nothing is agreed until everything is agreed." They and the Israelis likely will need that assurance in the future as well. It will be up to the U.S. negotiating team to uncover and deal with the full range of neces-sary assurances to make possible the next and most difficult steps on how to address the final status issues.

No less difficult will be deciding on how to deal with the divisions among the Palestinians—the PA in the West Bank and Hamas in Gaza—on which the Israelis will rightly want some un-derstanding. As president, Abbas holds full executive authority, but Hamas has de facto control in Gaza.

One possibility is a renewed effort by the Quartet to en-gage with Hamas on the Quartet's long-standing conditions for acceptance of Hamas. In its 2016 report the Quartet stated that "reuniting Palestinians under a single, democratic and le-gitimate Palestinian authority on the basis of the PLO platform and Quartet principles remains a priority. This is critical for the fulfillment of the national aspirations of the Palestinian people. The constraints of the occupation, the absence of elections, and budgetary pressures contribute to growing public discontent and undermine the popular legitimacy of Palestinian institutions and leadership. The division also damages Gaza's economic de-velopment, hinders basic service delivery, and impedes the re-construction process."[14] On several occasions in the past, Israel has negotiated with Hamas through intermediaries and modi-fied its policies on Gaza as a result. The Quartet effort could be coordinated with another review by Israel of the terms of its embargo on Gaza.

But at present Hamas apparently sees no need to accommodate Israeli or Quartet demands. They seem to view a strategy of violence to be more successful than Abbas's diplomatic approach. Reunification of Gaza and the West Bank may therefore have to await the circumstances that exist if and when Israel and the PA decide to make a serious effort to resolve their differences.

We recognize that there is little reason to be optimistic at this time about resolving the Israeli-Palestinian conflict. Our hope is that Israelis and Palestinians will weigh the risks of delay and inaction, however justifiable to them, against the benefits of an agreement, however imperfect. Some suggest that the situation on the ground must get worse before the folly of the conflict's current trajectory is undeniable to the leaders and peoples on both sides. But by then the current stalemate will seem easy. That is precisely why it is essential for the United States to propose clear, balanced, and reasoned principles and then to create the right incentives to encourage the parties to enter serious negotiations and reach an agreement.

We believe there is no such thing as a conflict that cannot be ended. Conflicts are created and conducted by human beings; they can be ended by human beings. We recognize the daunting difficulties that lie ahead. We acknowledge the long litany of failed past efforts. We are especially mindful of the many other conflicts and complexities in the region that work against an early resolution. Yet we firmly and realistically believe that there is a path to peace through a two-state solution and that all of us who care about the region and its people, in particular Israelis and Palestinians, must do whatever we can to advocate and work for an end to the conflict.

NOTES

INTRODUCTION

1. Yehuda Avner, *The Prime Ministers: An Intimate Narrative of Israeli Leadership* (New Milford, CT: Toby Press, 2010), 630–635.

2. Ibid.

3. Ibid.

4. *The Future of World Religions: Population Growth Projections, 2010–2050: Why Muslims Are Rising Fastest and the Unaffiliated Are Shrinking as a Share of the World's Population* (Washington D.C.: Pew Research Center, April 2, 2015), 7.

5. Sergio DellaPergola, a preeminent Israeli demographer, considers the estimate of 12.5 million Jews in Israel by 2050 to be an "optimistic scenario." The "pessimistic" figure is 9 million. Sergio DellaPergola, "The Jewish People in 2050: 2 Very Different

Scenarios," September 22, 2015, http://www.ynetnews.com/articles/0,7340,L-4702945,00.html.

6. *The Future of World Religions*, 154.

CHAPTER ONE: LEADERS IN DISAGREEMENT

1. William B. Quandt, *Peace Process: American Diplomacy and the Arab-Israeli Conflict Since 1967*. 3rd edition (Washington, DC: Brookings Institution Press, 2005), 254–255.

2. Isaac Alteras, *Eisenhower and Israel: U.S.-Israeli Relations, 1953–1960* (Gainesville: University Press of Florida, 1993), 1–2.

3. John B. Judis, "Seeds of Doubt: Harry Truman's Concerns about Israel and Palestine Were Prescient—and Forgotten," *New Republic*, January 15, 2014, https://newrepublic.com/article/116215/was-harry-truman-zionist.

4. Saudi Arabia sent forces that fought under Egyptian command.

5. Dwight D. Eisenhower, "Message from President Eisenhower to Prime Minister Ben Gurion," November 7, 1956, U.S. Department of State, Office of the Historian, https://history.state.gov/historicaldocuments/frus1955-57v16/d550.

6. Israel eventually withdrew from the Sinai in 1957. A UN peacekeeping force was interposed between Egypt and Israel and helped keep the Straits of Tiran open to Israeli ships.

7. John F. Kennedy, Memorandum of Conversation, Palm Beach, FL, December 27, 1962, U.S. Department of State, Office of the Historian, https://history.state.gov/historicaldocuments/frus1961-63v18/d121.

8. Nasser was a threat not just to Israel but to other Arab states as well. His aim was to unite the Arab world under his rule, in part by deposing some sitting leaders. This complicated arena left ample room for considerable maneuvering among regional actors and the United States and Soviet Union.

9. Warren Bass, *Support Any Friend: Kennedy's Middle East and the Making of the U.S.-Israel Alliance* (New York: Oxford University Press, 2004), 214–218.

10. Israel is widely believed to possess a substantial number of nuclear weapons but maintains a policy of ambiguity. Israeli officials say only that theirs will not be the first country to introduce nuclear weapons into the Middle East.

11. "U.S.-Israel Relations: Roots of the U.S.-Israel Relationship," Jewish Virtual Library, n.d., accessed June 20, 2016, http://www.jewishvirtuallibrary.org/jsource/US-Israel/roots_of_US-Israel.html.

12. Israel considered the closure of the Straits of Tiran an act of war.

13. Henry Kissinger, *White House Years*, reprint edition (New York: Simon & Schuster, 2001), 371.

14. Yitzhak Rabin, *The Rabin Memoirs*, expanded edition (Berkeley: University of California Press, 1996), 154.

15. Robert B. Semple Jr., "Nixon Stresses Commitment to Israel," *New York Times*, September 9, 1968.

16. Rabin, *The Rabin Memoirs*, 195.

17. Minutes of the Secretary of State's Staff Meeting, Washington, October 23, 1973, U.S. Department of State, Office of the Historian, https://history.state.gov/historicaldocuments/frus1969-76v25/d250.

18. Henry Kissinger, *Crisis: The Anatomy of Two Major Foreign Policy Crises* (New York: Simon & Schuster, 2003), 252.

19. Roger Stone, *Nixon's Secrets: The Rise, Fall, and Untold Truth about the President, Watergate, and the Pardon* (New York: Skyhorse, 2014), 399.

20. Gerald R. Ford, "Remarks of Welcome to Prime Minister Yitzhak Rabin of Israel," September 10, 1974, *American Presidency Project*, http://www.presidency.ucsb.edu/ws/index.php?pid=4701&st=Israel&st1=3.

21. Rabin, *The Rabin Memoirs*, 255.

22. Ibid., 257.

23. Also known as the Sinai II Agreement.

24. Jimmy Carter, "United Jewish Appeal Remarks at the Organization's National Young Leadership Conference," February 25,

1980, *American Presidency Project*, http://www.presidency.ucsb.edu/ws/?pid=32979.

25. Quandt, *Peace Process*, 182–183.

26. Bernard Reich, *Securing the Covenant: United States–Israel Relations after the Cold War* (Westport, CT: Praeger, 1995), 40.

27. George P. Shultz, *Turmoil and Triumph: My Years as Secretary of State* (New York: Charles Scribner's Sons, 1993), 54.

28. Katie Worth, "Netanyahu at War: The Highs and Lows of the 'Special Relationship,'" *Frontline*, January 6, 2016, http://www.pbs.org/wgbh/frontline/article/the-highs-and-lows-of-the-special-relationship/.

29. Thomas L. Friedman, "Baker, in a Middle East Blueprint, Asks Israel to Reach Out to Arabs," *New York Times*, May 23, 1989, http://www.nytimes.com/1989/05/23/world/baker-in-a-middle-east-blueprint-asks-israel-to-reach-out-to-arabs.html.

30. Quandt, *Peace Process*, 299.

31. William J. Clinton, "The President's News Conference with Prime Minister Yitzhak Rabin of Israel," March 15, 1993, *American Presidency Project*, http://www.presidency.ucsb.edu/ws/?pid=46339.

32. Peter Slevin and Jodi Enda, "Israel Defends Firm Tone on Peace: Arriving in Washington, Netanyahu Said His Country Drew Unfair Blame. A Tough Week of U.S. Mediation Is Seen," *Philadelphia Inquirer*, January 20, 1998, http://articles.philly.com/1998-01-20/news/25748109_1_netanyahu-nor-arafat-yasir-arafat-palestinians-last-night.

33. Storer H. Rowley, "Netanyahu Hints End Run on Clinton," *Chicago Tribune*, May 12, 1998, http://articles.chicagotribune.com/1998-05-12/news/9805120323_1_netanyahu-peacemaking-state-madeleine-albright.

34. George W. Bush, "Remarks by the President to the American Jewish Committee," May 2, 2001, http://georgewbush-whitehouse.archives.gov/news/releases/2001/05/text/20010504.html.

35. Suzanne Goldenberg, "Sharon on Collision Course with

America," *Guardian*, October 12, 2001, http://www.theguardian. com/world/2001/oct/12/afghanistan.israel.

36. Previous presidents made references to autonomy or to a homeland for Palestinians, but none proposed as a matter of U.S. policy the establishment of an independent sovereign state of Palestine.

37. "President Obama's Speech in Cairo: A New Beginning," White House, June 4, 2009, https://www.whitehouse.gov/blog/New Beginning/transcripts.

38. AIPAC, "Joint Military Exercises," 2016, accessed June 20, 2016, http://www.aipac.org/learn/us-and-israel/military-partnership/joint-military-exercises; U.S. Department of State, "Foreign Military Financing Account Summary," n.d., accessed June 20, 2016, http://www.state.gov/t/pm/ppa/sat/c14560.htm.

39. Rebecca Shimoni Stoil and AP, "Obama Approves $225 Million in Iron Dome Funding," *Times of Israel*, August 5, 2014, http://www.timesofisrael.com/obama-approves-225-million-in-iron-dome-funding/; Barbara Opall-Rome, "Israel Defense Minister: F-35 Will Preserve Qualitative Edge," *Defense News*, April 5, 2016, http://www.defensenews.com/story/defense/air-space/air-force/2016/04/05/f-35-israel-lockheed-martin/82666534/.

40. "Peres: Obama Is a Great President, Security Ties Are 'the Best We've Ever Had,'" *Haaretz*, March 2, 2012, http://www.haaretz. com/israel-news/peres-obama-is-a-great-president-security-ties-are-the-best-we-ve-ever-had-1.416030.

41. Lara Friedman, "Israel's Unsung Protector: Obama," *New York Times*, April 10, 2016, http://www.nytimes.com/2016/04/12/opinion/international/israels-unsung-protector-obama.html.

CHAPTER TWO: EARLY CONFLICT

1. Tom Segev, *One Palestine Complete: Jews and Arabs under the British Mandate* (New York: Metropolitan Books/Henry Holt, 1999), 129.

2. Sergio DellaPergola, *Demography in Israel/Palestine: Trends, Prospects, Policy Implications* (Jerusalem: Hebrew University of Jerusalem, Harman Institute of Contemporary Jewry, 2001), 5.

3. Several thousand Jews arrived from Yemen around the same time.

4. "The Great ideas of the eighteenth and nineteenth centuries have not passed by our people without leaving a mark. We feel not only as Jews; we feel as men. As men, we, too, wish to live like other men and be a nation like the others." Leon Pinsker, *Auto-Emancipation: An Appeal to His People By A Russian Jew,* 1882, translated from the German by Dr. D. S. Blondheim, Federation of American Zionists, 1916, available at http://www.jewishvirtual library.org/jsource/Zionism/pinsker.html.

5. Theodor Herzl, *Der Judenstaat* (1896), available at http://masorti youth.org/wp-content/uploads/2015/11/The-Jewish-State. pdf.

6. DellaPergola, *Demography in Israel/Palestine*, 5.

7. Ibid.

8. Henry McMahon, "The Hussein-McMahon Correspondence, No. 4," October 24, 1915, http://www.jewishvirtuallibrary.org/ jsource/History/hussmac1.html.

9. Arthur James Balfour, "The Balfour Declaration," November 2, 1917, http://www.mfa.gov.il/mfa/foreignpolicy/peace/guide/ pages/the%20balfour%20declaration.aspx.

10. Segev, *One Palestine Complete*, 129.

11. *Palestine Royal Commission Report* (London: H.M. Stationary Office, July 1937), 363, https://unispal.un.org/pdfs/Cmd5479. pdf.

12. Ibid.

CHAPTER THREE: MOVING IN OPPOSITE DIRECTIONS

1. Linda Sharaby, "Israel's Economic Growth: Success without Security," September 3, 2002, Rubin Center, http://www.rubin center.org/2002/09/sharaby-2002-09-03/.

2. Avner, *The Prime Ministers*, 545.

3. *How's Life? 2015: Measuring Well-Being* (Paris: OECD Publishing, 2015), http://dx.doi.org/10.1787/how-s-life-2015-en.

4. Council of the European Union, "Council Conclusions on the Middle East Peace Process," December 8, 2009, http://www.euro parl.europa.eu/meetdocs/2009_2014/documents/wgme/dv/2 00/200912/20091216councilcon081209_en.pdf.

5. Peter Beaumont, "EU Parliament Backs Palestinian State 'in Principle,'" *Guardian*, December 17, 2014, http://www.theguardian. com/world/2014/dec/17/eu-parliament-backs-palestine-state; Stephen Castle and Jodi Rudoren, "A Symbolic Vote in Britain Recognizes a Palestinian State," *New York Times*, October 13, 2014, http://www.nytimes.com/2014/10/14/world/europe/british-parliament-palestinian-state.html?_r=0.

6. Hand in hand with support for the establishment of the state of Palestine in the West Bank and Gaza has come more vocal and determined opposition to Israeli settlement activity. In 2015, over intense Israeli opposition, the EU issued guidelines on labeling and identifying Israeli products made in the West Bank. The European Council on Foreign Relations, a think tank that frequently informs EU policy, believes that those guidelines are not enough. The Council now proposes that the EU bar banking, loans, and mortgages to West Bank settlements, and deny tax-exempt status to European charities that deal with Israeli settlements. (Hugh Lovatt and Mattia Toaldo, "EU Differentiation and Israeli Settlements," European Council on Foreign Relations, July 22, 2015, http://www.ecfr.eu/publications/summary/eu _differentiation_and_israeli_settlements3076.)

CHAPTER FOUR: FROM MADRID TO CAMP DAVID

1. George Bush, "Remarks at the Opening Session of the Middle East Peace Conference in Madrid, Spain," October 30, 1991, http://www.presidency.ucsb.edu/ws/?pid=20163.

2. Israel Ministry of Foreign Affairs, "Statement by Prime Minister Shamir on the PNC Decisions," November 15, 1988, http://

mfa.gov.il/MFA/ForeignPolicy/MFADocuments/Yearbook7/ Pages/398%20Statement%20by%20Prime%20Minister%20 Shamir%20on%20the%20PNC.aspx.

3. Greer Fay Cashman, "Oslo Accords Not Root of Terrorism, Says Rabin Son at Memorial Commemoration," *Jerusalem Post*, October 15, 2013, http://www.jpost.com/National-News/ Oslo-Accords-not-root-of-terrorism-says-Rabin-son-at-memo rial-commemoration-328815.

4. Yitzhak Rabin, "Remarks by Late Prime Minister Yitzhak Rabin at Tel-Aviv Peace Rally," November 4, 1995, http://www.mfa. gov.il/mfa/mfa-archive/1995/pages/remarks%20by%20 late%20pm%20rabin%20at%20tel-aviv%20peace%20rally. aspx.

5. Mel Bezalel, "Who Is Ben Nitay, and Why Does He Look So Much Like Binyamin Netanyahu?," *Jerusalem Post*, March 29, 2009, http://www.jpost.com/Israel/Who-is-Ben-Nitay-and-why-does-he-look-so-much-like-Binyamin-Netanyahu.

6. Batsheva Sobelman and Laura King, "How Did the Polls In Israel Get It So Wrong?," *LA Times*, March 18, 2015, http:// www.latimes.com/world/middleeast/la-fg-israel-polls-wrong-20150318-story.html.

7. Jane Perlez, "Impasse at Camp David: The Overview; Clinton Ends Deadlocked Peace Talks," *New York Times*, July 25, 2000, http://www.nytimes.com/2000/07/26/world/impasse-at-camp-david-the-overview-clinton-ends-deadlocked-peace-talks. html?pagewanted=all.

8. Council on Foreign Relations, "Mitchell Report on Israeli-Palestinian Violence," April 30, 2001, http://www.cfr.org/israel/ mitchell-report-israeli-palestinian-violence/p13836.

9. Gilead Sher, *The Israeli-Palestinians Peace Negotiations, 1999–2001: Within Reach* (New York: Routledge, 2006), 196–200.

10. Ibid.

11. Bill Clinton, *My Life* (New York: Knopf, 2004), 936–44.

12. George W. Bush, "President Bush Calls for New Palestinian

Leadership," June 24, 2002, https://georgewbush-whitehouse
.archives.gov/news/releases/2002/06/text/20020624-3.html.

13. James Bennet, "Sharon Laments 'Occupation' and Israeli Settlers
Shudder," *New York Times*, June 1, 2003, http://www.nytimes
.com/2003/06/01/world/sharon-laments-occupation-and
-israeli-settlers-shudder.html?pagewanted=all.

14. Ariel Sharon, "Speech by PM Sharon at the Herzilya Conference,"
December 4, 2002, http://mfa.gov.il/MFA/PressRoom/2002/
Pages/Speech%20by%20PM%20Sharon%20at%20the%20
Herzliya%20Conference%20-%204.aspx.

CHAPTER FIVE: ANNAPOLIS

1. While he was acquitted of several of the charges against him, Olmert was ultimately convicted on one count of breach of trust in
2012 and one count of bribery in 2014 and sentenced to prison
for nineteen months.

2. George W. Bush, "President Bush Attends Annapolis Conference," November 27, 2007, http://2001-2009.state.gov/p/nea/
rls/rm/2007/95695.htm.

3. "Talking Points and Questions," September 16, 2008, *Al Jazeera Investigations*, accessed June 21, 2016, http://transparency.aljazeera
.net/en/projects/thepalestinepapers/201218203351640212.
html.

4. Elliott Abrams, *Tested By Zion: The Bush Administration and the
Israeli-Palestinian Conflict* (Cambridge: Cambridge University
Press, 2013), 291.

5. Condoleezza Rice, *No Higher Honor: A Memoir of My Years in
Washington* (New York: Crown, 2012), 724.

6. Condoleezza Rice, "Remarks at the United Nations Security
Council," December 16, 2008, http://2001-2009.state.gov/
secretary/rm/2008/12/113242.htm.

7. Roee Nahmias, "Hamas: Willing to Renew Truce," *Ynet
News*, December 23, 2008, http://www.ynetnews.com/
articles/0,7340,L-3642815,00.html.

8. Israel Ministry of Foreign Affairs, "The Operation Against Hamas in Gaza: The Israeli Perspective," September 15, 2009, http://mfa.gov.il/MFA/ForeignPolicy/Terrorism/Pages/Gaza_Facts_website_launched_15-Sep-2009.aspx.

9. "Gaza 'Looks Like Earthquake Zone,'" BBC, January 20, 2009, http://news.bbc.co.uk/2/hi/middle_east/7838618.stm.

10. Pinchas Wolf, "The War's Damage: 1,900 Claims for Direct Hits," *Walla News,* January 21, 2009 (in Hebrew), http://finance.walla.co.il/item/1421716.

11. Shimon Shiffer, "Olmert's Legacy," *Yediot Aharonot,* January 29, 2009 (in Hebrew).

12. "Netanyahu Refuses to Evacuate Settlements" UPI, January 30, 2009, http://www.upi.com/Top_News/2009/01/30/Netanyahu-refuses-to-evacuate-settlements/10481233337878/.

CHAPTER SIX: CONTESTED TERRITORY

1. Donald Macintyre, "Netanyahu: The Leader Who Struts Like a Superpower," *Independent,* February 6, 2009, http://www.independent.co.uk/news/world/middle-east/netanyahu-the-leader-who-struts-like-a-superpower-1570710.html.

2. International Crisis Group, "Palestine Divided," Middle East Report No. 25, December 17, 2008, http://www.crisisgroup.org/en/regions/middle-east-north-africa/israel-palestine/B025-palestine-divided.aspx.

3. International Crisis Group, "Gaza's Unfinished Business," Middle East Report No. 85, April 23, 2009, http://www.crisisgroup.org/~/media/Files/Middle%20East%20North%20Africa/Israel%20Palestine/85%20Gazas%20Unfinished%20Business.

4. In October 2009, Congress further tightened the restrictions, blocking assistance to "any power-sharing government of which Hamas is a member." The United States would not be able to provide the PA with a single dollar of assistance if even a single member of the government was affiliated with Hamas or any other terrorist organization.

5. Nadav Shragai and Agencies, "Peace Now: 32% of Land Held for Settlements Is Private Palestinian Property," *Haaretz*, March 14, 2007, http://www.haaretz.com/news/peace-now-32-of-land-held-for-settlements-is-private-palestinian-property-1.215530.

6. Dean Rusk, "Airgram From the Department of State to the Embassy in Israel," April 8, 1968, https://history.state.gov/historic aldocuments/frus1964-68v20/d137.

7. Shlomo Slonim, *Jerusalem in America's Foreign Policy: 1947–1997* (The Hague, Netherlands: Kluwer Law International, 1998), 220.

8. William Scranton, "U.S. Position on Israeli Settlements in the Administered Areas," March 23, 1976, http://mfa.gov.il/MFA/ForeignPolicy/MFADocuments/Yearbook2/Pages/161%20US%20position%20on%20Israeli%20settlements%20in%20the%20admi.aspx.

9. Bernard Gwertzman, "U.S. Assails Israel For Sticking to Settlement Plans," *New York Times*, November 5, 1982, http://www.nytimes.com/1982/11/05/world/us-assails-israel-for-sticking-to-settlement-plans.html.

10. Daniel C. Kurtzer, et al, *The Peace Puzzle: America's Quest for Arab-Israeli Peace, 1989-2011* (Ithaca, NY: Cornell University Press, 2013), 23.

11. George H. W. Bush, "Remarks on Fast Track Legislation and a Question-and-Answer Session with Reporters," May 23, 1991, http://www.presidency.ucsb.edu/ws/?pid=19619.

12. Quandt, *Peace Process*, 312–314.

13. "PM Seeking Ways to 'Deal With' Outposts," *Arutz Sheva*, Israel National News, August 10, 2004, http://www.israelnational news.com/News/News.aspx/67097.

14. Talya Sason, "Summary of the Opinion Concerning Unauthorized Outposts," Israel Ministry of Foreign Affairs, March 10, 2005, http://www.mfa.gov.il/mfa/aboutisrael/state/law/pages/summary%20of%20opinion%20concerning%20unauthorized%20outposts%20-%20talya%20sason%20adv.aspx.

15. Benjamin Netanyahu, "Remarks by President Obama and Israeli Prime Minister Netanyahu in Press Availability," May 18, 2009, https://www.whitehouse.gov/the-press-office/remarks-presi dent-obama-and-israeli-prime-minister-netanyahu-press-availa bility.

16. Lally Weymouth, "Binyamin Netanyahu's Outlook," *Washington Post,* February 28, 2009, http://www.washingtonpost.com/wp-dyn/content/article/2009/02/27/AR2009022702278_3.html.

17. Ora Cohen and Reuters, "Lieberman: Obama-Netanyahu Meeting Went Better Than You Think," *Haaretz,* May 21, 2009, http://www.haaretz.com/news/lieberman-obama-netanyahu-meeting-went-better-than-you-think-1.276459.

CHAPTER SEVEN: OVERCOMING THE TRUST DEFICIT

1. The president met with the king in Riyadh on June 4, 2009. Along with the Palestinians and other Arabs, the Saudis wanted a freeze on settlements.

2. Adam Entous, "Netanyahu Defies Obama on Israeli Settlement Freeze," Reuters, May 24, 2009, http://www.reuters.com/article/us-israel-palestinians-settlements-idUSTRE54N12320090524.

3. Barak Ravid, "Netanyahu: We'll Build Only in Existing Settlements," *Haaretz,* May 24, 2009, http://www.haaretz.com/netan yahu-we-ll-build-only-in-existing-settlements-1.276616.

4. Entous, "Netanyahu Defies Obama on Israeli Settlement Freeze."

5. Ibid.

6. "Israel Won't Yield to U.S. Demands, Won't Halt Settlement Construction," *Haaretz,* May 23, 2009, http://www.haaretz.com/israel-won-t-yield-to-u-s-demands-won-t-halt-settlement-con struction-1.276570.

7. In 2016, Prime Minister Netanyahu appointed Dayan as Israel's consul general in New York.

8. Ori Lewis, "Israeli Settlers Reject Obama Call to Halt Building," Reuters, May 19, 2009, http://uk.reuters.com/article/2009/05/19/uk-israel-palestinians-reaction-idUKTRE54I22120090519.

9. Daniel C. Kurtzer et al., *The Peace Puzzle: America's Quest for Arab-Israeli Peace, 1989–2011* (Ithaca, NY: Cornell University Press, 2013), 114.

10. Barak Ravid, "Israeli Ministers: No West Bank Settlement Freeze," *Haaretz*, May 31, 2009, http://www.haaretz.com/israeli-ministers-no-west-bank-settlement-freeze-1.276992. Just as we complained about Israeli and Palestinian leaks, they complained about American leaks. There were such leaks, but they did not come from our office. I brought to that office the policy I had established as Senate majority leader: Anyone who leaks information will be immediately dismissed.

11. Many Americans who criticized Obama for seeking a settlement freeze were silent when Bush earlier made the same request.

12. Jackson Diehl, "Abbas's Waiting Game on Peace with Israel," *Washington Post*, May 29, 2009, http://www.washingtonpost.com/wp-dyn/content/article/2009/05/28/AR2009052803614.html.

13. "Full Text of Netanyahu's Foreign Policy Speech at Bar Ilan," *Haaretz*, June 14, 2009, http://www.haaretz.com/news/full-text-of-netanyahu-s-foreign-policy-speech-at-bar-ilan-1.277922.

14. Amit Segel, "Netanyahu's Father Reveals His Secret," *Mako Channel 2 News*, July 8, 2009, http://www.mako.co.il/news-military/politics/Article-77cd5b4ae4b5221006.htm&sCh=3d385dd2dd5d41108tpId=978777604 (in Hebrew).

15. Barak Ravid and Avi Issacharoff, "Netanyahu to Okay New West Bank Homes Before Freeze," *Haaretz*, September 4, 2009.

CHAPTER EIGHT: MUCH PROCESS, NO PROGRESS

1. Three other members of the UN fact-finding mission continue to stand by the report. They responded to Goldstone's op-ed with their own, writing, "Members of the mission, signatories to this statement, find it necessary to dispel any impression that subsequent developments have rendered any part of the mission's report unsubstantiated, erroneous or inaccurate." Hina Jilani,

Christine Chinkin, and Desmond Travers, "Goldstone Report: Statement Issued By Members of UN Mission on Gaza War," *Guardian*, April 13, 2011, https://www.theguardian.com/commentisfree/2011/apr/14/goldstone-report-statement-un-gaza.

2. Richard Goldstone, "Reconsidering the Goldstone Report on Israel and War Crimes," *Washington Post*, April 1, 2011, https://www.washingtonpost.com/opinions/reconsidering-the-goldstone-report-on-israel-and-war-crimes/2011/04/01/AFg111JC_story.html.

3. Barack Obama, "Remarks By the President at Beginning Of Trilateral Meeting With Israeli Prime Minister Netanyahu and Palestinian Authority President Abbas," September 22, 2009, https://www.whitehouse.gov/the-press-office/remarks-president-beginning-trilateral-meeting-with-israeli-prime-minister-netanyah.

4. Karin Laub, "Mahmoud Abbas Faces Outrage over Deferred Gaza War-Crimes Vote in UN," Cleveland.com, October 4, 2009, http://www.cleveland.com/world/index.ssf/2009/10/mahmoud_abbas_faces_outrage_ov.html.

5. Khaled Abu Toameh, "Abbas Blames Aides for Motion's Removal," *Jerusalem Post*, reprinted, American Task Force on Palestine, October 6, 2009, http://www.americantaskforce.org/daily_news_article/2009/10/06/1254801600_14; Avi Issacharoff, "Hamas Accuses Abbas of Treason for 'Justifying' Gaza War," *Haaretz*, October 5, 2009, http://www.haaretz.com/news/hamas-accuses-abbas-of-treason-for-justifying-gaza-war-1.6656.

6. Heather Sharp, "Goldstone Fall-out Plagues Abbas," *BBC News*, October 9, 2009, http://news.bbc.co.uk/2/hi/middle_east/8297698.stm.

7. Donald Macintyre, "Women Prisoners Go Free in Return for a Glimpse of Hostage," *Independent*, October 2, 2009, http://www.independent.co.uk/news/world/middle-east/women-prisoners-go-free-in-return-for-a-glimpse-of-hostage-1797018.html.

8. Ethan Bronner, "Palestinian Authority's Future Is in Question,"

New York Times, November 9, 2009, http://www.nytimes.com/2009/11/10/world/middleeast/10mideast.html.

9. UN Office for the Coordination of Humanitarian Affairs, Occupied Palestinian Territory, "West Bank Movement and Access Update," November 2009, https://www.ochaopt.org/documents/ocha_opt_movement_access_2009_november_english.pdf.

10. UN Office for the Coordination of Humanitarian Affairs, Occupied Palestinian Territory, "West Bank Movement and Access: Special Focus," June 2010, https://www.ochaopt.org/documents/ocha_opt_movement_access_2010_06_16_english.pdf.

11. George Mitchell, "Briefing by Special Envoy for Middle East Peace," November 25, 2009, http://www.state.gov/r/pa/prs/ps/2009/nov/132447.htm.

12. Ibid.

13. Council of the European Union, "Council Conclusions on Middle East Peace," December 12, 2009, http://eeas.europa.eu/delegations/israel/press_corner/all_news/news/2009/20091208_01_en.htm.

14. Yasmine Saleh, "Arab League Gives Mideast Talks 4-Month Window," Reuters, March 3, 2010, http://www.reuters.com/article/us-palestinians-israel-idUSLDE6221BV20100303.

15. Obama consistently prevented UN action against Israel. During his presidency no UN Security Council resolution critical of Israel has passed. By comparison, the Security Council adopted at least seven critical resolutions under President Johnson, fifteen under Nixon, fourteen under Carter, twenty-one under Reagan, nine under George H. W. Bush, three under Clinton, and six under George W. Bush (Friedman, "Israel's Unsung Protector").

16. On June 27, 2016, Israel and Turkey agreed to a process to again normalize the relations between their two countries.

17. Barak Ravid, "Identity of Secret Mediator in Israeli-Palestinians Talks Revealed," *Haaretz*, November 27, 2014, http://www.haaretz.com/israel-news/.premium-1.628971.

18. In 2013 Netanyahu requested that the secret channel be reacti-
vated. The United States agreed. So the same people met in the
same so-called secret process, the same leaks followed, and the
result was the same.

19. Barack Obama, "Remarks by the President on the Middle East
and North Africa," May 19, 2011, https://www.whitehouse.gov/
the-press-office/2011/05/19/remarks-president-middle-east-
and-north-africa.

CHAPTER NINE: ISRATINE

1. Muammar Qaddafi, "The One-State Solution," *New York Times*,
January 21, 2009, http://www.nytimes.com/2009/01/22/
opinion/22qaddafi.html.

2. Carlo Strenger, "Requiem for a Two-State Solution to the Israeli-
Palestinian Conflict," *Haaretz*, August 29, 2012, http://www.
haaretz.com/blogs/strenger-than-fiction/requiem-for-a-two-
state-solution-to-the-israeli-palestinian-conflict-1.461445.

3. This figure includes Israeli Druze, an Arabic speaking population
who adhere to a religious sect with Islamic origins. Not counting
the Druze population, the Arab demographic figure stands at 5.8
million. Either way, Jews comprise less than half of the current
population between the Jordan River and the Mediterranean Sea.
Nir Hasson, "How Many Palestinians Actually Live in the West
Bank," *Haaretz*, June 30, 2013, http://www.haaretz.com/israel-
news/.premium-1.532703.

4. Mairav Zonszein, "Binyamin Netanyahu: 'Arab Voters Are Heading to the Polls in Droves,'" *Guardian*, March 17, 2015, https://
www.theguardian.com/world/2015/mar/17/binyamin-netan
yahu-israel-arab-election.

5. Lidar Gravé-Lazi, "Israeli University Heads Warn of 'Erosion'
of Democracy at Knesset Event," *Jerusalem Post*, May 8, 2016,
http://www.jpost.com/Israel-News/Israeli-university-heads-
warn-of-erosion-of-democracy-at-Knesset-event-453458.

6. Maayan Lubel, "Breaking Taboos: East Jerusalem Palestinians

Seek Israeli Citizenship," August 5, 2015, http://www.haaretz.com/israel-news/1.669643.

7. Jodi Rudoren, "Tradition of Not Voting Keeps Palestinians Politically Powerless in Jerusalem," *New York Times*, October 21, 2013, http://www.nytimes.com/2013/10/22/world/middleeast/tradition-of-not-voting-keeps-palestinians-politically-powerless-in-jerusalem.html?_r=0.

8. Mazal Mualem, "Could Jerusalem Get a Palestinian Mayor?" *Al Monitor*, February 12, 2016, http://www.al-monitor.com/pulse/originals/2016/02/israel-interview-haim-ramon-diplomatic-plan-jerusalem.html.

9. Caroline Glick, *The Israeli Solution: A One-State Plan for Peace in the Middle East* (Danvers, MA: Crown Forum, 2014). Glick is the deputy managing editor of the *Jerusalem Post*.

10. R. M. Schneiderman, "Former Israeli Security Chief Pushes for Unilateral Withdrawal," *Daily Beast*, March 21, 20012, http://www.thedailybeast.com/articles/2012/03/21/former-israeli-security-chief-pushes-for-unilateral-withdrawal.html.

11. Yair Rosenberg, "Michael Oren: If Peace Talks Fail, Israel Should Withdraw from West Bank," *Tablet*, January 13, 2014, http://www.tabletmag.com/scroll/159210/michael-oren-if-peace-talks-fail-israel-should-withdraw-from-west-bank.

12. Barak Ravid, "Herzog Presents New Diplomatic Plan: Separation From Jerusalem's Palestinian Villages," *Haaretz*, January 19, 2016, http://www.haaretz.com/misc/iphone-article/.premium-1.698391.

13. Interview of Dani Dayan by Alon Sachar, Tel Aviv, October 23, 2012.

14. Dani Dayan, "Israel's Settlers Are Here to Stay," *New York Times*, July 25, 2012, http://www.nytimes.com/2012/07/26/opinion/israels-settlers-are-here-to-stay.html?_r=0.

15. Dayan interview.

16. David K. Shipler, "Israel Rejects Reagan Plan for Palestinians' Self-Rule: Terms It 'A Serious Danger,'" *New York Times*,

September 3, 1982, http://www.nytimes.com/1982/09/03/world/israel-rejects-reagan-plan-for-palestinians-self-rule-terms-it-serious-danger.html?pagewanted=all.

17. Dayan interview.

18. Adnan Abu Amer, "Despite Mounting Violence, IDF-PA Security Cooperation Unlikely to End," translated by Cynthia Milan, *Al Monitor*, October 7, 2015, http://www.al-monitor.com/pulse/originals/2015/10/palestine-authority-israel-security-coopera tion-negotiations.html#.

19. "Anger and Hope: A Conversation With Tzipi Livni," *Foreign Affairs*, July/August 2016, https://www.foreignaffairs.com/inter views/2016-06-08/anger-and-hope.

20. Former chiefs of staff of the Israeli Defense Forces Shaul Mofaz, Dan Halutz, Gabi Ashkenazi, Benny Gantz, and Ehud Barak; former directors of Israel's Shin Bet Avi Dichter, Yuval Diskin, Ami Ayalon, Jacob Perry; and former heads of Israel's Mossad Tamir Prado, Danny Yatom, Shabtai Shavit, Efraim Halevy. "In a Turbulent World Israel's Security Chiefs Agree: Separation Into Two States Is Essential for Israel's Security," advertisement in the *New York Times* by the S. Daniel Abraham Center for Middle East Peace, July 27, 2016, http://centerpeace.org/wp-content/uploads/2015/11/Bluelight_CMEP_Chiefs_0716_Tearsheet.pdf.

21. Livni interview, *Foreign Affairs*.

22. Peter Beaumont, "PLO Leadership Votes to Suspend Security Cooperation with Israel," *Guardian*, March 5, 2015, http://www.theguardian.com/world/2015/mar/05/plo-leadership-votes-to-suspend-security-cooperation-with-israel.

23. Yaakov Lappin, "IDF Drill Prepares for Large Scale Unrest in West Bank, Collapse of Security Coordination with PA," *Jerusalem Post*, March 1, 2015, http://www.jpost.com/Israel-News/IDF-drills-responses-to-terror-attack-scenarios-in-West-Bank-392545.

24. Peter Beaumont, "US Officials and Israeli President Blast

Withholding of Palestinian Tax Revenues," *Guardian*, January 6, 2015, http://www.theguardian.com/world/2015/jan/06/us-israel-reuven-rivlin-palestinian-tax-revenues.

25. Israel Ministry of Foreign Affairs, "The Hussein-Arafat Accord," February 11, 1985, http://www.mfa.gov.il/mfa/foreignpolicy/mfadocuments/yearbook7/pages/42%20the%20hussein-arafat%20accord-%2011%20february%201985.aspx.

26. Jordan had not conducted parliamentary elections since 1967 because of Israel's occupation of the West Bank districts and an inability to hold elections there. Hussein imposed martial law in 1967 that was still in place at the time. A serious economic crisis in the late 1980s provoked substantial domestic protests in Jordan. The Palestinian-origin population wanted more political say, and non-Palestinian Jordanians were gravely uneasy with the confederation concept to begin with. Relinquishing Jordan's claims to the West Bank was a necessary first step to ending martial law, holding parliamentary elections in 1989, and legalizing political parties, all of which were fundamental to restoring domestic stability. None of that was possible so long as Jordan retained its claim to an Israeli-occupied West Bank.

27. Robert M. Danin, "Israel Among the Nations," *Foreign Policy*, July/August 2016, https://www.foreignaffairs.com/articles/middle-east/2016-06-08/israel-among-nations.

28. Ibid.

29. The other members of the Commission were Süleyman Demirel, the former president of Turkey; Thorbjørn Jagland, the former foreign minister of Norway; Warren B. Rudman, the former U.S. senator from New Hampshire; and Javier Solana, the former head of foreign policy for the European Union. The Commission's report was submitted to President George W. Bush on May 1, 2001.

30. Nick Gray, "Europe's Love-Hate Relationship With Israel," *The Commentator*, December 19, 2013, http://www.thecommentator

.com/article/4476/europe_s_love_hate_relationship_with_
israel.

31. "Report of the Middle East Quartet," July 1, 2016, http://www
.state.gov/p/nea/rls/rpt/259262.htm.

CHAPTER TEN: A PATH TO PEACE

1. Donald Trump, "Remarks by President Trump and Prime Minister
Netanyahu of Israel in Joint Press Conference," February 15, 2017,
https://www.whitehouse.gov/the-press-office/2017/02/15
/remarks-president-trump-and-prime-minister-netanyahu-israel
-joint-press.

2. "Right-Wing Lawmakers Rejoice after Netanyahu-Trump Summit," *Times of Israel*, February 15, 2017, http://www.timesofisrael
.com/right-wing-lawmakers-rejoice-after-netanyahu-trump
-summit/.

3. Peter Beaumont, "Trump in Apparent U-Turn on Israeli Settlement
Growth," *Guardian*, February 10, 2017, https://www.theguardian
.com/world/2017/feb/10/trump-apparent-u-turn-israeli
-settlement-growth.

4. Donald Trump, "Remarks by President Trump and President
Abbas of the Palestinian Authority in Joint Statement," May 3, 2017,
https://www.whitehouse.gov/the-press-office/2017/05/03
/remarks-president-trump-and-president-abbas-palestinian
-authority-joint.

5. Ian Black, "The 'Ultimate Deal'?," *Guardian*, May 24, 2017,
https://www.theguardian.com/world/2017/may/24/israel
-palestine-trump-arab-peace-initiative.

6. George W. Bush, "President Bush Discusses Israeli-Palestinian
Peace Process," White House, January 10, 2008, https://
georgewbush-whitehouse.archives.gov/news/releases/2008/01
/20080110-3.html.

7. Another effort came from the Baker Institute at Rice University
in Houston. Headed by Edward Djerejian, a distinguished former

U.S. diplomat whose career has been devoted to Middle East policy, the Center produced detailed reports, accompanied by precise maps, setting forth possible approaches to the territorial dispute between the parties.

8. Barack Obama, "Remarks by the President on the Middle East and North Africa," May 19, 2011, https://obamawhitehouse.archives.gov/the-press-office/2011/05/19/remarks-president-middle-east-and-north-africa.

9. Bush, "President Bush Discusses Israeli-Palestinian Peace Process."

10. Ethan Bronner, "Olmert Memoir Cites Near Deal for Mideast Peace," *New York Times*, January 27, 2011, http://www.nytimes.com/2011/01/28/world/middleeast/28mideast.html?_r=0.

11. Obama, "Remarks by the President on the Middle East and North Africa."

12. While the Palestinians are largely free to negotiate and reach agreement on other issues, Jerusalem is of intense interest to Muslims across the globe, as well as to several Arab countries that have historical connections to the city, including Jordan, Morocco, and Saudi Arabia. It is unlikely that the Palestinians would ever act on Jerusalem without their approval.

13. Omer Zanany, *The Annapolis Process (2007–2008): An American Policymaker's Guide to the Israeli-Palestinian Conflict: A Case Study of the Annapolis Process* (Tel Aviv: Tel Aviv University, 2015), 67.

14. "Report of the Middle East Quartet," July 1, 2016, https://unispal.un.org/DPA/DPR/unispal.nsf/0/6E9212B45B0CEF-4985257FE3004DB4CC.

INDEX

Page numbers in *italics* refer to maps.

ABOUT THE AUTHORS

GEORGE J. MITCHELL served as a Democratic senator from Maine from 1980 to 1995 and Senate majority leader from 1989 to 1995. He was the primary architect of the 1998 Good Friday Agreement for peace in Northern Ireland, chairman of The Walt Disney Company, US Special Envoy for Middle East Peace, and the author of the Mitchell Report on the use of performance-enhancing drugs in baseball, as well as the books *The Negotiator* and *A Path to Peace*. He was awarded the Presidential Medal of Freedom in 1999.

ALON SACHAR has worked to advance Middle East peace under two U.S. administrations. He served as an adviser to Daniel B. Shapiro, the U.S. Ambassador to Israel, from 2011 to 2012 in Tel Aviv and to President Obama's Special Envoys for Middle East Peace, George J. Mitchell and David Hale, from 2009 to 2011. In those capacities, Alon participated in negotiations with Israelis, Palestinians, and Arab states. From 2006 to 2009, he served in the State Department's Bureau of Near Eastern Affairs, focusing on the U.S. bilateral relationships with Israel and the Palestinians, as well as Arab-Israeli relations. Alon has also worked out of the U.S. Consulate in Jerusalem, which serves as the U.S. diplomatic mission to the Palestinians. Today, Alon practices law in California, where he was born and raised.